Managing Digital Enterprise

Jun Xu

Managing Digital Enterprise

Ten Essential Topics

ATLANTIS
PRESS

Jun Xu
Southern Cross Business School
Southern Cross University
Gold Coast
Australia

ISBN 978-94-6239-093-5 ISBN 978-94-6239-094-2 (eBook)
DOI 10.2991/978-94-6239-094-2

Library of Congress Control Number: 2014951669

Printed on acid-free paper

Preface

In line with the potential opportunities and the rapid development of digitization, facilitated by the dramatic advancements in digital technologies, extensively connected networks, and wider adoption of computing devices (especially mobile devices), more and more organizations are realizing the strategic importance of digitization (e.g., sustainable growth of the organization, competitive advantage development, and enhancement) and are embarking on digital enterprise.

Digital enterprise is a large subject that can be discussed in-depth from many different perspectives, including business models of digital enterprise, technologies enabling digital enterprise, strategy planning and implementation, products and services of digital enterprise, marketing and advertising of digital enterprise, digital payment systems, business processes and operations of digital enterprise, laws and regulations associated with digital enterprise, security and privacy issues of digital enterprise, and digital enterprise systems and applications (e.g., Big Data and Advanced Analytics, Cloud Services, The Internet of Things, Mobile Computing, and Social Media). This book titled *Managing Digital Enterprise: Ten Essential Topics* is about digital enterprise and managing the digital enterprise, and focuses primarily on the important knowledge and essential understanding of digital enterprise management required by managers and decision-makers in the organization.

This book comprises ten chapters. Chapter 1 introduces the digital world we live in, defines digital enterprise, discusses types of digital enterprise and elements of digital enterprise management, looks at some challenges and issues of digital enterprise, and spells out some emerging trends and future directions of digital enterprise. Chapter 2 reviews technology infrastructure for digital enterprise, enterprise systems supporting digital enterprise, and measures and tools for addressing security and privacy issues associated with digital enterprise, then discusses emerging technologies of Big Data and Data Analytics, Cloud Computing, and The Internet of Things, and concludes with talent management for digital enterprise.

Chapter 3 discusses digital transformation, looks at digital enterprise strategy framework, reviews some success factors of digital enterprise, and introduces a model of sustainable digital business. Chapter 4 provides an overview of e-tailing, discusses issues of e-tailing, reviews success factors of e-tailing, and presents some emerging trends and future directions of e-tailing.

Chapter 5 provides an overview of e-services, then discusses e-learning, e-government, digital publishing and e-health respectively, and concludes with 3D-design and 3D-printing. Chapter 6 explains B2B digital enterprise, discusses supply chains and B2B digital enterprise for supply chains, reviews issues and success factors of managing digital supply chains, and presents some emerging trends and future directions of digital supply chains.

Chapter 7 introduces the definition and different types of digital platforms, reviews social media platforms, and discusses some issues and success factors of digital platforms. Chapter 8 highlights the importance of understanding digital customers, looks at digital advertising methods, presents measures for evaluating effectiveness of digital advertising, and discusses some issues and success factors of digital marketing and advertising.

Chapter 9 presents an overview of payment systems, discusses B2C and B2B digital payment systems, addresses mobile payment systems, highlights success factors and challenges/issues of digital payment systems, and suggests some emerging trends and future directions of digital payment systems. Chapter 10 introduces the mobile era, explains the concept of digital enterprise and its major applications, discusses key mobile technologies, and examines some key issues and success factors of mobile enterprise, and points out some emerging trends and future directions of mobile enterprise.

I would like to thank John Hammond, Southern Cross University, Australia, Dr. Daniel O'Sheedy, Enero Group, Australia, and Dr. Chad Lin, Curtin University, Australia for their kind assistance in reviewing the book. Finally, I would like to thank Atlantis Press and Springer for opportunity of working on the book, and thank Zeger Karssen and Willie van Berkum, Atlantis Press, for overseeing the publishing process of the book and for giving me such a wonderful publishing experience.

Gold Coast, Australia, August 2014 Jun Xu

Contents

1 Foundation of Digital Enterprise 1
1.1 The Digital World We Live In 1
1.1.1 Digitization and Its Impacts 3
1.2 Defining Digital Enterprise 4
1.3 Types of Digital Enterprise 5
1.4 Elements of Digital Enterprise Management 5
1.5 Challenges and Issues 6
1.5.1 Security 6
1.5.2 Privacy 9
1.5.3 Value of Personal Data 11
1.5.4 Digital Divide 11
1.5.5 Internet Governance 12
1.5.6 Less-Human and Work-Life Balance 12
1.5.7 Long Tail Versus Power Law 13
1.5.8 Integration Challenge 13
1.6 Emerging Trends and Future Directions 14
1.6.1 Emerging Technologies and Technological Trends 14
1.6.2 Emerging Markets and Industries 14
1.6.3 Digital Global Flows 15
1.6.4 Multiple-Screen Culture 16
1.6.5 Digital Identity Management 16
1.6.6 Ten Working Forces in 2020 17
1.6.7 Technology-Enabled Trends 18
1.6.8 The Robotic Age 19
1.6.9 Digital Cities 20
1.6.10 Green Technologies 20
1.6.11 Big Data, Cloud Computing, Social Business, and Mobile Business 21
References 21

2 Technology Foundation and Talent Management for Digital Enterprise 27
2.1 Digital Enterprise Technology Infrastructure 27
2.2 Enterprise Systems Supporting Business Processes 27
2.2.1 Integration 30
2.3 Managing Security and Privacy Threats 30
2.4 Big Data and Data Analytics 32
2.4.1 Data-Led Transformation 37
2.5 Cloud Computing 39
2.6 The Internet of Things 41
2.7 Talent Management for Digital Enterprise 42
References 46

3 Digital Enterprise Strategy Planning and Implementation 51
3.1 Digital Transformation 51
3.1.1 Organization's Readiness for Digital Transformation 51
3.1.2 Digital Transformation Capabilities 53
3.2 Digital Enterprise Strategy Framework 55
3.3 Success Factors of Digital Enterprise 55
3.3.1 Selection of Products and Services 61
3.3.2 Sound Business Model and Business Practices 61
3.3.3 Being a Global Player 62
3.3.4 Being the Best Player in Your Field 62
3.3.5 Being Small Could Be Beautiful 63
3.3.6 Establishing a Data-Driven Decision-Making Culture in the Organization 63
3.3.7 Working on Having a Good Understanding of the Impact of Digital Capital 63
3.3.8 Keeping in Mind of Developing a Digital Ecosystem 64
3.3.9 Demonstrating Digital Leadership 64
3.3.10 Making Required Organizational Adjustments 65
3.3.11 Digital Talent Management and Digital Skills Development 66
3.3.12 Open Innovation and Organizational Learning Strategy 66
3.3.13 Justification and Evaluation of Digital Investments 67
3.4 A Sustainable Digital Business Model 68
References 73

4 B2C Digital Enterprise: E-Tailing 77
4.1 Overview of E-Tailing 77
4.2 Issues of E-Tailing 78
4.2.1 Channel Conflict 78
4.2.2 Pricing 78
4.2.3 Personalization 79
4.3 Success Factors of E-Tailing 79
4.3.1 The Multi-channel Strategy 80
4.3.2 Developing Effective Supply Chains for Multiple-Channel Services 81
4.3.3 Addressing People's Needs 83
4.3.4 Excellent Customer Services 83
4.3.5 Effective and Dynamic E-Tailing Site 86
4.3.6 Education and Trust Building 88
4.4 Emerging Trends and Future Directions 89
References 93

5 E-Services 97
5.1 Overview of Providing Services Online 97
5.2 E-Learning 99
5.3 E-Government 102
5.4 Digital Publishing 105
5.5 E-Health 112
5.6 3D-Design and 3D-Printing 115
References 115

6 B2B Digital Enterprise and Supply Chain 119
6.1 B2B Digital Enterprise 119
6.2 Supply Chains 120
6.3 B2B Digital Enterprise and Supply Chain 121
6.4 Issues and Success Factors of Digital Supply Chain Management 123
6.5 Emerging Trends and Future Directions of Digital Supply Chains 126
References 127

7 Digital Platforms 131
7.1 Definition and Classification of Digital Platforms 131
7.2 Social Media Platforms 132
7.3 Challenges/Issues and Success Factors of Digital Platforms 139
References 141

8 Digital Marketing and Advertising 145
8.1 Understanding Digital Customers 145
8.2 Digital Advertising Methods 149
8.3 Evaluating the Effectiveness of Digital Advertising 149
8.4 Issues and Success Factors of Digital Advertising 154
References 156

9 Digital Payment Systems 159
9.1 Overview of Payment Systems 159
9.1.1 Country's Cashless Journey 160
9.2 B2C and B2B Digital Payment Systems 161
9.3 Mobile Payment Systems 163
9.3.1 Contactless Cards/NFC Payments 164
9.4 Challenges/Issues and Success Factors of Digital Payment Systems 166
9.4.1 Security of Digital Payment Systems 167
9.4.2 Payment Fraud Management 167
9.4.3 The Hype of Bitcoin 169
9.4.4 Required Legal Framework and Policies 170
9.4.5 Required Collaboration Among Stakeholders 171
9.5 Emerging Trends and Future Directions 171
References 173

10 Mobile Enterprise 177
10.1 The Mobile Era 177
10.1.1 The Mobility Culture 177
10.1.2 Mobile Workforce 178
10.1.3 Mobile Economy 179
10.2 Definition and Major Applications of Mobile Enterprise 181
10.3 Key Mobile Technologies 182
10.3.1 iOS, Windows Phone and Android 183
10.3.2 Bring Your Own Device 184
10.3.3 Mobile Payment Systems 184
10.3.4 Mobile Applications 185
10.4 Issues and Success Factors of Mobile Enterprise 188
10.4.1 Key Issues 188
10.4.2 Success Factors 189
10.5 Emerging Trends and Future Directors 189
References 196

Chapter 1
Foundation of Digital Enterprise

This chapter introduces the digital world we live in, defines digital enterprise, discusses types of digital enterprise and elements of digital enterprise management, looks at some challenges and issues of digital enterprise, and spells out some emerging trends and future directions of digital enterprise.

1.1 The Digital World We Live In

We are in the digital economy in which digitization is an essential part of the way we live, work, and conduct business. The world we live in has seen many dramatic digital changes in recent years:

- It is reported that in 1990, there were 100 million PCs worldwide, 10 million mobile phone users, and less than 3 million Internet users; but by 2010 there were 1.4 billion personal computers, 5 billion mobile phone users, and 2 billion Internet users (El-Darwiche et al. 2012).
- According to studies of 40 countries done by leading consulting firm McKinsey (reported in Bughin and Manyika 2013), in 2005, investment in digital capital, which includes tangible assets (e.g., servers, routers, online platforms, and fundamental Internet software) and intangible assets (e.g., intellectual property), represented only 0.8 % of GDP for those countries but will reach more than 3.1 % in 2013. Meanwhile the accumulating global value of digital capital investments has reached more than US$6 trillion in 2013, which is equivalent to 8.5 % of nominal world GDP. In addition, more global digital capital investments have been made in intangible assets than in tangible assets. In more highly digitized countries, such as Israel, Japan, Sweden, the U.K., and the U.S., two-thirds of their digital capital investments are in intangible assets.
- According to Gartner (2014), by 2020, more than 7 billion people and businesses, and at least 30 billion devices will be connected to the Internet.
- In 2013 there were 6.8 billion mobile-cellular subscriptions with 7.1 billion global population, 2.7 billion global Internet users (around 40 % of world's population), and 41 % of households (around 750 million households) in the

J. Xu, *Managing Digital Enterprise*, DOI 10.2991/978-94-6239-094-2_1

world connected to the Internet. In comparison, in 2005, there were 2.2 billion mobile-cellular subscriptions with 6.5 billion global population, 1 billion global Internet users (around 15 % of world's population), and 18.4 % of households in the world connected to the Internet (International Telecommunication Union 2013).

- We now live in a world of "The Global Grid": everyone and everything is connected. On this global grid, every company is now a global company and has the potential to leverage the power of more than 4 billion connected minds (Bisson et al. 2010), and it is reported that there will be more than 50 billion connected devices in the world by 2020 (Dutta et al. 2012, p. 3).
- It is suggested that the installed base of smartphones exceeded that of PCs in 2011 and is growing more than three times faster than personal computers, and the expected shipment of smartphones between 2011 and 2015 could be around 4 billion, and the total download of mobile applications reached 8 billion in 2010 and should surpass 100 billion by 2015. It is also reported (cited in Berman and Bell 2011) that by the end of 2011, smart phones and tablet-computers will overtake personal computer shipments; and downloads of mobile applications (Apps) are expected to surge from 11 billion in 2010 to 77 billion in 2014 (Bold and Davidson 2012, pp. 71–72).
- In 2010 enterprises and consumers stored 13 exabytes (or 13 billion gigabytes) of new data on devices and the projected annual growth in global data generated is 40 % (just imaging the information produced by more than 4 billion mobile phones, by 30 million network sensor nodes, social networks. Do you know there are more than 30 billion pieces of content (photos, notes, blogs, web links, and news stories) shared on Facebook every month and 2.9 billion hours of video are watched at Youtube every month? (Manyika et al. 2011).
- By the end of 2013, the number of wirelessly connected devices could reach 8 billion (more than the global population of 7.2 billion); by 2020, 50 billion wireless devices could be connected to the Internet while the projected population will be less than 8 billion; and from 2012 to 2017, machine-to-machine data traffic is estimated to grow 24 times and reach 6X1017 bytes per month (Haynes and Nguyen 2014, p. 68).
- Global digital data will reach 44 zettabytes (or 44 trillion gigabytes) in 2020 up from 4.4 zettabytes in 2013 (EMC Corporation 2014). It is said more data was created between 2008 and 2011 than in all history before 2008 (Biggs et al. 2012, p. 48); and 90 % of the world's data was created in the last two years with over 2.5 quintillions (or 2.5 billion gigabytes), and digital universe (including all digital data created, replicated, or consumed) has been growing by a factor of 30 from 2005 to 2020, doubling every two years (Pepper and Garrity 2014, p. 35). In the past, data storage was expensive and a lot of data have been thrown away. However the price of storage is dropping significantly; by 2020, storing a petabyte of data will only cost US$4 (Siegele 2012).
- Global B2C e-commerce (digital transactions) could reach US$1.2 trillion and global B2B digital transactions could reach US$12.4 trillion by the end of 2012 (World Trade Organization 2013).

- According to Meeker (2014), global compute cost had been declining 33 % annually for the period of 1990–2013 and the cost of per 1 million transistors had decreased from US$527 in 1990 to US$0.05 in 2013; global storage cost had been declining 38 % annually for the period of 1990–2013 and the cost of per gigabytes had decreased from US$569 in 1990 to US$0.02 in 2013; global bandwidth cost had been declining 27 % annually for the period of 1990–2013 and the cost of per 1,000 Mbps had decreased from US$1,245 in 1990 to US$16 in 2013; and average global smart phone price had been declining 5 % annually for the period of 2008–2013 and the price had decreased from US$430 in 2008 to US$335 in 2013.

1.1.1 Digitization and Its Impacts

Past research (e.g., El-Darwiche et al. 2012; Sabbagh et al. 2012a,b; Friedrich et al. 2013a) suggests that the national economic growth is associated with the adoption of information and communications technology (ICT), and suggest countries that have achieved mass adoption of digital technologies and ICT applications by individuals, businesses, and governments (in other words, advanced level of digitization) have realized significant economic, social, and political benefits; and it further points out that countries with most advanced digitization development which is measured by the level of digitization, could derive 20 % more in economic benefits than those who are in the beginning stage; and every 10 % increase in digitization could increase 0.60 % of GDP per capita (Sabbagh et al. 2012a, p. 17). On top of economic benefits, digitization could have social contributions (e.g., 10 % increase in digitization could reduce the unemployment rate by 0.84 %) and governance impacts (e.g., 10 % increase in digitization could raise the e-government development index by 0.10 points) (Sabbagh et al. 2012a, p. 17). More precisely, in 2011, digitization contributed US$192.6 billion to GDP and created 6 million jobs (Friedrich et al. 2013b, p. 3). On a related note, The Boston Consulting Group suggests (reported in Dean et al. 2012) that the Internet contributed 4.1 % of GDP in the G-20 countries in 2010; and McKinsey Global Institute suggests (reported in Manyika et al. 2013, p. 21) the Internet accounted for 3.7 % GDP of developed economies, 1.9 % GDP of emerging economies, and 1.1 % GDP of Africa. In addition, according to one recent research conducted by consulting firm McKinsey (reported in Hazan et al. 2011), from 2005 to 2009, the Internet accounted for 21 % of the combined GDP growth of nine developed economies (being Sweden, Germany, United Kingdom, France, South Korea, United States, Italy, Canada, and Japan).

Digitization can be measured across six key attributes (Sabbagh et al. 2012b, p. 122):

- Ubiquity (the extent to which consumers and enterprises have universal access to digital services and applications): measured by fixed broadband penetration, mobile phone penetration, mobile broadband penetration, personal computers, population penetration, and 3G mobile connection penetration.

- Affordability (the extent to which digital services are priced in a range that makes them available to as many people as possible): measured by fixed line installation cost, fixed cost per minute, mobile connection fee, mobile prepaid tariff, and fixed broadband Internet access tariff.
- Reliability (the quality of available digital services): measured by investment per subscriber (mobile broadband and fixed line).
- Speed (the extent to which digital services can be accessed in real time): measured by international Internet bandwidth and broadband speeds
- Usability (the ease of use of digital services and the ability of local ecosystems to boost adoption of these services): measured by Internet retail as % of total retail, E-government web measure index, % of individuals using the Internet, Data as % of wireless ARPU (average revenue per user), domains by country per 100 inhabitants, IP addresses per 100 inhabitants, social network unique visitors per month, and average SMS usage per customer.
- Skills (the ability of users to incorporate digital services into their lives and businesses): measured by the number of engineers per 100 inhabitants, % of labor force with more than secondary education.

Meanwhile the impact of digitization could be looked at from three perspectives (Sabbagh et al. 2012b, p. 126):

- Economy (the impact of digitization on the growth of economy): it is measured by GDP growth, job creation, and innovation.
- Society (the impact of digitization on the society well-being of a country): it is measured by quality of life and access to basic services.
- Governance (the impact of digitization on the public sector): it is measured by transparency of government operations and business activities, E-government, and education.

1.2 Defining Digital Enterprise

Digital enterprise is a widely used term, but it means different things to different people! And there are no agreed universal definitions. It could be defined primarily from a communications and technical perspective focusing on the technology that enables and improves information and transaction communications. It also could be looked at from a business perspective, focusing on the digitization of business transactions and work-flows. It also can be examined from a service perspective, highlighting the use of technology to cut service costs while improving quality and speed of service. It also could be discussed from other perspectives, such as learning, collaborative, community, and so on. All of these definitions are valid.

In this book, digital enterprise is defined as 'using digital technologies and networks in the activities of buying and selling goods and services, servicing customers, collaborating with business partners, conducting communications and transactions within the organization' (adapted from Turban et al. 2012, p. 38). Meanwhile we have seen such terms as digital enterprise, digital business, digital commerce, electronic business, electronic commerce, online business, Internet-based business; in this book, these terms are treated as equivalent terms and are used interchangeably.

1.3 Types of Digital Enterprise

There are different ways of categorizing digital enterprise (digital business/digital commerce/electronic business/electronic commerce/online business/Internet-based business). One way of categorizing is to look at the degree of digitization (measured by the product/service sold, the process, and the delivery method (Turban et al. 2010, p. 48). Digital enterprises can be either pure online/digital or click-and-mortar businesses (having both digital/online and non-digital/offline operations/channels). Another way is to focus on the type of transaction taking place. Transactions could be conducted among businesses (business-to-business), between an organization and its retail customers (i.e., consumers) (business-to-consumer), within an organization (intra-business), between consumers (consumer-to-consumer), between peers (peer-to-peer), between members of networks and communities (you-and-me), and between the government and its citizens (government-to-citizen). In this book, the approach of categorizing digital enterprise as per the type of transaction is adopted; and major types of digital enterprise consist of:

- Business to consumer (B2C) digital enterprise.
- Business to business (B2B) digital enterprise.
- E-Services (including B2C services, E-leaning, E-government, E-publishing, E-health, and other e-services).
- Digital platforms (including consumer to consumer (C2C) sites/platforms, online communities, social networks, and online portals (including corporate and customer portals).

1.4 Elements of Digital Enterprise Management

Effective management of digital enterprise requires close attention to various elements of digital enterprise, including (1) understanding current status, challenges/issues, and future directions of digital enterprise; (2) addressing digital enterprise enabling technologies (including hardware, software, and networks); (3) recruiting, developing, and retaining required talent and skills; (4) having good management

Table 1.1 Elements of digital enterprise management and corresponding book chapters

Elements/dimensions of digital enterprise management	Corresponding chapters in this book
Understanding current status, challenges/issues, emerging trends, and future directions of digital enterprise	This chapter: Foundation of Digital Enterprise
	Chapter 10: Mobile Enterprise
Addressing digital enterprise enabling technologies	Chapter 2: Technology Foundation and Talent Management for Digital Enterprise
Recruiting, developing, and retaining required talent and skills	Chapter 2: Technology Foundation and Talent Management for Digital Enterprise
Having good management practices	Chapter 3: Digital Enterprise Strategy Planning and Implementation
Managing chosen digital enterprise model(s)	Chapter 4: B2C Digital Enterprise: E-tailing
	Chapter 5: E-Services
	Chapter 6: B2B Digital Enterprise and Supply Chain
	Chapter 7: Digital Platforms
Ensuring the delivery of associated support services for digital enterprise	Chapter 8: Digital Marketing and Advertising
	Chapter 9: Digital Payment Systems

Source Developed by the Author

practices (e.g., strong leadership, effective strategy planning and execution, right business processes, fostering organizational culture and structure); (5) managing chosen digital enterprise model(s); and (6) ensuring the delivery of associated support services for digital enterprise. Table 1.1 presents the key elements of digital enterprise management and corresponding chapters in this book.

1.5 Challenges and Issues

In this section, some significant challenges and issues associated with digital enterprise/digital business are discussed, including security, privacy, value of personal data, digital divide, Internet governance, less-human and work-life balance, long tail versus power law, and integration challenge.

1.5.1 Security

Cybersecurity is a critical issue for individuals, organizations, and even national security. Security is and will remain a major issue for digital enterprise/e-business participants. It is estimated that over the next five to seven years, US$9 trillion to

21 trillion of global economic-value creation relies on the robustness of the cybersecurity environment (Bailey et al. 2014). As a result of the interconnectedness at the global scale, attackers could achieve a wide range of effects with little input and easily make large-scale disruptions, and it can be said that "a threat to the Internet increasingly means a threat to everything" (World Economic Forum 2014a, p. 39). It is also well said that "The more digital we are, the more vulnerable to attacks we become" (Startupsmart.com.au 2014). There are more than 5 billion devices connected to the Internet (a perpetrator needs only a single weakness in order to attack a system), accessing and serving up to 500 billion gigabytes of information and transmitting 2 trillion emails per day. Furthermore 75 % of emails are spam even though the spam rate has been dropping in recent years; every minute 42 new strains of malware (short for malicious software including viruses, worms, and Trojans) are generated, an average of 8,600 new websites with malicious code are developed each day, and half of the results for the top 100 daily search terms lead to malicious sites (Laseter and Johnson 2011). Some major cyber technical attacks include: Malware, Unauthorized access, Denial of Services attack, Spam and Spyware, Hijacking (servers and pages), and Botnets (Turban et al. 2012, p. 500; Laudon and Laudon 2012, p. 246). Malware is number one cyber security concern. Another major issue is SPAM. Even though we do have solutions (e.g., Junk-mail filters, Automatic junk-mail deleters, Blocking certain URLs and e-mail addresses), it is really challenging to control spamming since spammers send millions of e-mails, shifting Internet accounts to avoid detection and use different methods to find their victims.

The financial losses (including such costs as loss of customer business, legal defense services, investigations and forensics, audit and consulting fees, deployment of detection software, services and polices, damage to brand and reputation, court settlements) from a cyberattack can be substantial (Oxford Economics 2014, p. 28). For example, according to RSA Anti-Fraud Command Center (reported in Enterprise Management Associates 2012), phishing attacks alone cost businesses US$1.3 billion in 2011). Meanwhile in Australia, the estimated cost of cybercrime could be as high as US$2 billion annually (Startupsmart.com.au 2014). In addition, the 2011 U.S. Cost of a Data Breach Study by Symantec and the Ponemom Institute (reported in Westby 2012, p. 11) indicated that data breach cost firms an average of US$5.5 million per incident, and another recent study by the Ponemom Institute (reported in Westby 2012, p. 11) pointed out a data breach could cost organizations 17–30 % loss of brand and reputation, and such damage to corporate image could take them more than a year to recover. Organizations have to take cyberattacks seriously; otherwise they may face the consequence of going out of business. Today's attackers are well organized and well informed, and they take advantage of the latest advances in crimeware and hacking skills (Enterprise Management Associates 2012).

Any type of digital activity involves a number of players who use a variety of network and application services that provide access to a variety of data sources. A perpetrator needs only a single weakness in order to attack a system. While some attacks require sophisticated techniques and technologies (such as Denial of Service

(DoS) attacks, Distributed Denial of Service (DDoS) attacks, Crimeware and Malware, Web Applications attacks, Point-of-Sale (POS) intrusions (e.g., Phishing, Offline Cracking, Use of Stolen Credit Cards, RAM Scraping, Brute Force, Card Skimming)), most attacks are not sophisticated (e.g., preying on poor security practice and human weaknesses) (Turban et al. 2012, pp. 500–502; Verizon 2014). Meanwhile, insiders' breaches could be more frequent and more harmful than those of outsiders.

As a result of the emerging trend of The Internet of Things in many industries (towards the trend of The Internet of Everything?!), the concept of cyber-security/ digital security has gone beyond of the normal boundary (e.g., buying or trading goods online, providing services online) and has extended to more traditional industries (e.g., oil and gas, manufacturing, warehousing and logistics, transportations). For example, it is estimated that global cost resulting from cyber-attacks against oil and gas infrastructure could reach US$1.9 billion by 2018; and the oil tankers and container vessels, which move around 90 % of the goods around the global, could be easily hacked by attacking their navigation systems (e.g., Global Positioning System (GPS), marine Automatic Identification System (AIS), and Electronic Chart Display and Information System (ECDIS) for viewing digital nautical) and other digital components, which were largely developed prior to the contemporary digital era (Wagstaff 2014).

Effective security management of information technology is very critical to the success of a business. Security of today's networked enterprises is a major management challenge. Networked computer systems are highly vulnerable to various threats and failures, ranging from natural failure of hardware and software to misuse by information systems professionals and end users; and security weaknesses could be identified and explored in many parts of business operations and many perspectives of the organization (Bailey et al. 2012; Laudon and Laudon 2005, p. 523). The explosive growth of the Internet use by individuals and businesses has been accompanied by rising concerns of security breach and identity theft. Corporate and personal information is at a higher risk of theft and misuse than ever before as a result of the global connectedness.

However organizations have not given sufficient attention to security issues. According to Carnegie Mellon 2012 CyLab's global survey on how boards and senior management are governing their organizations' information assets (digital assets) (reported in Westby 2012, p. 5), "57 % of them are not analyzing the adequacy of cyber insurance coverage or undertaking key activities related to cyber risk management to help them manage reputational and financial risks associated with the theft of confidential and proprietary data and security breaches". In addition, on top of potential legal implications (more and sophisticated regulations for protecting information and privacy are being established around the world), the reputational and financial losses arising from a breach could be significant. The results of the survey also showed that the majority of organizations still lag in establishing key positions for properly looking at privacy, risk and security risks (such as Chief Information Security Officer, Chief Security Officer, Chief Privacy Officer, and Chief Risk Officer). Bailey et al. (2014) argue senior leaders must be the front line against cyberattacks and lead the organization's cybersecurity initiatives by actively engaging in strategic decision making of enterprise risk management, driving consideration of the implications of cybersecurity across the whole organization, pushing required culture change and changes in user behavior, and ensuring effective governance of cybersecurity strategy and compliance of cybersecurity policies.

Security is everyone's business: businesses, consumers, government organizations, military/defense departments, universities, among many others. And a proactive (rather than reactive), systematic and integrated approach is needed to address cybersecurity issues.

1.5.2 Privacy

Privacy refers to 'the right to be left alone and the right to be free of unreasonable personal intrusions' (Turban et al. 2012, p. 727). One key issue of privacy is the personal data privacy. Personal data is "any data that can be attributed to an identifiable person either directly or indirectly" (Beardsley et al. 2014, p. 77). Very often the collected data about consumers are collected, used, sold or revealed inappropriately without getting the permission from them. Some recent examples include the reported controversial case of Facebook's 2012 experiment on its users without complying with consent standards, the U.S government's global surveillance activities disclosed by National Security Agency (NSA) whistle blower Edward Snowden, and the alleged involvement of many Internet companies and digital businesses including Google, Apple, Microsoft, Facebook, Twitter, Yahoo, AOL, Cisco, IBM, HP and others. Meanwhile the inappropriate handling of privacy concerns could have significant financial impact on businesses. For example, it is estimated that the NSA Spying Scandal could cost the Internet service provider industry up to US$180 billion net loss by 2016 (i.e., 25 % decline in the overall information technology services market) (According to Forrester analyst James Staten reported in Gustin 2013).

Consumers are increasingly concerned about the use of their personal data. For example, recent studies by USC Dornslife/Los Angeles Times and European Commission (reported in Beardsley et al. 2014, p. 74) suggest that: 78 % of US citizens viewed collecting consumers' information online is invading their privacy, 72 % of Internet users were worried about providing too much personal data, and 88 % of Europeans believed that their data would be better protected in large firms since they are mandated to name a data protection officer. The same notions were identified in a recent survey of 10,000 consumers aged 18 and over across 20 countries by Boston Consulting Group (BCG) (reported in Rose et al. 2013) wherein, it found that (1) for 75 % of consumers across all age groups in most countries, the privacy of personal data (especially such sensitive information as credit card, financial data, information about children, health/generic information, information about spouse, dialed phone number history, exact location, online surfing history, e-mail) remains a top issue; (2) consumers are more concerned about the privacy practices of financial institutions, social media, and search engine companies, and government agencies than other industries/sectors; and (3) generally speaking consumers are more willing to share the information about them if, and only if, they trust the companies can handle the data properly (e.g., not embarrassing them, not damaging their interests, not harming them). Based on the results of the BCG survey, it is suggested that companies need to work on mastering data stewardship (i.e., by establishing guiding principles for collecting and using data, translating principles into codes of conduct, creating processes to ensure compliance, and developing external trust metrics) and on engaging customers (i.e., by clarifying how data is being managed, clearly spelling out how data is being used, providing transparency into new uses of personal data, and publishing trust metrics). Meanwhile consumers would like to have more control of their personal data, and an opt-in approach has been requested by many consumers. For example, according to a recent survey of 1,000 U.S. consumers regarding issues of retailer's in-store tracking via their smartphones (reported in Leggatt 2014), 77 % of consumers believed that it is not acceptable to track their behavior in-store via their smartphones, 67 % believed opt-in is a way for retailers to operate a tracking program, and 63 % would not opt-in even in their favorite store (they just don't want to be tracked in-store!).

A vast array of personal information has been shared on social media, and the emerging trend of wearable devices (e.g., connected glasses; watches, wristbands, Wi-Vi systems which can see through walls to track moving people) could expose more of your personal information (e.g., your movements, your activities, your locations, your body conditions); coupled with your other online activities and offline transactions (e.g., via loyalty programs, social memberships, transaction history in the stores), we will soon have no secrets (Caruana 2014; the author's own knowledge).

On the other hand, privacy laws need to evolve with the changing nature of digital business, and have to be re-evaluated and constantly updated to address the fast growing data volume (collected data) and the changing approaches of utilizing the collected data (e.g., Big Data and Advanced Analytics); the unclear and out-of-date privacy laws would hamper the free flow or use of data for economic and social benefits (Lund et al. 2013, p. 84; World Economic Forum 2014, p. 25). On a related note, regulations and guidelines are needed to clearly determine the ownership of the data (e.g., answering such questions as: To what extent users own their own data and how it can be shared? To what extent computing device manufacturers or telecom operators or software suppliers or websites or application developers own the users' data and how they can use the data?) (Lund et al. 2013, p. 85). Consumers can protect their own privacy by taking care where and to whom they reveal personal details and controlling the use of cookies. For organizations, some measures they could take include: reviewing their privacy policies at least once a year, limiting collection, retention and access personal information to minimum necessary, conducting risk management assessing internal and external risks of all stored personal information, continuously monitoring data privacy program, requiring suppliers and business partners to comply their privacy policies, providing employees with mandatory training on privacy policy, requiring employees to certify in writing that they are complying with privacy policies, imposing disciplinary measures for privacy policy breaches, and looking at appointing a Chief Privacy Officer or similar executive in the senior management team (Oxford Economics 2014, pp. 8, 16).

1.5.3 Value of Personal Data

A challenge in the Big Data era is to decide the value of personal data, and without good understanding of the value of personal data, it is very difficult to measure the impact and contribution of personal data and to have a fair value exchange between the organization who uses the personal data and the owners of the data (Haynes and Nguyen 2014, p. 69). So far there are no established methods and frameworks for such purposes, and in the future, governments and their regulatory representatives, industry sectors, researchers, and consumer groups need to work together to develop innovative and evidence-based methods for measuring the value of personal data. A close but different example could be how the value of the number of users and/or what users do online is decided when Internet-based companies are raising venture capital (Strategy + Business 2013; the author's own knowledge).

1.5.4 Digital Divide

Today more than 70 % of the world's citizens live in societies which are in the early stage of digitization (Mainardi 2012). The Networked Readiness Index reflects the degree to which economies leverage ICT for enhanced competitiveness and is measured by four dimensions of environment (political and regulatory environment, business and innovation environment), readiness (infrastructure and digital content, affordability, skills), usage (individual usage, business usage, and government usage), impact (economic impacts and social impacts) (Bilbao et al. 2014, pp. 3–34; Dutta et al. 2012, pp. 3–7). Most of the advanced economies (e.g., top 10 countries of Sweden, Singapore, Finland, Denmark, Switzerland, Netherlands, Norway, United States, Canada, and United Kingdom in 2012; top 10 countries of Finland, Singapore, Sweden, Netherlands, Norway, Switzerland, United States, Hong Kong, United Kingdom, and Korea Republic in 2014) have a high Networked Readiness Index, and many developing countries (especially in certain parts of Asia and Africa-such as the bottom ten countries of Haitia, Yemen, Angola, Mauritania, Chad, Burundi, Swaziland, Burkina Faso, Madagascar, and Lesotho in 2012; bottom ten countries of Chad, Burundi, Myanmar, Guinea, Angola, Haiti, Mauritania, Timor-Leste, Yemen, and Madagascar in 2014) have very low ICT readiness with the main reason being the insufficient development of ICT infrastructure, which still remains very costly. The digitization scores, which are measured from six perspectives of ubiquity (the level of access to digital services and applications), affordability (pricing), reliability (the quality of connection), speed (the rate of data throughput), usability (how easy is to get online and use online applications/services), and skills (the ability of users to incorporate digital applications and services into their lives and businesses) (Sabbagh et al. 2012b, p. 123), indicate the same trend. For example, those top ten countries in terms of the Networked Readiness Index are at the advanced level of digitization while the bottom ten countries in terms of the Networked Readiness Index are at the low level of digitization (Sabbagh et al. 2012b, p. 124).

Meanwhile, for Baby Boomers, Generation Y, Generation X, Generation C, So called "Digital Natives", 21st Centuries, and beyond, they have different attitudes towards digital technologies and different habits of usage. For example Kleiner (2012) argues for the digital generation (those under 25 and are always-on), the digital channel is definitely preferred way of doing everything, and having to go offline is viewed as an annoyance.

1.5.5 Internet Governance

Open access approaches and infrastructure sharing are likely to be the foundation for future networks (Biggs et al. 2012, p. 51). Some countries (e.g., Australia, Malaysia, Qatar, Singapore) have embarked on creating entirely new national broadband networks (deploying fiber optic technology throughout the core network), and investments in those networks are huge (e.g., Australia's NBN will cost AU$43 billion). Currently we are in a mixed mode policy environment where self-regulation, through a variety of Internet policy and technical bodies, co-exists with limited government regulation. As Eric Smith, Former CEO and now Chairman of Google argues (reported in Manyika 2008), it will not be easy to establish international agreement on Internet governance (for example, what is appropriate or legal in one country could be inappropriate and illegal in another country) since various legal and political challenges will be involved. It is not true that the Internet cannot be controlled—in fact, the Internet can be very easily controlled, monitored, and regulated from a central location (such as is done by China, Singapore, and others). Primary questions are: (1) who will control the Internet and (2) what elements will be controlled and how.

1.5.6 Less-Human and Work-Life Balance

"Nobody knows you are a dog on the web". Have we become less human and more represented only by a series of the number 0 and the number 1? Have the technologies and the Internet made us stupid? Have we lost our ability of writing and thinking and over relied on computing devices and the Internet? At the same time, nowadays the line between leisure and work has become blurred. The technologies and the networks have made the work and the home life inseparable. Today, mobile devices have been an inseparable part of our life, and so much so that many of us are addicted to our mobile devices. For example, a recent study commissioned by Nokia (reported in Spencer 2013) indicated that people are so dependent on their mobile phones, that they will check their mobile phones every six-and-half minutes and up to 150 times a day.

1.5.7 Long Tail Versus Power Law

As Eric Smith, Former CEO and now Chairman of Google argues (reported in Manyika 2008) while organizations need both tails (referring to long tail theory suggested by Chris Anderson in his book titled 'The Long Tail: why the Future of Business is Selling Less for More") and heads, the majority of revenue remains in the head (i.e., some core products and services for a business). He also suggests the Internet will likely follow the power law and lead to more concentration (i.e., a few major players and brands). His views are supported by Elberse (2008), who suggests organizations should focus on their most popular products and services since most of the revenue will come from them, and the niche products (in the long tail) should not be the focus unless the organization wants to satisfy the appetite of its heavy and frequent customers, who are interested in products and services in both the head and then the tail.

1.5.8 Integration Challenge

Giving the phenomenon of the Internet of Things, there are many computing devices, household applications, mobile devices, industrial equipment, sensors, cameras, embedded devices, vehicles, and ships using different software and standards and sitting on different platforms. How to ensure they communicate to each other in an integral way or integrate them together will be a tough challenge (Heck and Rogers 2014). Without effective integration, advanced technologies will be useless (e.g., without successfully integrating data from various sources in different formats and thus ensuring appropriate data cleansing and organization, Big Data will be meaningless and can only produce inaccurate and irrelevant results (i.e., Garbage in and Garbage out). Some established approaches (such as standardization, modularization, developing common technical platforms, using simple building blocks, and adopting open source tools and open standards) are useful in dealing with integration issues.

1.6 Emerging Trends and Future Directions

In the 21st century, organizations are facing more uncertainty than ever. Technological change is one of the primary sources of this uncertainty. Haag et al. (2008, p. 430) state that good understanding of emerging trends and new technologies can provide organizations with valuable strategic advantages. Those organizations that can most effectively grasp the deep currents of technological evolution are in the better position to protect them against sudden and fatal technological obsolescence.

1.6.1 Emerging Technologies and Technological Trends

Some emerging technologies and technological trends include (Brynjofesson and McAfee 2012; Kappelman et al. 2013; Laudon and Traver 2014, p. 791; Laudon and Laudon 2014, pp. 206–229; Baltzan 2013, pp. 428–440; the author's own knowledge): (1) Inexpensive industry robots for industrial and life purposes; (2) Real time voice recognition and translation software, and digital assistants; (3) Sophisticated automated response systems, Automatic computing, and Smarter computers trained by machine learning; (4) Autonomous vehicles (e.g., self-moving cars and trucks); (5) Social computing; (6) Mobile computing; (7) Big Data and Advanced Analytics; (8) Business intelligence; (9) Cloud computing; (10) On-demand and Internet-driven enterprise systems (e.g., Customer relationship management, Enterprise resources planning systems, Enterprise application integration, Supply Chain Management, and Knowledge Management); (11) Security and Disaster Recovery tools; (12) Collaboration tools; (13) Digital platforms; (14) Virtualization; (15) Web services and Service-oriented Architecture; (16) Laser and other open-space wireless networks; (17) Bring Your Own Device (BYOD); (18) Open source software and standards; (19) Integration and Lean management tools; (20) Grid computing; (21) Green computing; (22) More innovative (e.g., wireless charging, using body heat to power mobile devices, solar panel for charging mobile devices) and powerful batteries (e.g., is it possible to make small and safe nuclear batteries for our daily uses?); (23) Open-air 3D screen and projectors controlled by our mobile devices so we can have screens with different sizes and resolutions anywhere and anytime; (24) Digital currency; (25) Wireless and automatic Biometric Identification Systems (e.g., is it possible to use our DNA as our identification?); (26) Smart home/building, smart meters, and other smart appliances; and (27) Hybrid human body with digital implants and/or digital parts.

1.6.2 Emerging Markets and Industries

As a result of the large population (i.e., around 85 % of global population) and lower digitization level (i.e., half of average Digitization Scores of developed countries) (El-Darwiche et al. 2012), there is bright future and many digital opportunities in emerging economies, including investing digital capabilities and infrastructure or developing innovative and localized products and services or expanding into remote and rural areas/regions. In developed countries, digital opportunities are available in the lesser digitized industries. According to Booz and Company's 2012 Industry Digitization Study of 15 industries in Europe (reported in Friedrich et al. 2013b), the five most digitized industries are (in order with the industry with highest digitization index points being the first): Financial Services and Insurance, Automotive, Computers and Electronics, Media and Telecommunications, and Equipment and Machinery while the five least digitized industries are (in the order with industry with the lowest digitization index points being the first): Construction, Hotels and Restaurants, Consumer Goods, Transportation and Logistics, and Real Estate, Rental and Leasing. The midfield industries, those industries with mid-range index points, (in order with the industry with highest digitization index points being the first) are: Trade and Retail, Chemicals, Basic Manufacturing, Business and Administrative Services, and Utilities. The Industry Digitization Index is calculated from four perspectives of input (i.e., the extent of digital processes in the procurement stage of the business), processing (i.e., the degree to which business processes are digitally integrated), output (i.e., the extent of digital processes in the sales function and customer-facing activities), and infrastructure (i.e., the degree of the sophistication of the underlying digital technologies and networks). Digital opportunities (e.g., increasing the level of digitization) are available in the industries with lower Industry Digitization Index points.

However developed countries may not always trump emerging economies in digitization. For example, by surveying 354 companies from 19 countries including both emerging and developed economies in 2012, Weill and Woerner (2013) unveil that emerging economies are investing more in digitization, digitizing more core-business activities, achieving better outcomes (e.g., being more innovative and faster to market, delivering better financial performance). Some possible reasons could be the firms in emerging economies jumped on the technology curve at a later point so they could invest less on developing and maintaining legacy systems, spend more on building new systems (e.g., cloud computing and mobile computing) and on digitizing core business activities, use more modules, learn the lessons from the developed world and effectively apply lessons learned, and realize better outcomes. The survey results also indicate that emerging market firms grew three times faster than firms in the same industries of developed countries.

1.6.3 Digital Global Flows

Digital technologies and networks are transforming all types of global flows, and significant growth of digital components of these global flows has been observed in a few areas (Manyika et al. 2014):

- 18-fold increase in global cross-border Internet traffic between 2005 and 2012.
- 90 % of commercial sellers on eBay export to other countries versus less than 25 % of traditional small businesses.
- In 2013 E-commerce contributed to 12.1 % of total cross-border goods trade while the figure was 5 % in 2005.
- The share of Skype calls out of total international calls increased to 39 % in 2013 up from 3 % in 2005. And international Skype call minutes have increased by 500 % since 2008.
- The share of digitally enabled services out of total services trade increased to 63 % in 2103 up from 51 % in 2005.
- Large U.S.-based Internet and Social Media firms have achieved the fastest growth of international revenue outside the United States, and have been growing their annual international revenue 6–7 times as fast as more traditional sectors in the U.S.

1.6.4 Multiple-Screen Culture

In many countries, people have developed the culture/habit of viewing multiple screens (e.g., TVs, Laptops, PCs, Smartphones, and Tablets) simultaneously (Meeker 2014). According to a recent Nielson research in the U.S.(reported in Meeker 2014), while watching TV, 84 % of mobile device owners used their mobile devices for various activities (e.g., surfing the web, shopping, checking sports scores, looking for information, emailing and texting, reading discussions, social networking). People who use multiple screens at the same time tend to spend more digital time, for example, according to the research by comScore and London Olympics Lab for NBC (reported in Meeker 2014), 2012 London Olympics fans followed the Olympics Games by (1) spending 259 min on TV only per day, (2) Or spending 268 min on TV and 50 min on PC (including notebook) per day, (3) Or spending 300 min on TV and 59 min on PC and 51 min on Mobile Phone per day, (4) Or spending 367 min on TV and 55 min on PC and 40 min on Mobile Phone and 47 min on Tablet per day.

1.6.5 Digital Identity Management

Nowadays we have many user names and passwords for our work and our personal life. For security, privacy, and regulatory control, our digital identities (represented by user names and passwords) have to be properly managed, and they must be unique (i.e., the identity only refers to a single entity and can't be reused and duplicated), verifiable (i.e., the ability to authenticate that the user is who he/she claims to be), and non-repudiable (i.e., confirming the integrity of the identity and subsequent communications-once the transaction or the communication is done, the buyer and sender can't deny) (Deloitte Consulting 2012). Meanwhile even though businesses and corporations have been working on addressing the issues of the growing number of digital identities (such as using single sign-on or one digital identity (represented by one set of user name and password) to login multiple Google accounts and multiple accounts in the work place; applying federated identity management which links digital identity and attributes, stored across multiple distinct identity management systems (e.g., matching your credit card information and delivery address with the information on your driver's license or social security card) (Wikipedia.org 2014), there are still quite a few digital identities for us and they could cause serious security and privacy concerns for individuals and organizations. So is it possible to develop a universal digital identity for each individual? The author (Jun Xu) believes there is a possibility even though it would be very difficult. To move towards that direction, significant investments and efforts have to be put into developing required technologies, platforms, and standards, developing appropriate policies (and updating them regularly since digital technologies and therefore digital identities are moving targets) and ensuring rigorous compliance, and more importantly the individual's own awareness and responsibility of protecting their digital identities. In addition, all the stakeholders (including businesses, governments, individuals, industry associations, consumer groups, technology firms, telecom firms, financial institutions, and many others) have to closely work together. One interesting development in recent years is the combination of digital identification with human elements (e.g., digital user name/ account with vein scan or iris scan). On a related note, a two-step login (using two sets of user-name and password in two steps) is a very practical effective way for individual users (e.g., one set of user name and password to login into your mobile device and use another set of user name and password to login into mobile applications). Of course, if it is practicable (likely in the future since the cost of identifying individual DNA is getting lower and lower), using your own DNA as your unique identification would be an ideal option.

1.6.6 Ten Working Forces in 2020

According to research into the workplace of the future, Fredette et al. (2012, pp. 116–117) suggest ten working forces in 2020:

- Demographics: there will be five generations working side by side.
- The knowledge economy: except domain knowledge, a significant more complex set of interdisciplinary skills will be required.
- Globalization: by 2020, companies will rely on global marketplace rather than domestic or even international marketplace to fuel growth.
- The digital workplace: employees will find it easier to create and access digital assets of the organization.
- Mobile technology: organizations could do more via mobile devices.

- Culture of connectivity: Hyper-connectivity will result in a connectivity culture in business and in our personal life.
- Participation: improved collaboration and knowledge/information sharing will foster a participating society.
- Social learning: Learning 3.0 (also called social learning), which incorporates social media, gaming, real-time feedback and simulation, would be used for teaching and learning purposes.
- Corporate social responsibilities: an increased cultural intelligence and a deeper appreciation of the relationship between business and society.
- The Millennial generation: This generation has grown up with hyper-connectivity and embracing it is an integral part of their life.

1.6.7 Technology-Enabled Trends

Bughin et al. (2010) present ten technology-enabled business trends executives need to understand and respond to:

- Wide adoption of distributed co-creation: organizations need to effectively use online communities to develop, market, and support products and services.
- Making the network the organization: networked organizations need to embrace open innovation and take full advantage of the opportunities of tapping into a world of talent" (i.e., accessing expertise within and outside the organization). They also need to break down silos in the organization and focus on the orchestration of the tasks rather than existing organizational structure and the ownership of workers.
- Deeper collaboration: organizations need to leverage the productivity of knowledge workers by having technologies such as video conferencing, shared workspaces, virtual teams, and virtual organizations.
- The growing Internet of Things: organizations need to utilizing the ability of capturing, computing, communicating, and collaborating information at large scale in real time provided by radio frequency identification tags, sensors and similar things embedded in the devices to improved capabilities of information collection and analysis and monitoring and responding.
- Using Big Data for experimenting and business intelligence: organizations need to effectively collect data from various sources (especially social data), analyze data, understand the implications of the results of data analysis, and use such information for improving operations, and enhancing business performance.
- Paying close attention to Green and Sustainable information systems: organizations need to actively work on reducing carbon emission from computing facilities (e.g., by adopting virtualization technologies to reduce the number of servers, using natural air for the cooling of data centers, using renewable energy (such as hydroelectric power, wind and solar energy) for powering data centers, only using environmental friendly components to build computing devices) and

using information systems for reducing environmental stress (e.g., via smart meters to better allocate energy usage, smart grids to improve the efficiency of transmission and distribution of energy, smart buildings to monitor and optimize energy uses, powerful analytic software to improve logistics and routing for planes, trains, trucks to reduce the carbon footprint of transportation).
- Wide adoption of the service model of paying only for what you use (as per usage): organizations (large and small) could actively pursue cloud computing and outsourcing options as a result of the global connectedness and the available technologies for effectively organizing, monitoring, measuring, customizing and billing for computing assets.
- The age of multisided business model (generating revenue from giving something free): organizations need to leverage on the network effects and learn to create value (e.g., revenue or insights on customers via large volume information collected) from large traffic and large customer base developed from free services.
- Creating opportunities from the bottom of the pyramid: organizations need to have the skills to identify and prosper from extreme market conditions e.g., customer demand for low prices, poor infrastructure, hard-to-access suppliers and low cost curve for talent) by developing technology-enabled solutions (e.g., deploying mobile payment systems for African countries in which Internet access is a luxury for many people; developing B2B online platforms like www.alibaba.com for buyers to source cheap products and services from low cost suppliers; virtual research and service teams by tapping into low cost talent in some developing countries).
- Using technology for government services and community support: technology-enabled solutions such as e-government, smart community, e-learning, e-health, e-police, smart water grids should be provided to the public, but it should be a joint effort of government agencies, communities, organizations and individuals.

It is further suggested that only understanding and adopting these technology-enabled trends is not sufficient, as organizations need to strategically work on their organizational culture and structure as well as management practices to meet these new demands. In addition, the significance and approach for fostering unfamiliar collaboration with non-traditional partners should be clearly communicated to all the parties involved.

1.6.8 The Robotic Age

Advanced technologies have been commoditizing work, and digitizing many routine, repetitive or dangerous tasks performed in the past by human beings. While we are debating issues such as (Hurst 2013): How much automation is it necessary? What is human? Why do we work? What does make us happy? Can robots develop metacognitive skills (including empathy, intuition, social intelligence, ability to think systematically, applied imagination, design thinking, and learning); robots can certainly be used to provide some assistance in certain areas. For example, given the issue of the aging population in many countries (especially in developed economies), more and more robots will be the companions of the elderly and will be used to assist in or perform certain surgeries and take care of patients by the regular checking and updating from doctors, specialists, and nurses connected via networks.

1.6.9 Digital Cities

By 2050 there will be 70 % of the global population residing in cities; digital cities could enable the government to deliver better city services for more people (Shehadi et al. 2014). Digital cities need to have five elements (Shehadi et al. 2014):

- End users including residents/visitors, government, and businesses.
- Access points including smart urban transport, digital signage, wearable devices, phones, tablets/e-readers, PCs, Kiosks, smart applications, and smart TVs.
- Digital services provided including Healthcare, Government, Education, Transport, Energy and Utilities, Public Safety and Security, Real Estate, and Media.
- Convergence (or a central integrated layer for coordinating data among multiple applications) including service delivery platform, integrated operation centers, content management, interconnected services/API, and cyber-security.
- Infrastructure including broadband devices, in-building solutions, building automation, main distribution frame, fixed communication (fiber/copper), mobile communications (WCDMA/WiMAX/Wi-Fi), private networks (IP networks/VoIP networks), and data centers.

1.6.10 Green Technologies

Green technologies are also an emerging trend. Do you know 'performing two Google searches can generate a similar amount of carbon dioxide as boiling the kettle for a cup of tea'? (Leake and Woods 2009). In 2007, IT accounted for all 1.4 % of global CO_2 emissions, with 34 % from servers (including cooling), 57 % from PCs and monitors, and 9 % from printers (Trepant et al. 2010). It is reported that U.S. firms spend close to US$6 billion on the power needed to run data centers and another US$3.5 billion to air-condition them (Trepant et al. 2008).

Trepant et al. (2008) suggest organizations (such as Google notably) have used alternative sources of energy (e.g., wind, hydraulic) to power their data centers and have adopted technologies (such as server virtualization) to efficiently utilize servers to achieve savings in energy and reduce carbon emissions. Consolidating data centers is another effective solution (Trepant et al. 2010). According to

Babcock (2010, p. 10), it is estimated Google could have 500,000–600,000 servers across its 12 international data centers; and Microsoft is building the largest data center on earth with 300,000 servers. Babcock also suggests energy could make up 20 % of the running cost of a data center (p. xiii). Other approaches organizations could adopt include: having an EIP (environmental impact planning) system to monitor the environmental impacts of their business activities, using power management software on PCs, and implementing advanced cooling systems (Trepant et al. 2008, 2010). Green technology (Eco-technology) solution/approach not only reduces the costs for the organization (i.e., reducing the environmental impact of computing devices), but also shifts IT from a cost player to a revenue player when more and more consumers are considering the environmental impact of the products they purchase. In addition, by applying green IT solutions to other sectors could help their CO_2 reduction efforts (e.g., reducing unnecessary travel by using telecommuting technologies, replacing brick-and-mortar shops with online stores, automating some routine tasks, smart building applications, fleet and traffic management systems, smart metering, smart billing, smart motor systems, E-services, and more accurate and timely decision making by Big Data capabilities), and it is estimated that the IT enabled reduction in CO_2 emissions will be five times greater than the CO_2 emissions of the entire ICT sector (Trepant et al. 2010).

1.6.11 Big Data, Cloud Computing, Social Business, and Mobile Business

Big Data, Cloud Computing, Social Business and Mobile Business have been adopted by many organizations, but they are still in the early development stage and it will take time to reach industry/sector-wide adoption and their applications have been going beyond consumer facing industries (e.g., financial services, marketing and advertising, retail) to other sectors (e.g., manufacturing, natural resources). More discussion for Big Data and Cloud Computing is found in Chap. 2 of this book, more discussion for Social Business is found in Chap. 7, and more discussion regarding Mobile Business is revealed in Chap. 10 of this book.

References

Babcock, C. (2010). *Management strategies for the cloud revolution: How could computing is transforming business and why you can't afford to be left behind.* New York: McGraw-Hill.

Bailey, T., Kaplan, J., & Weinberg, A. (2012, July). Playing war games to prepare for a cyberattack. *McKinsey Quarterly*, 1–6.

Bailey, T., Kaplan, J., & Rezek, C. (2014, June). Why senior leaders are the front line against cyberattacks. *Insights & Publications*. McKinsey & Company. Retrieved July 8, 2014, from http://www.mckinsey.com/insights/business_technology/why_senior_leaders_are_the_front_line_against_cyberattacks.

Bailey, T., Miglio, A. D., & Richter, W. (2014). The rising strategic risks of cyberattacks. *McKinsey Quarterly*, (2), *17–22.*

Baltzan, P. (2013). *Business driven technology* (5th ed.). New York: McGraw-Hill.

Beardsley, S., Enriquez, L., Grijpink. F., Sandoval, S., Spittaels, S., & Strandell-Jansson, M. (2014). Building trust: The role of regulation in unlocking the value of Big Data. In B. Bilbao-Osorio, S. Dutta & B. Lanvin (Eds.), *The global information technology report 2014: Rewards and risks of big data* (pp. 73–86). INSEAD & World Economic Forum.

Berman, S. J., & Bell, R. (2011). *Digital transformation: Creating new business models where digital meets physical* (pp. 1–17). IBM Global Business Service Executive Report, IBM Institute for Business Value.

Biggs, P., Johnson, T., Lozanova, Y., & Sundberg, N. (2012). Emerging issues for our hyper-connected world. In S. Dutta & B. Bilbao-Osorio (Eds.), *The global information technology report 2012: Living in a hyper-connected world* (pp. 47–56). INSEAD & World Economic Forum.

Bilbao-Osorio, B., Crotti, R., Dutta, S., & Lanvin, B. (2014). The networkded readiness index 2014: Benchmarking ICT uptake in a wold of Big Data. In B. Bilbao-Osorio, S. Dutta & B. Lanvin (Eds.), *The global information technology report 2014: Rewards and risks of big data* (pp. 3–34). INSEAD & World Economic Forum.

Bisson, P., Stephenson, E., & Patrick Viguerie, S. (2010, June). The global grid. *McKinsey Quarterly, 1–7.*

Bold, W., & Davidson, W. (2012). Mobile broadband: Redefining Internet access and empowering individuals. In S. Dutta & B. Bilbao-Osorio (Eds.), *The global information technology report 2012: Living in a hyper-connected world* (pp. 67–77). INSEAD & World Economic Forum.

Bughin, J., Chui, M., & Manyika, J. (2010, Summer). Ten tech-enabled business trends executives need to watch to succeed. *McKinsey on Business Technology*, (20), 4–17.

Bughin, J., & Manyika, J. (2013, July). Measuring the full impact of digital capital. *McKinsey Quarterly, 1–8.*

Brynjofsson, E., & McAfee, A. (2012). Winning the race with ever-smarter machines. *MIT Sloan Management Review, 53*(2), 53–60.

Caruana, A. (2014, March 7). Wearable Tech-Can your life by hacked. *Cso.com.au.* Retrieved 20, 2014, from http://www.cso.com.au/article/539954/wearable_tech_-_can_your_life_hacked_/.

Dean, D., Digrande, S., Field, D., Lundmark, A., O'Day, J., Pineda, J., & Zwillenberg, P. (2012). *The internet economy in the G-20: The $4.2 trillion growth opportunity.* The Boston Consulting Group.

Deloitte Consulting. (2012). *Tech Trends 2012: Elevate IT for digital business.* Retrieved December 10, 2013, from http://www.deloitte.com/assets/Dcom-UnitedStates/Local%20Assets/Documents/us_cons_techtrends2012_013112.pdf.

Dutta, S., Bilbao-Osorio, B., & Geiger, T. (2012). The networked readiness index 2012: Benchmarking ICT progress and impacts for the next decade. In S. Dutta & B. Bilbao-Osorio (Eds.), *The global information technology report 2012: Living in a hyper-connected world* (pp. 3–34). INSEAD & World Economic Forum.

El-Darwiche, B., Singh, M., & Genediwalla, S. (2012, Autumn). Digitization and Prosperity. *Strategy + Business,* (68), 1–10.

Elberse, A. (2008, July–August). Should you invest in the long tail. *Harvard Business Review*, 88–96.

EMC Corporation. (2014, April). Executive summary: Data growth, business opportunities, and the IT imperatives. *EMC/IDC Digital Universe Report 2014.* Retrieved May 10, 2014, from http://www.emc.com/leadership/digital-universe/2014iview/executive-summary.htm.

Enterprise Management Associates. (2012, March). The industrialization of fraud demands a dynamic intelligence-driven response. *Enterprise Management Associates White Paper*, 1–12.

Fredette, J., Marom, R., Setinert, K., & Witters, L. (2012). The promise and peril of hyperconnectivity for organizations and societies. In S. Dutta, & B. Bilbao-Osorio (Eds.), *The global information technology report 2012: Living in a hyper-connected world* (pp. 113–119). INSEAD & World Economic Forum.

Friedrich, R., El-Darwiche, B., Singh, M., & Koster, A. (2013a). Digitization for economic growth and job creation regional and industry perspective. *Perspective*, 1–17. Booz & Company.

Friedrich, R., Koster, A., Groene, F., & Maekelburger, B. (2013b). The 2012 industry digitization index. *Perspective*, 1–13. Booz & Company.

Gartner. (2014, April 10). Gartner says digital business will spot opportunities in a matter of seconds. Press Release. *Gartner.com*. Retrieved April 18, 2014, from http://www.gartner.com/newsroom/id/2705317.

Gustin, S. (2013, December 10). NSA spying scandal could cost U.S. Tech giants billions. Technology & Media. *Business.time.com*. Retrieved January 20, 2014, from http://business.time.com/2013/12/10/nsa-spying-scandal-could-cost-u-s-tech-giants-billions/.

Haag, S., Baltzan, P., & Phillips, A. (2008). *Business driven technology* (2nd ed.). Boston, USA: McGraw-Hill Irwin.

Hazan, E., Manyika, J., & Pelissie du Rausas, M. (2011, Autumn). Sizing the Internet's economic impact. *McKinsey on Business Technology*, (24), 18–21.

Haynes, P., & Nguyen, C. (2014). Re-balancing socioeconomics asymmetry in a data-driven economy. In B. Bilbao-Osorio, S. Dutta & B. Lanvin (Eds.), *The global information technology report 2014: Rewards and risks of big data* (pp. 67–72). INSEAD & World Economic Forum.

Heck, S., & Rogers, M. (2014). Are you ready for the resource revolution. *McKinsey Quarterly*, (2), 32–45.

Hurst, D. K. (2013, July 20). A robot ate my job. *Business Literature, Strategy + Business*. Retrieved December 12, 2013, from http://www.strategy-business.com/article/13305c?gko=9206c.

International Telecommunication Union (ITU). (2013, February). The World in 2013: ICT facts and figures. *International Telecommunication Union*, Switzerland. Retrieved April 6, 2014, from http://www.itu.int/en/ITU-D/Statistics/Documents/facts/ICTFactsFigures2013-e.pdf.

Kappelman, L., Luftman, J., McLean, E., & Johnson, V. (2013). Key issues of IT organizations and their leadership: The 2013 SIM IT trends study. *MIS Quarterly Executive, 12*(4), 227–240.

Kleiner, A. (2012, June 25). Brand transformation on the Internet. *Strategy + Business*. Retrieved July 20, 2012, from http://www.strategy-business.com/article/00117?pg=all).

Laseter, T., & Johnson, E. (2011, Winter). A better way to battle Malware. *Strategy + Business*, (65), 1–6.

Laudon, K. C., & Laudon, J. P. (2005). *Essentials of management information systems: Managing the digital firm* (6th ed.). Upper Saddle River: Prentice Hall.

Laudon, K. C., & Laudon, J. P. (2012). *Management information systems: Managing the digital firm* (12th ed.). Upper Saddle River: Prentice Hall.

Laudon, K. C., & Laudon, J. P. (2014). *Management information systems: Managing the digital firm* (13th ed.). Upper Saddle River: Prentice Hall.

Laudon, K. C., & Traver C. G. (2014). *E-commerce 2014: Business, technology, and society* (10th ed.). Upper Saddle River: Prentice Hall.

Leake, J., & Woods, R. (2009, January 13). Revealed: The environmental impact of Google searches. *Energy Bulletin*. Retrieved January 20, 2014, from http://www.resilience.org/stories/2009-01-13/google-footprint-jan-13.

Leggatt, H. (2014, April 9). Consumers do not want to be stalked in-store via smartphone. *Bizreport.com*. Retrieved May 8, 2014, from http://www.bizreport.com/2014/04/consumers-do-not-want-to-be-stalked-in-store-via-smartphone.html.

Lund, S., Manyika, J., Nyquist, S., Mendonca, L., & Ramaswamy, S. (2013). *Game changes: Five opportunities for US growth and renewal*. McKinsey Global Institute.

Mainardi, C. (2012). Forward. In S. Dutta & B. Bilbao-Osorio (Eds.), *The global information technology report 2012: Living in a hyper-connected world* (p. vii). INSEAD & World Economic Forum.

Manyika, J. (2008, September). Google's views on the future of business: An Interview with CEO Eric Schmidt. *McKinsey Quarterly*. Retrieved August 2, 2012, from https://www.mckinseyquarterly.com/Googles_view_on_the_future_of_business_An_interview_with_CEO_Eric_Schmidt_2229.

Manyika, J., Chui, M., Brown, B., Bughin, J., Dobbs, R., Roxburgh, C., et al. (2011). *Big data: The next frontier for innovation, competition, and productivity*. McKinsey Global Institute, McKinsey & Company.

Manyika, J., Cabral, A., Moodley, L., Moraje, S., Yeboah-Amankwah, S., Chui, M., et al. (2013, November). *Lions go digital: The internet's transformative potential in Africa* (pp. 1–112). McKinsey Global Institute, McKinsey & Company.

Manyika, J., Bughin, J., Lund, S., Nottebohm, O., Poulter, D., Jauch, S., & Ramaswamy, S. (2014). *Global flows in a digital age: How trade, finance, people, and data connect the world economy*. McKinsey Global Institute, McKinsey & Company.

Meeker, M. (2014, May). 2014 Internet Trends. *2014 CODE Conference Presentation*, Kleiner, Perkins, Caufield & Byers. Retrieved July 10, 2014, from http://www.kpcb.com/internet-trends.

Oxford Economics. (2014, August). *Global information security survey: Initial findings* (pp. 1–36).

Pepper, R., & Garrity, J. (2014). The Internet of everything: How the network unleases the benefits of Big Data. In B. Bilbao-Osorio, S. Dutta & B. Lanvin (Eds.), *The global information technology report 2014: Rewards and risks of big data* (pp. 35–42). INSEAD & World Economic Forum.

Rose, J., Barton, C., Souza, R., & Platt, J. (2013, November 6). The trust advantage: How to win with big data. *BCG Perspective*. Retrieved January 10, 2014, from https://www.bcgperspectives.com/content/articles/information_technology_strategy_consumer_products_trust_advantage_win_big_data/.

Sabbagh, K., El-Darwiche, B., Friedrich, R., & Singh, M. (2012a). Maximizing the impact of digitization. *Strategy*, 1–31.

Sabbagh, K., Friedrich, R., El-Darwiche, B., Singh, M., & Ganediwalla, S. (2012b). Maximizing the impact of digitization. In S. Dutta & B. Bilbao-Osorio (Eds.), *The global information technology report 2012: Living in a hyper-connected world* (pp. 113–119). INSEAD & World Economic Forum.

Shehadi, R. T., Acker, O., Karam, D., & Lee, K. K. (2014). Building next-generation sustainable cities: A road map for economic, social, and environmental sustainability. *Strategy*, 1–19.

Siegele L. (2012, January). Welcome to the yotta world. The World in 2012. *The Economist*, 122.

Spencer, B. (2013, February 11). Mobile users can't leave their phone alone for six minutes and check it up to 150 times a day. *Dailymail.co.uk*. Retrieved December 18, 2014, from http://www.dailymail.co.uk/news/article-2276752/Mobile-users-leave-phone-minutes-check-150-times-day.html.

Startupsmart.com.au. (2014, May 5). The more digital we are, the more vulnerable to attacks we become. *Startsmart.com.au*. Retrieved May 20, 2014, from http://www.startupsmart.com.au/planning/the-more-digital-we-are-the-more-vulnerable-to-attacks-we-become-csiro-report/2014050512221.html.

Strategy + Business (2013, June 28). Share the digital wealth. Business Literature. *Strategy-business.com*. Retrieved December 10, 2013, from http://www.strategy-business.com/article/ac00050?pg=all.

Trepant, H., Chow, G., & Baker, E. H. (2008, Winter). The eco IT solution. *Strategy + Business*, (53), 1–3.

Trepant, H., Shehadi, R., & Karam, D. (2010). Demystifying Green IT seeding advantage. *Perspective*, 1–9. Booz & Company.

Turban, E., King, D., Lee, J., Liang, T. P., & Turban, D. (2012). *Electronic commerce: A managerial and social networks perspective 2012* (International ed.). Upper Saddle River, NJ: Prentice Hall.

Turban, E., Lee, J. K., King, D., Liang, T. P., & Turban, D. (2010). *Electronic Commerce: A Managerial Perspective 2010* (International ed.). Upper Saddle River, USA: Prentice Hall.

Verizon. (2014). *2014 Data Breach Investigations Report*, 1–57.

Wagstaff, J. (2014, April 24). All at sea: Global shipping fleet exposed to hacking threat. *Reuters.com*. Retrieved May 10, 2014, from e.g., matching your credit card information and delivery address with the information on your driver's license or social security card.

Weill, P., & Woerner, S. L. (2013, October). The new digital divide: Emerging trump developed economies. *Research Briefing*, *XIII*(10), 1–4. MIT Sloan Center for Information Systems Research.

Westby, J. R. (2012). How boards & senior executives are managing cyber risks. *Governance of Enterprise Security: CyLab 2012 Report*, 1–28. Carnegie Mellon University CyLab.

Wikipedia.org. (2014, May 28). Federated Identity. *Wikipedia.org*. Retrieved July 28, 2014, from http://en.wikipedia.org/wiki/Federated_identity.

World Economic Forum. (2014). *Insight report: Global risks 2014* (9th ed., pp. 1–59).

World Trade Organization (WTO). (2013). *E-commerce in developing countries: Opportunities and challenges for small and medium-sized enterprises*. World Trade Organization, Switzerland. Retrieved April 7, 2014, from http://www.wto.org/english/res_e/booksp_e/ecom_brochure_e.pdf.

Chapter 2
Technology Foundation and Talent Management for Digital Enterprise

This chapter reviews technology infrastructure for digital enterprise, enterprise systems supporting digital enterprise, and measures and tools for addressing security and privacy issues associated with digital enterprise, then discusses emerging technologies of Big Data and Data Analytics, Cloud Computing, and The Internet of Things, and concludes with talent management for digital enterprise.

2.1 Digital Enterprise Technology Infrastructure

The subject area of digital enterprise (like any other specialist area) is riddled with terminology. Much of the terminology relates to the underlying technologies. It is important to understand that digital enterprise applications are built on top of a number of technologies and required infrastructure. The underlying technologies provide a layered, integrated infrastructure which enables digital enterprise/applications to be deployed. The layered structure means that each layer depends on the layer below and cannot function without the lower layers. Table 2.1 shows the digital enterprise infrastructure.

2.2 Enterprise Systems Supporting Business Processes

Many companies have moved from mainframe legacy systems, which focus on traditional business functions or only supporting the internal business processes, to integrated cross-functional enterprise applications, which emphasize accomplishing fundamental business processes in concert with customers, suppliers, partners, and employees. Integrated systems, such as enterprise resource planning systems, knowledge management systems, supply chain management systems, and customer relationship management systems, allow the same data (especially from a central database) to be used for multiple applications; information output from one function can easily become data input to another function. Many organizations view cross-

J. Xu, *Managing Digital Enterprise*, DOI 10.2991/978-94-6239-094-2_2

Table 2.1 Digital enterprise technology infrastructure

Basic technologies	Functions	Application examples
Digital enterprise applications	Support business processes of organizations (e.g., B2B, B2C, and intra-organizational communication) and activities of individuals (e.g., communication, networking, community building, knowledge sharing, online shopping, online selling, and online information search) as well as the government's functions	Digital platforms, electronic marketplaces, E-procurement applications, sales force automation applications, digital retailing, digital banking, digital publishing, digital learning, digital auctions, search engines, social networks, virtual communities, and digital government
Interfacing, sharing, integration and aggregation applications	Tie different services together and integrate with business partners' applications	Service oriented architecture (SOA), Web services, virtualization, grid computing, cloud computing, utility computing, software-as-a-service, mobile computing, social computing, semantic web, web science, middleware, enterprise architecture, and enterprise application integration (EAI)
Common business services applications	Provide services required for digital transactions and functions	Digital security, digital authentication, IP addresses (IPv6), storage repositories, digital payment systems, and smart cards
Transportation services technologies	Publish and distribute information in different formats (i.e., in text, audio, fax, video) on the digital networks	Hyper-text transfer protocol (HTTP), transmission control protocol/Internet protocol (TCP/IP), electronic Data interchange (EDI), E-mail, world wide web (WWW), hypertext markup language (HTML), java, natural language, extensible markup language (XML), HTML5, virtual reality modelling language (VRML), and open source standards
Telecommunication networks and data storage facilities	Connect different devices together and enable digital communication	The internet (copper cable or fiber optics), TV Networks, telephone networks, mobile networks (3G or 4G), electricity grids, smart grids, wireless networks (including balloons, drones, satellites, laser, open space, underwater, and cloud-based wireless

(continued)

Table 2.1 (continued)

Basic technologies	Functions	Application examples
		networks as well as wireless personal area networks (WPANs)), mesh networks, intranets, extranets, virtual private networks (VPNs), local area networks (LANs), wide area networks (WANs), and data centers and data farms

Source Adapted from Xu and Quaddus (2009, p. 27); the author's own knowledge

functional enterprise systems as a strategic way to use information technology/information systems to share information resources and improve the efficiency and effectiveness of business processes, thus helping attain their strategic objectives. Table 2.2 presents key enterprise/cross-functional information systems that enterprises (especially large enterprises) can put in place. Such systems typically include enterprise resources planning (ERP) systems, customer relationship management (CRM) systems, supply chain management (SCM) systems, and knowledge management (KM) systems. A major trend of enterprise/cross-functional information systems is the move (partially or wholly) to the cloud. On top of such concerns of limited functionality, the potential loss of internal control, performance reliability, and security, organizations also need to look at such factors as implementation size, solution complexity, capital costs, operating costs, total costs, and implementation time when they are embarking on cloud services (Utzig et al. 2013).

Table 2.2 Key enterprise/cross-functional information systems in the organization

Key enterprise systems	Purposes and emphasis of the systems
ERP systems	Enterprise resource planning (ERP) systems focus on improving the efficiency of a company's internal business processes, such as production, logistics and distribution, human resources, accounting and financial processes
CRM systems	Customer relationship management (CRM) systems mostly deal with understanding, acquiring, enhancing relationships with customers, and retaining customers
SCM systems	Supply chain management (SCM) systems primarily provide the enterprise with the solutions in optimising the efficiency of its supply chain (especially its procurement and sourcing activities) and enhancing its relationship with its suppliers
KM systems	Knowledge management (KM) systems (also called organizational memory/organizational learning systems) aim at organising, storing, sharing and applying existing knowledge within and outside the organisation and creating new knowledge for the organization. Even though KM systems could assist in managing both tacit and explicit knowledge, the emphasis really is on managing the tacit dimension of knowledge

Source Developed from O'Brien and Marakas (2011, p. 275); the author's own knowledge

2.2.1 Integration

When organizations are embarking on exciting opportunities and capabilities offered by various technologies and leveraging advantages from multiple channels (e.g., call centers, stores/branches, online operations, mobile applications, videos, fax machines, agents and third parties), one critical factor is integration. They need to appropriately integrate various applications/systems with their information systems infrastructure or/and existing applications/systems and unify different channels to share information across the organization. Technologies such as service-oriented architecture, which can create a unified business-service layer for channels and front-end processes to share (customer) information, could be useful in this regard and help win or retain customers. For example, if a customer called before walking into a store, and this information is not managed and shared across the organization and the multiple channels, then the opportunity of wining the customer could be gone (Wang 2010). One particular relevant point at the moment is to integrate personal mobile devices (e.g., smart phones, tablets) into the IS/IT infrastructure so the owners of those mobile devices could securely and smoothly access the required information and make use of corporate applications (Kleiner 2012).

The next generation of Internet standards such as HTLM5 will provide the access to all programs and applications via a web browser from any device anywhere anytime. HTML5 arguably is the most significant evolution yet in web standards, and it could locally store 1,000 times more data in browsers than they currently do (Korkmaz et al. 2011). It allows programs/applications to run through web browsers and communicate different multimedia content without requiring plug-in software and other workarounds.

2.3 Managing Security and Privacy Threats

To deal with various security challenges arising from the use of information technology and protect our information resources requires a variety of security tools and defensive measures and a coordinated security management program, including hardware, software, policies, and procedures. Some security measures and tools adopted by organizations include: Biometrics (e.g., Vein ID, finger prints, Iris Scan, face recognition, speech recognition), password, swipe card and other tools for physical access control, Malware and virus protection software/applications, Virtual private networks, Firewalls, Identity management and access control systems, Encryption (e.g., secure socket layer (SSL) protocol), Digital certificate, Digital signature, Tokenization and Key Management, Intrusion detection systems, Vulnerability scanning tools, Online access control, Security event correlation tool, Third-party Internet monitoring and analysis, Patch management tools, Network security protocols, Data backup, Data loss prevention systems (for monitoring data moving on the corporate network), Governance, risk and compliance (GRC) tools,

Information security plan, Regular security plan testing, Security plan compliance audit, Information systems control and audit, Risk Management and Cyber Risk Insurance, Security and Privacy risks committees, Mobile device management software, VoIP, Mobile, Social, and Cloud computing security policy, C-level positions (e.g., Chief Information Officer, Chief Security/Information Security Officer, Chief Privacy Officer, Chief Risk Officer, Chief Trust Officer), and locks/keys/physical security for computer hardware, (O'Brien and Marakas 2011, pp. 534, 538; Laudon and Laudon 2005, p. 542; Laseter and Johnson 2011; Westby 2012; Xu and Quaddus 2013, pp. 6–11; Oxford Economics 2013, pp. 18–22). Meanwhile, the larger the organization and the more sensitive of the information (i.e., information in certain government intelligence gathering agencies), the increased risk and costs of security breaches, the more comprehensive, systematic, integrated and sophisticated security (and privacy) measures need to be put into place. Westby (2012, p. 26) provides some recommendations for governing enterprise security management:

- Establishing a board Risk Committee for managing enterprise risks (including IT risks) and recruit directors with security, IT governance and cyber risk expertise.
- Ensuring privacy and security roles are separated and their responsibilities are appropriately assigned.
- Establishing a cross-organizational team and discuss privacy and security issues at least once every moth.
- Creating a culture of security and respect for privacy and view security and privacy as a corporate social responsibility.
- Ensuring the quality of security program by regularly reviews and taking into consideration of best practices and industry standards.
- Ensuring the security and privacy requirements to third parties and vendors.
- Conducting annual audit of enterprise security program by relevant committees and act on identified gaps.
- Requiring regular security and privacy reports for board and senior executives.
- Assessing cyber risks and potential loss valuations and reviewing adequacy of cyber insurance coverage.
- Allocating sufficient resources for security and privacy programs.

Haag et al. (2008, pp. 330–339) suggest organizations can implement information security lines of defense through people first and technology second. They point out that most information security breaches result from people misusing an organization's information either advertently or inadvertently. Their views are supported by Laseter and Johnson (2011), who believe that many of the security breaches are done by insiders. The first line of defense an organization should follow is to create an information security plan detailing the various information security policies. Steps to creating an information security plan include (Haag et al. 2008, p. 333):

1. Developing the information security policies.
2. Communicating the information security policies.

3. Identifying critical information assets and risks.
4. Testing and re-evaluating risks.
5. Obtaining stakeholder support.

Information systems should be periodically examined, or audited, by a company's internal auditing staff or external auditors from professional accounting firms. Such audits should review and evaluate whether proper and adequate security measures and management policies have been developed and implemented (Laudon and Laudon 2005, p. 542).

According to a recent global survey of 12,052 senior executives by PWC (reported in Oxford Economics 2013, p. 30), some of the greatest obstacles to improving the overall strategic effectiveness of an organization's information security function include (in order): insufficient capital expenditure, lack of an actionable vision or understanding of future challenges, lack of an effective information security strategy, absence or shortage of in-house technical expertise, lack of leadership, insufficient operating expenditures, and poorly integrated or overly complex information and IT systems.

Good digital enterprise security management must take into consideration technology solutions, organizational policies and procedures, and laws and industry standards. Furthermore given the fact that a large number of security breaches are committed by insiders, education, and prevention programs should be heavily emphasized even though technological solutions and monitoring and controlling measures could be useful. It should be clearly spelt out that people are the first defense line, and technology is the second defense line. In addition, an effective cyber-security risk analysis and management process should be put in place and such process should include such steps as: (1) identifying risks, (2) prioritizing top risks, (3) conducting risk assessment, (4) selecting risk management options, (5) developing risk management strategy, (6) designing crisis management strategy (for unpredicted events), (7) implementing the developed strategies, and (8) monitoring progress and updating strategies (World Economic Forum 2014a, p. 42). Cyber-security risk management also needs to be an integral part of enterprise-wide risk management and governance processes and be an integral part of people's life in the organization (e.g., the biggest security vulnerabilities often exist in people's everyday uses of email and the Internet) (Bailey et al. 2014).

On a related note, the above-mentioned technologies and approaches for managing security are effective in dealing with privacy concerns as well.

2.4 Big Data and Data Analytics

Gathering and analyzing large (or very large)-scale data is quickly becoming popular among organizations for reasons such as large volume data from multiple channels and various sources, the need to better understand customers better, and the tangible benefits of gaining competitive advantages by doing this (e.g., the success of the data initiatives of Amazon, Google) (Bughin et al. 2011). Big data can be defined as "data sets whose size is beyond the ability of typical database software tools to capture, store, manage and analyze" (Manyika et al. 2011, p. 1). Big data is different from the traditional concept of data in four perspectives (Dijcks 2012; Brown et al. 2011):

- Bigger volume: in 2010 enterprises and consumers stored 13 exabytes or 14 billion gigabytes) of new data on devices and the projected annual growth in global data generated is 40 % (just imaging the information produced by more than 4 billion mobile phones, by 30 million network sensor nodes, social networks. Do you know there are more than 30 billion piece of content (photos, notes, blogs, web links, and news stories) shared on Facebook every month and 2.9 billion hours of video are watched at Youtube every month?). It is estimated that there will be more than 50 billion connected devices in the world by 2020 (Dutta et al. 2012, p. 3). Have you imagined living in a yotta world (1,000 trillion gigabytes data in which your every move will be digitized and added to the data flow of the world)? (Siegele 2012). According to the latest EMC/IDC Digital Universe Report (reported in EMC Corporation 2014a), global digital data will reach 44 zettabytes (or 44 trillion gigabytes) in 2020 from 4.4 zettabytes in 2013. It is said more data were created between 2008 and 2011 than in all history before 2008 (Biggs et al. 2012, p. 48); and 90 % of the world's data was created in the last 2 years, and digital universe (including all digital data created, replicated, or consumed) has been growing by a factor of 30 from 2005 to 2020, doubling every 2 years. In the past, data storage was expensive and a lot of data have been thrown away (Pepper and Garrity 2014, p. 35). However the price of storage is dropping significantly, and by 2020, storing a petabyte data will only cost US$4 (Siegele 2012). According to Meeker (2014), global compute cost had been declining 33 % annually for the period of 1990–2013 and the cost of per 1 million transistors had decreased from US$527 in 1990 to US$0.05 in 2013; global storage cost had been declining 38 % annually for the period of 1990–2013 and the cost of per gigabytes had decreased from US$569 in 1990 to US$0.02 in 2013; global bandwidth cost had been declining 27 % annually for the period of 1990–2013 and the cost of per 1,000 Mbps had decreased from US$1,245 in 1990 to US$16 in 2013; and average global smart phone price had been declining 5 % annually for the period of 2008–2013 and the price had decreased from US$430 in 2008 to US$335 in 2013.
- Higher velocity: for example even at 140 characters per tweet, Twitter generated data volume is large than 8 terabytes per day as a result of high velocity or frequency. Do you know Youtube videos are uploaded 100 h/per min, Twitter delivers 500 million tweets per day, and Facebook has 150 billion friend connections (World Economic Forum 2014b, p. 9). And it is reported that 90 % of the world's data are generated in the last 2 years (Conway 2012).
- More data variety (including traditional and non-traditional data and structured and unstructured data (i.e., social media data)): it is estimated that 95 % of the world data is unstructured data, which makes big data more meaningful and

challenging (Oracle 2012). In the future, 80 % of enterprise data (from both traditional and non-traditional sources) will be unstructured (SAP AG 2012).
- Higher economic value: huge financial gains can be realized via Big Data and more powerful and accurate decision-making and thus significantly improving business operations and organizational performance.

Big Data could exist in various formats (including video, image, audio, text/numbers), and include various types of data, including traditional enterprise data (e.g., customer, transaction, operation information), machine-generated/sensor data (e.g., call details records, weblogs, information from smart meters and smart devices, manufacturing sensors, network sensors, cameras and CCTVs, bar codes, embedded devices, equipment logs), and social data (e.g., information from blogs including micro-blogging sites such as Twitter, social networks). Start-up firms like Lexalytics and Klout have been established to understand social data (Dijcks 2012). We are in the Big Data era for reasons such as the cheaper and cheaper data devices (for example, for a few hundred dollars, you can buy a disk that can store all of the world's music (Brown et al. 2011)), the wide adoption of mobile phones and other mobile devices, and the great connectedness as a result of the availability of extensive networks across the globe.

Big Data could create value for organizations in several ways (Manyika et al. 2011, pp. 5–6): (1) creating transparency and improving efficiency via easier access to more data across the organization; (2) improving productivity and organizational performance through quicker, deeper and more accurate discovery, prediction and analysis; (3) better segmentation with more tailored customization actions; (4) better (automation) support in decision making; (5) enhancing existing products and services and creating new ones through better understanding customers' needs and stronger capabilities in identifying opportunities for new products and services; and (6) becoming a key basis of competition and growth through the use of Big Data for organizations as well as (7) better pricing strategies (for example, it has been suggested that on average, a 1 % price increase could translate into an 8.7 % increase in operating profits) (Baker 2014). Meanwhile, Professor Tom Davenport (reported in Baker 2014) has suggested that developing new products and services from Big Data is the most interesting and valuable initiative for organizations. Specifically Big Data could bring huge financial value to various sectors, for example (Brown et al. 2011; Manyika et al. 2011, p. 8; Plansky et al. 2013; Lund et al. 2013, p. 12):

- US$300 billion value per year to US health care sector.
- More than 60 % increase in net margin to US retail sector.
- EUR€250 billion value per year to Europe public sector administration.
- Up to 50 % decrease in product development and assembly costs to manufacturing sector.
- US$100 billion and US$700 billion value for service providers and end users in the sector of global personal location data.

- US$175 billion revenue from commercializing data in 2013 and up to US$300 billion in the next 3–5 years across financial areas of capital markets, commercial banking, consumer finance and banking, and insurance.
- Up to US$325 billion annual GDP increase in retail and manufacturing sectors and up to US$285 billion productivity gains in health care and government services by 2020 in the U.S.
- Huge benefits to sports industry?!: Have you watched the popular movie Moneyball? (Stafford 2012; Lohr 2012).

In 2012, the U.S. had one third of the world's data (followed by Western Europe (19 %), China (14 %), and India (4 %)), and it has been leading the development of Big Data (Lund et al. 2013, pp. 11–12). Some notable examples of using Big Data for competitive advantages include: Google, Amazon, Apple, Zipcar, and Netflix. Hagström and Gill (2012, p. 102) point out that the combination of hyper-connectivity, Big Data, and powerful analytics, has enhanced organizational ability to know, dialogue, and innovate.

Meanwhile some techniques for analyzing Big Data include: A/B testing, Association rule learning, Classification, Cluster analysis, Crowdsourcing, Data fusion and data integration, Data mining, Ensemble learning, Genetic algorithms, Machine learning, Natural language processing, Neural networks, Network analysis, Optimization, Pattern recognition, Predictive modelling, Regression, Sentiment analysis, Signal processing, Spatial analysis, Supervised learning and unsupervised learning, Simulation, Time series analysis, Visualization, and many others (Manyika et al. 2011, pp. 27–31). Some technologies and applications for Big Data are: Big table, Data warehouse, Cassandra, Cloud computing, Distribute system, Dynamo, Google file system, HBasem, Hadpoop, MapReduce, Metadata, Stream processing, Visualization, and many others (Manyika et al. 2011, pp. 31–33).

On top of the required techniques and technologies and talent to take advantage of the potential Big Data, organizations also need to (1) put in appropriate data policies in place (especially addressing data sourcing, accessing and disseminating issues and critical but complex (as a result of the size and the sources of data) data security and privacy issues); (2) make necessary organizational adjustments (including structural and cultural changes, end user education); and (3) ensure top management's skills and support for Big Data use in the organization. Meanwhile the data quality is one of the most critical factors (if not the most critical factor) for using Big Data for decision making; in order to avoid the problem of "Garbage in and Garbage out", organizations need to work hard on the sources of the data (sources/data partners must be reliable) and on the acquisition/collection of data (e.g., right questions and research design; good understanding of data constraints; and ensuring real-time or timely data) (Chui and Fleming 2011). Meanwhile to maximize the value of Big Data, Organizations should let the business case guide the data analytics and minimize the cost of Big Data by targeting analyses generating tangible business results (Lund et al. 2013, p. 87). Another two critical areas associated with Big Data are having a culture that supports analytics and data-driven business making (including such things as (1) analytics are valued,

(2) creativity and innovation are valued, and (3) people are willing to work together and share in the organization) and putting data governance (especially focusing on privacy, security and compliance issues) into place (Halper 2014). Organizations also need to be effective in articulating Big Data and data analytics (e.g., having more effective measures, telling success stories better) (Vesset and Morris 2013). In addition, much of the data collected is unstructured in nature and is difficult to analyze, so the ability of effectively dealing with some unique dimensions of unstructured data have to be developed. For example, how can computers interpret our feelings, attitude and intentions in our messages? or how can computers deal with the tacit dimension of the knowledge sitting in our brain?); and the capabilities of continuous and high-speed decision making need to be developed as well as a result of the sheer speed of the flow of data (Baker 2014).

However while the huge potential and benefits are recognized, its role and influence should not be overstated. It should be remembered that human beings are decision-makers, and the machine or data is viewed as the basis upon which better decisions are made. Big Data could make our decision making process more scientific (Lohr 2012), but the role of our experience and intuition, which is impossible (or extremely hard) for the machine to emulate and acquire, should never be diminished. On a related note, we need to be aware that while we are talking about Big Data at the moment, we mostly refer to the data collected digitally via different channels and various devices (e.g., wired and wireless networks, mobile devices, desktop PCs, sensors, cameras, machines and equipment). However such digitally collected data could not provide all the required information to the organization (for example, some observational (or broadly speaking qualitative) research/data could not be collected and interpreted in a digital way); and Big Data approach may not be suitable or available to some organizations (for example, firms in some emerging markets where access to abundant information is very limited resulting from poor technology infrastructure and other factors; and similarly firms in some specified industries, firms working in relatively sparse data environments, firms with no resources for expensive data acquisition, hardware, and software or technology infrastructure, could have limited access to Big Data) (Meer 2014). With the right process and mind-set, firms with either Little Data or Big Data, could take advantage of available data (virtually all sources of information available to the organization) to make better decision, improve products, and enhance customer experience; meanwhile some areas they need to look at include: (1) demonstrating the commitment to become more fact-based in the decision-making, (2) having the willingness to learn by doing (i.e., doing some qualitative studies, using trials and errors, conducting pilot studies before larger scale data collection and data analytics), and (3) being creative (e.g., quick iPad-assisted customer surveys in the store by retailers, asking more target and specified questions in the online registration forms, leveraging the data collected in call centers, adopting user panels of savvy customers for ideas, and using sales representatives in the field to collect market intelligence) (Meer 2014). Another related question organizations need to ask is whether real-time data, which could be very expensive, is really necessary? For many organizations the answer could be not so, and for them aggregating, organizing (i.e., giving structure to unstructured data), and analyzing data in a more leisurely approach via utilizing their existing infrastructure is a more practical way to go (Goodwin 2014b).

Furthermore, according to a recent research with some large Fortune companies by Wixom and Beath (2014), obstacles for firms to realize expected value from their data initiatives include: lack of common data platform and missing or broken business processes to support the common data platform, lack of user engagement, and lack of leadership or commitment for required change; and their suggestions for addressing these identified barriers are: having user-centric development (i.e., actively engaging users to develop tools and services), developing hybrids on staff (i.e., proactively nurturing business-savvy IT people and IT-savvy business people), and marketing internally (i.e., aggressively marketing and selling the value of data).

The Boston Consulting Group (reported in Argawal et al. 2014) proposes a framework for enabling Big Data in the organization, which looks at building up six capabilities:

- Identifying opportunities via creating a culture of innovation and experimentation (e.g., encouraging non-traditional ideas, fostering collaboration between data and business experts, adopting a test-and-learn approach).
- Building trust among consumers to enable broad use of their data (e.g., clearly communicating how data is used, providing choices and control, articulating the benefits of the data use).
- Developing technical platform and leveraging flexible, scalable, and efficient data systems (e.g., adopting a scalable and multipurpose data platform, utilizing/making most of the existing infrastructure, adjusting operational processes to leverage insights quickly).
- Shaping organization and developing capabilities to implement and take advantage of relevant data applications (e.g., establishing a Big Data Center of Excellence, gaining senior management's support/sponsorship, effectively managing data talent and skills).
- Participating in a Big Data ecosystem and identifying strategic partners that can help unlock new economic opportunities (e.g., understanding the opportunities for the organization in the ecosystem, identifying strategic partners, starting small but scaling quickly).
- Relationship building and having an open culture to support collaborating and sharing (e.g., having strong capabilities of managing partners, ensuring seamless integration, working on win-win arrangements and contracts).

2.4.1 *Data-Led Transformation*

Data-lead transformation involves monetizing data assets, integrating outside data with internal information, and developing data analytics to (Plansky et al. 2013):

- Leveraging enhanced data for core business (e.g., exploring new opportunities to enhance existing services through new data sources, developing new data platforms, delivering enhanced services).
- Generating new insights (e.g., having more and better understanding of customers, improving ROI of marketing efforts).
- Entering adjacent businesses (e.g., monetizing existing analytics capabilities, commercializing infrastructure to sell platforms as a service, partnering with adjacent players across the business value chain, identifying and monetizing new data sources).
- Developing new products and services (e.g., creating new sets of analytics and data products and services).

Some key design principles and required capacities for implementing data transformation strategy include (Plansky et al. 2013):

- Understanding your customers and investing in continuous improvement of addressing their needs.
- Having good understanding of your data and systematically organizing your data (e.g., cataloguing and mapping available data).
- Exploring the opportunities of the whole value chain of the organization and developing new opportunities from the data ecosystems and from the partnerships with relevant stakeholders.
- Sizing the value of opportunities of commercializing data and working on the scale, efficiency, and effectiveness of data initiatives.
- Enhancing the organization's IS/IT infrastructure and building a sophisticated, transparent, and flexible data infrastructure to unlock or maximize the value of its data.

El-Darwiche et al. (2014, pp. 46–48) present a Big Data Maturity model, which includes four stages:

- Stage 1 Performance management (e.g., looking at what can be read from the data by applying such tools as financial reporting, regulatory/compliance reporting, dashboards for management reporting, and performance measurement via key performance indicators/metrics).
- Stage 2 Functional area excellence (e.g., looking at what can be learned from the data to become better by applying such approaches and tools as smart pricing, targeted mailings, customer segmentation, customer value analysis, choice analysis, website clickstream analysis, loyalty schemes, customer satisfaction measures, supply chain balancing, facility optimization, fraud monitoring/prevention, traffic optimization, crime monitoring, patient treatment control, route optimization for fleet, and optimization of staff utilization).
- Stage 3 Value proposition enhancement (e.g., looking at how data can become a value driver of the business by applying such approaches and services as providing real-time targeted advertising and customized recommendations, providing personalized customer experience and services, providing online

telematics services, and using Big Data for preventative health monitoring and disease detection).
- Stage 4 Business model transformation (e.g., looking at how data can be used to fundamentally reinvent the business by applying such approaches as generating new revenue by selling data, having data-centric business models, quantitatively managing investment funds, and using crowdsourcing to augment internal data).

Meanwhile, in order to successfully execute the Big Data Maturity model, some key required internal capabilities are (El-Darwiche et al. 2014, pp. 49–50):

- Developing a clear Big Data strategy.
- Proving the value of data in pilot schemes.
- Identifying the owner for Big Data in the organization and appointed formal senior position (e.g., Chief Data Officer, Chief Data Scientist).
- Recruiting, training, and retaining data talent.
- Making Big Data an integral part of the operation of the organization.
- Establishing data-driven decision culture and proactively promoting such culture.

Governments have to take Big Data seriously. They need to work on a regulatory framework for data privacy (e.g., looking at such areas as the limitation of personal data collection, the specification of the purpose of the data collection, the protection of collected data, the prevention of data loss or unauthorized access, and the right of individuals to obtain information about collected data), deploy required ICT infrastructure, provide education/training, address public perception and awareness, and develop Big Data ecosystem (El-Darwiche et al. 2014, pp. 48–50).

2.5 Cloud Computing

Cloud computing basically is renting computing resources (including software, networks, servers, storage, processing, operation systems, applications, services) as per usage on the networks (especially the Internet), and it can deploy in the models of private cloud (solely for one firm and could be managed by the organization or a third party on its premise or off its premise), public cloud (is made to the general public or a large industry group and is owned by an organization selling cloud services), and hybrid cloud (the combination of private and public clouds) (Compuware Corporation 2010; Trend Micro 2010). By adopting cloud-computing, organizations could (1) better utilize there IS/IT investments; (2) have better flexibility, quicker responses to changes, enhanced ability for information systems to scale up, better ability of disaster recovery and business continuity; and (3) focus on their core business (especially for small and medium firms). One good example (reported in Roberts et al. 2010) is that by using Amazon's cloud computing facilities, The New York Times digitalized and catalogued more than 100 years of archived articles for its web in a 24-h period, avoiding the need to configure and run a set of servers for a onetime effort. In line with the rapid progress and huge potential of Cloud computing, major ICT firms have committed significant resources to cloud computing developments.

Some typical technologies associated with cloud computing include virtualization and service-oriented architecture. It could be argued that the approach of clouding computing is not really new (i.e., thinking about the example of mainframe computer to individual users of it). The difference is between sharing computing resources on the networks [there are more than 50 million servers and most of them operates only at 15 % of capacity (Intel Corporation 2011; Harvard Business Review 2010)] and sharing the main-frame computer. Some characteristics of cloud computing consist of: (1) on-demand self-service (for example, required computing resources could be run automatically without human interaction once the parameter and instruction are set); (2) broad network access (for example, cloud services can be accessed by various devices such as mobile devices, personal computers, laptops); (3) resource pooling (the provider's computing resources are pooled to serve multiple clients simultaneously by using a multi-tenant model); (4) rapid elasticity (the ability of quickly scaling out and scaling in according to the changes in demand); and (5) measured service (adopting metering capability for transparency in monitoring, controlling and reporting) (Compuware Corporation 2010).

Cloud service models include (Trend Micro 2010; Intel Corporation 2011; Compuware Corporation 2010):

- Cloud Software as a Service (SaaS): providing the customer with the capability to use the provider's applications sitting on a cloud infrastructure. Examples of SaaS include Google's Gmail system and Microsoft's Office 365.
- Cloud Platform as a Service (PaaS): providing the customer with the capability to deploy applications on the cloud platform using programming languages and tools supported by the cloud provider, who has full control of the cloud infrastructure. Examples include Microsoft's Windows Azure and Google App engine.
- Cloud Infrastructure as a Service (IaaS): the customer has the ability to access processing, storage, networks and other fundamental computing resources and run arbitrary software such as operating systems and applications. But such computing resources controlled by the customer are typically for securing their own virtual machines and applications and data residing on them, the cloud provider still controls the underlying cloud infrastructure. Examples include Amazon EC2 and vCloud.

Meanwhile some major concerns of cloud computing are: security, privacy, availability and performance (Trend Micro 2010; Compuware Corporation 2010; Intel Corporation 2011). Security and privacy issues are very critical and typical for cloud computing since you have put your critical information/data in other people's properties and you have no good idea and have no effective control regarding what is going to happen to your data/information. Furthermore issues such as multi-tenancy (you are completely unaware of your neighbor's identity, security profile or intention), data access control and protection (the cloud provider could easily move around your data for their purposes), data romance (there is no clear standard on how the cloud provider should recycle memory and disk space. So it is likely the next user of your ex-rented cloud computing resources could have your critical and confidential data), and data privacy issues (for example, data losses/leakage and breaches are top security concerns of cloud computing, especially for public cloud), further highlight the need for effective security management of information/data in the cloud.

Organizations need to put effective security management process and tools (e.g., encryption, control, and auditing) in place to protect the information in the cloud. Availability and performance issues are logical concerns when you are relying on other people's services. At the moment, even you host applications/systems in your organization, the availability is around 99 % since the networks are controlled by the telecoms who cannot guarantee 100 % availability, and while you put your applications/systems with the cloud service provider, the availability may become 99 % × 99 % × 99 %... since problems may come from each part of the cloud chain. One effective way to deal with such issues is to sign a service level agreement (SLA) with a cloud service provider. Another concern is the hidden costs in the cloud, and organizations need to pay close to attention to data transfer charges, which could increase dramatically once required cloud service and computing power grow to a certain level (Harvard Business Review 2010). Some other concerns include the need for adapting business processes to cloud applications, addressing the issues of integration and interoperability, establishing technology governance processes for cloud applications, and developing the required skills for managing cloud applications (Roberts and Sikes 2011).

2.6 The Internet of Things

The Internet of Things refer to objects embedded with sensors and actuators and linked with wired and wireless networks (Chui et al. 2010), and they can viewed as a part of the Big Data discussed previously in this chapter. They have the ability to sense the environment and deliver large volume of data through networks. According to Bisson et al. (2010), there are more than 35 billion Internet Things. And the number is growing very quickly. The Internet of Things could include cameras, sensors, routers, manufacturing equipment, traffic lights, rail cars, escalators, weather stations, vehicles, and others. Unlike end-user devices (e.g., desktop PCs, laptops, smart phones, tablets), connected devices are used for real-time monitoring, control, and integration (Sadauskas 2014).

The Internet of Things could assist organizations' efforts in various areas (Chui et al. 2010; EMC Corporation 2014b):

- Creating new business models and revenue streams: providing new value-added products and service to customers and addressing their heads in more efficient and innovative ways, identifying new business opportunities and revenue sources.

- Establishing better global visibility and therefore better global business: making it easier for enterprises to track effectiveness and efficiency of their global operations and supply chains and understanding their global customers.
- Tracking behavior: monitoring the behavior of persons, things, or data through space and time (e.g., targeted advertising based on the location of the users of smart phones; real-time information of movement of packages from the warehouse to end user).
- Having enhanced situational awareness and real-time information: realizing real-time and accurate information of physical environment (e.g., utilizing sensor networks that combine video, audio and vibration detectors to identify unauthorized individuals and crime suspects), and improving operational efficiency and enhancing customer loyalty by capturing and responding to real-time information.
- Supporting decision making via sensor-driven business analytics: supporting long-range and more complex planning and decision making (e.g., remote monitoring and controlling oil and gas operations; remote monitoring and controlling medical procedures).
- Optimizing resource consumption and management: monitoring and controlling resource consumption across network (e.g., managing consumption (and pricing) of water, electricity and energy via networked sensors and automatic feedback mechanism).
- Improving operations and processes: automation of processes by having much better information granularity (e.g., automation of chemical plants by utilizing sensors and actuators along the production lines), enabling organizations to capably make dynamic decisions on pricing, logistics, sales, and support deployment.
- Enhanced ability (especially in open environments with great uncertainty): rapid and real-time sensing and response systems (e.g., sensors in the two cars could detect and avoid potential collision between them).

The Internet of Things could contribute greatly to the economy. For example, the Internet of Things could contribute to Australia's GDP by US$6.5 billion over 4 years (Sadauskas 2014). On a different note, while there are extremely large amounts of data being collected via The Internet of Things, it is reported that only one half of 1 % of the collected data gets analyzed in any way at all, and it is argued that knowing how to analyze and use the collected data (whether a small or large amount) to make better decision is the key skill required (Baker 2014).

2.7 Talent Management for Digital Enterprise

We are in the digital economy in which digitization is an essential part of the way we live, work and conduct the business. In line with the potential opportunities and the rapid development of digitization, many organizations have set up designated positions for leading their digitization initiatives (even though their roles and responsibilities could vary based on the industry and the organization and even the location), such as Chief Digital Officer, Starbucks.; Digital Prophet, AOL; Head of Strategy & Programs for Digital Innovation, Philips; EVP, Digital Strategy & Emerging Business, Discovery Communications; VP, Digital Banking Strategy, Wells Fargo; EVP, Digital Media, BET Networks; VP, Digital Strategy, BAE Systems; VP, Digital Marketing & Media, GSN; Director, Digital Marketing & Communication, PBS; VP, Innovation, Deutsche Telelkom; VP, Digital, Technology R & D, UFC; VP, Digital Strategy, Dell; CTO, Digital Operations, Education Week; VP, Audience Insights, TiVO; Director, Digital Strategy, Rodale Grow; Director, Online Strategy & Media, The Story Stuff Project; Global Head of Social Media, Bloomberg; among many others.

In association with the Big Data phenomenon, there is a shortage of people who have the required skills to deal with Big Data. For example, it is reported the U.S. alone faces a shortage of 140,000–190,000 people with deep analytical skills and 1.5 million data-savvy (being able to analyze Big Data and make decisions from Big Data) managers which are equivalent to 50–60 % gap in supply of required talent (Manyika et al. 2011, p. 3; Brown et al. 2011). It can be assumed in the future titles/positions such as "data strategist", "data scientist", "chief data officer", "data expert", "data specialist", "data technology officer/expert/specialist", "business intelligence specialist", and similar titles, will become common terms for organizations. A more general term of "digital workforce" (Chui and Fleming 2011) has been suggested in recent years, and it includes people with different skills (from programming, computing modelling simulation, data analysis to analytical thinking and many others) for the current digital economy (also called knowledge economy). In addition, for knowledge workers (coined by Peter Drucker) such skills as organizing, accessing, processing, visualizing, understanding, analyzing and extracting the value from (large volume) information available in the organization are essential for doing their tasks effectively in the twenty first century (Manyika 2009). On a related note, according to a recent report by career website www.Careercast.com (reported in Kensign 2014), a Mathematician is the best job of 2014 in the U.S. While mathematics is the important foundation for many disciplines, the phenomenon of Big Data has further enhanced its importance (at least to some extent). Meanwhile, the results of a 2014 McKinsey Global Survey of 850 C-level executives from various industries (reported in Josh and Willmott 2014) suggest that on top of the very much needed data and analytics talent, other digital expertise required by organizations include (in order): mobile or online development, project/program management, cloud and distributing computing, joint business and IT expertise, enterprise application architecture, cybersecurity, agile development, partner and vendor management, and data architecture.

Another critical dimension is recruiting, training and retaining good staff with digital expertise and skills. Agarwal et al. (2006) suggest that in order to retain good IS/IT staff, organizations need to work on such areas as: work environment, career development, community-building initiatives, money incentives and employment incentives. For many people, achievement (e.g., making bigger impact on more people) is the most important motivator for them at work. The results of a recent survey by www.SmartCompany.com.au (reported in Ash 2014) prove this notion and indicate that the motivators for people at work include (in the order): achievement (70.8 % of the participants), money (64.7 %), creative output (41.2 %), great team (29.4 %), retirement (23.5 %), and status (11.8 %). One emerging trend is to hire and develop digital workforces, who have the skills to access, organize, understand, analyze, communication, and utilize the large volume of data for decision-making and for creation of new ideas (Chui and Fleming 2011; Manyika 2009). Having a digital talent management strategy in place is crucial for the success of the digital enterprise. One good example is comScore, a leading Internet analytics firm with a 1,200 global workforce possessing varying levels of skills and responsibilities of data analytics (reported in Wixom et al. 2013). comScore's strategy involves: investing significant time and resources in supporting and collaborating with universities (especially in the areas of business and IT where future talent can be sought), providing additional in-house data analytics training for new university hires, establishing groups across the company to foster a broad analytics savvy workforce, co-locating teams that need to communicate regularly, and adopting matrix organizational structures to bring together people with diverse skillsets. In addition to the traditional approach of recruiting university graduates, some organizations have taken a step further and started working on their digital talent pipeline from the school. For example, Deloitte now hires talent directly from schools and help students receive a university degree (reported in Goodwin 2014a). Organizations need to work on provide employees with multiple ways of acquiring skills (e.g., on the job training, company-wide formal training, observing others, attending own training outside of the work, information leaning such as reading articles and books, watching videos, and speaking with colleagues) and with different training strategies (e.g., mobile delivery of training, social media tools for training, massive open online courses (MOOCs), and gamification of training) (Accenture 2013).

Meanwhile, in line with the rapid development of computing technologies, the wide penetration of the Internet, and the large scale adoption of digitization by individuals, businesses, communities, governments, the demand for digital skills and talent will be no doubt increasing dramatically, and well as the need for more IS/IT skills and talent. The shortage of IS/IT skills and talent has not been commonly recognized, which could be a major hindering factor for future developments. The recent survey of 3,169 respondents from 105 countries by IDG Connect (2011) has highlighted this concern, and most of the participants of the survey indicated there is a lack of senior technical skills in the market. The survey also asked the respondents' opinions for IS/IT employment problems in their area. Some reasons identified from the survey include:

- Economy uncertainty: in bad times, hiring is always slow.
- Poor training: the results of the survey indicate IS/IT training issue is more of an issue for participants from developing countries in Asia, Middle East, Africa, and South America. In fact, many universities and colleges around the world

that used to offer information systems training programs downsized or even closed down their IS/IT faculties/departments after 2000.

- IS/IT talent brain-drain issues: the survey results indicate it is a major issue (more than 50 % participants believed) for Africans, South Americans and Asians. It has been an on-going issue for developing countries. Their best information systems talent prefer to go overseas for better pay and/or working conditions. But in recent years, to some extent, it has changed. For example, many information systems talents in China now would stay in China as a result of rapidly rising pay and many more opportunities in China.
- The challenge of updating skills constantly as a result of a very changing information systems industry: this issue is really making people in Asia think twice when they are planning to embark on IS/IT careers. In additional, the need for soft skills (e.g., interpersonal and communication skills, project management skills, language skills) was also pointed out by some respondents. This is so true. In addition, the challenge of updating skills constantly coupled with factors such as poor IS/IT training and IS/IT brain drain could lead to the identified shortage of senior technical skills.
- Generation Y work ethics: the majority of respondents across all regions agree that Generation Y IS/IT professionals (at the entry level) have different work ethics to older generations.

Another concern associated with IS/IT skills and talent management is the lack of soft skills among IS/IT people who highly (if not overly) enjoy their technical skills. But IS/IT people don't work alone in the organization, and they are there to work with the business side of the organization and are an integral part of the organization. Organizations should equip IS/IT people with such skills as effective working habits, better emotional intelligence and enhanced skills of persuading and influencing people to make them more communication-minded. In addition to the organization's capabilities of managing the required digital talents, the country differences also play an important role in attracting and retaining talents. Generally speaking, high-income countries are doing better than low-income countries. For example, according to INSEAD Global Talent Competitive Index (reported in Evans et al. 2013), the top 20 most talent competitive countries are (in order): Switzerland, Singapore, Denmark, Sweden, Luxemboug, Netherlands, United Kingdom, Finland, United States, Iceland, Canada, Norway, Belgium, Australia, Germany, New Zealand, Ireland, United Arabs Emirates, and France. Meanwhile according to a recent survey of talent challenges in emerging markets by Sylvia Ann Hewlett Associates and Booz and Company (reported in Divakaran et al. 2012), the lack of skilled employees along with rapidly rising salary expectations are constraining firms' ability to operate and expand in emerging markets (especially in BRIC countries of Brazil, Russia, India, and China). In responding to such challenges, Booz and Company (reported in Divakaran et al. 2012) provides some good suggestions:

- Being innovative in talent sourcing (e.g., building talent pipeline through university partnerships; partnering with outsourcing service providers; tapping non-traditional talent sources (such as crowdsourcing)).
- Cultivating a GLOCAL (global plus local) culture (e.g., investing in strong global brand; tailoring the employee value proposition for the local culture; and embracing local norms, behaviors, mind-sets, and commitments).
- Investing in global talent competencies (e.g., adopting a global career model, recruiting people who have the experience and willingness to work globally; implementing global training and development; developing a global knowledge management system).

Meanwhile in recent years, some firms have adopted the strategy of "acqui-hiring" (i.e., acquiring a firm mainly for its talents and skills rather than their products) (Brown et al. 2013).

References

Accenture. (2013). *Accenture 2013 Skills and Employment Trends Survey: Perspectives on Training-Key Findings*. Retrieved May 6, 2014, from http://www.accenture.com/SiteCollectionDocuments/PDF/Accenture-2013-Skills-And-Employment-Trends-Survey-Perspectives-On-Training.pdf.

Agarwal, R., Brown, C. V., Ferratt, T. W., & Moore, J. E. (2006). Five mindsets for retaining IT staff. *MIS Quarterly Executive, 5*(3), 137–150.

Argawal, R., Baltassis, E., Brock, J., & Platt, J. (2014, May). *Enabling big data: Building the capabilities that really matters* (pp. 1–13). New York: The Boston Consulting Group.

Ash, E. (2014, May 06). What do you work for, *SmartCompany.com.au*. Retrieved May 9, 2014, from http://www.smartcompany.com.au/people/41812-what-do-you-work-for.html.

Bailey, T., Miglio, A. D., & Richter, W. (2014). The rising strategic risks of cyberattacks. *McKinsey Quarterly, 2*(2014), 17–22.

Baker, E. (2014, March 31). Look outward with big data: A Q&A with Tom Davenport, *Strategy + Business*. Retrieved May 8, 2014, from http://www.strategy-business.com/article/00245?pg=all.

Biggs, P., Johnson, T., Lozanova, Y., & Sundberg, N. (2012). Emerging issues for our hyper-connected world. In S. Dutta & B. Bilbao-Osorio (Eds.), *The global information technology report 2012: Living in a hyper-connected world* (pp. 47–56). INSEAD & World Economic Forum.

Bisson, P., Stephenson, E., & Patrick Viguerie, S. (2010, June). The global grid. *McKinsey Quarterly*, 1–7.

Brown, B., Chui, M., & Manika, J. (2011, October). Are you ready for the ear of big data. *McKinsey Quarterly*, 1–12.

Brown, B., Sikes, J., & Willmott, P. (2013, August). Bullish on digital: McKinsey global survey results, *Insights & Publications*. McKinsey & Company. Retrieved December 10, 2013, from http://www.mckinsey.com/insights/business_technology/bullish_on_digital_mckinsey_global_survey_results.

Bughin, J., Livingston, J., & Marwaha, S. (2011, Autumn). Seizing the potential of big data. *McKinsey on Business Technology* (24), 8–13.

Chui, M., & Fleming, T. (2011, November). Inside P & G's digital revolution. *McKinsey Quarterly*, 1–11.

Chui, M., Löffler, M., & Roberts, R. (2010). The internet of things. *McKinsey Quarterly, 2*(2010), 1–9.

Compuware Corporation. (2010). Performance in the Cloud. *White Paper: Cloud Computing 2010* (pp. 1–6). Compuware Corporation USA.

Conway, R. (2012, January). Where angels will tread: The World in 2012. *The Economist*, 123.

Dijcks, J. P. (2012, January). Big data for the enterprise, *An Oracle White Paper*. Oracle Corporation, USA.

Divakaran, A., Mani, M., & Post, L. (2012). Building a global talent pipeline finding, developing, and retaining tomorrow's manufacturing workforce, *Perspective*, 1–9. Booz & Company.

Dutta, S., Bilbao-Osorio, B., & Geiger, T. (2012). The networked readiness index 2012: Benchmarking ICT progress and impacts for the next decade. In S. Dutta & B. Bilbao-Osorio (Eds.), *The global information technology report 2012: Living in a hyper-connected world* (pp. 3–34). Geneva: INSEAD & World Economic Forum.

EL-Darwiche, B., Koch, V., Meer, D., Shehadi, R. T., & Tohme, W. (2014). Big data maturity: An action plan for policymakers and executives. In B. Bilbao-Osorio, S. Dutta, & B. Lanvin (Eds.), *The global information technology report 2014: Rewards and risks of big data* (pp. 35–42). Geneva: INSEAD & World Economic Forum.

EMC Corporation. (2014a, April). Executive Summary: Data Growth, Business Opportunities, and the IT Imperatives. *EMC/IDC Digital Universe Report 2014*. Retrieved May 10, 2014, from http://www.emc.com/leadership/digital-universe/2014iview/executive-summary.htm.

EMC Corporation. (2014b, April). The Internet of Things, *EMC/IDC Digital Universe Report 2014*. Retrieved May 10, 2014, from http://www.emc.com/leadership/digital-universe/2014iview/internet-of-things.htm.

Evans, P., Lanvin, B., & Wachter, S. (2013, November 26). The world's most talent competitive countries. *INSEAD Knowledge*. Retrieved May 8, 2014, from http://knowledge.insead.edu/talent-management/the-worlds-most-talent-competitive-countries-3006.

Goodwin, B. (2014a). Skills shortage loom as development comes back in-house. *Computerweekly.com*. Retrieved March 18, 2014, from http://www.computerweekly.com/feature/CW500-Skills-shortages-loom-as-development-comes-back-in-house.

Goodwin, B. (2014b). Thinking outside the big storage box. *Computerweekly.com*. Retrieved March 18, 2014, from http://www.computerweekly.com/feature/CW500-Thinking-outside-the-big-storage-box.

Haag, S., Baltzan, P., & Phillips, A. (2008). *Business driven technology* (2nd ed.). Boston, USA: McGraw-Hill Irwin.

Hagström, M., & Gill, N. (2012). The wisdom of the cloud: Hyper-connectivity, big data, and real-time analytics. In S. Dutta & B. Bilbao-Osorio (Eds.), *The global information technology report 2012: Living in a hyper-connected world* (pp. 97–103). Geneva: INSEAD & World Economic Forum.

Halper, F. (2014, April 22). Big data: Two steps in the right direction. *The Data Warehousing Institute*. Retrieved May 8, 2014, from http://tdwi.org/articles/2014/04/22/big-data-two-steps-in-the-right-direction.aspx.

Harvard Business Review. (2010, June). Idea watch: cloud computing. *Harvard Business Review*, 24–30.

Intel Corporation. (2011). *The New CIO Agenda: Inter Cloud Computing Insights 2011* (pp. 1–14). Intel Corporation USA.

IDG Connect. (2011, Summer). *IDG Connect Special Report: The Global IT Skills Landscape* (pp. 1–8). IDG Connect International.

Josh, G., & Willmott, P. (2014). The digital tipping point. *McKinsey Global Survey Results* (pp. 1–8). Chennai: McKinsey & Company.

Kensign, K. (2014). The best jobs of 2014. *Careercast.com*. Retrieved May 28, 2014, from http://www.careercast.com/jobs-rated/best-jobs-2014.

Kleiner, A. (2012, Spring). The thought leader interview: Bob Carrigan (CEO IDG Communications). *Strategy + Business*, (66), 1–8.

Korkmaz, B., Lee, R., & Park, L. (2011, April). How new internet standards will finally deliver a mobile revolution. *McKinsey Quarterly*, 1–9.

Laseter, T., & Johnson, E. (2011, Winter). A better way to battle Malware. *Strategy + Business*, (65), 1–6.

Laudon, K. C., & Laudon, J. P. (2005). *Essentials of management information systems: Managing the digital firm* (6th ed.). New Jersey: Prentice Hall.

Lohr, S. (2012, February 11). The age of big data. *The New Your Times*. Retrieved August 11, 2012, from http://www.nytimes.com/2012/02/12/sunday-review/big-datas-impact-in-the-world.html?pagewanted=all.

Lund, S., Manyika, J., Nyquist, S., Mendonca, L., & Ramaswamy, S. (2013, July). *Game changers: Five opportunities for US growth and renewal* (pp. 1–158). McKinsey Global Institute, McKinsey & Company.

Manyika, J. (2009, January). Hal varian on how the web challenges managers. *McKinsey Quarterly*. Retrieved July 23, 2012, from https://www.mckinseyquarterly.com/Strategy/Innovation/Hal_Varian_on_how_the_Web_challenges_managers_2286.

Manyika, J., Chui, M., Brown, B., Bughin, J., Dobbs, R., Roxburgh, C., & Byers, A. H. (2011). *Big data: The next frontier for innovation, competition, and productivity*, McKinsey Global Institute, McKinsey & Company.

Meeker, M. (2014, May 28). 2014 internet trends. *2014 CODE Conference Presentation*, Kleiner, Perkins, Caufield & Byers. Retrieved July 10, 2014, from http://www.kpcb.com/internet-trends.

Meer, D. (2014, Summer). When big data isn't an option. *Strategy + Business*, (75), 1–3.

O'Brien, J. A., & Marakas, G. M. (2011). *Management information systems* (10th ed.). New York, USA: McGraw-Hill.

Oracle. (2012). Driving innovation through analytics. *Executive Strategy Series*. Oracle Corporation, USA.

Oxford Economics. (2013). *Global information security survey: Initial findings*, August 2013, pp. 1–36.

Pepper, R., & Garrity, J. (2014). The internet of everything: How the network unleashes the benefits of big data. In B. Bilbao-Osorio, S. Dutta, & B. Lanvin (Eds.), *The global information technology report 2014: Rewards and risks of big data* (pp. 35–42). Geneva: INSEAD & World Economic Forum.

Plansky, J., Solomon, J., Karp, R., & Drisko, C. (2013). The data gold rush companies need the right models and capabilities to monetize data, *Perspective*, 1–8. Booz & Company.

Roberts, R., Sarrazin, H., & Sikes, J. (2010). Reshaping IT management for turbulent times. *McKinsey on Business Technology*, (21), 2–9.

Roberts, R., & Sikes, J. (2011, Spring). How IT is managing new demands: McKinsey Global Survey results, *McKinsey on Business Technology*, (22), 24–33.

Sadauskas, A. (2014, April 30). Internet of things could boost Australia's GDP by $6.5 billion. *Smartcompany.com.au*. Retrieved May 8, 2014, from Internet of Things could boost Australia's GDP by $6.5 billion.

Sap, A. G. (2012). Harnessing the power of big data in real time through in-memory technology and analytics. In S. Dutta & B. Bilbao-Osorio (Eds.), *The global information technology report 2012: Living in a hyper-connected world* (pp. 89–96). Geneva: INSEAD & World Economic Forum.

Siegele L. (2012, January). Welcome to the yotta world, the world in 2012. *The Economist*, 122.

Stafford, P. (2012). How big data can turn the smallest business into Moneyball? *Smartcompany.com.au*. Retrieved August 16, 2012, from http://www.smartcompany.com.au/information-technology/051244-best-of-the-web-how-big-data-can-turn-the-smallest-business-into-moneyball.html?utm_source=SmartCompany&utm_campaign=8ca827ec42-TechCompany_16_August_201216_08_2012&utm_medium=email.

Trend Micro. (2010, July). The need for cloud computing security. *Trend Micro White Paper* (pp. 1–7). USA: Trend Micro Inc.

Utzig, C., Holland, D., Horvath, M., & Manohar, M. (2013). ERP in the cloud: Is it ready? Are you? *Perspective*, 1–9. Booz & Company.

Vesset, D., & Morris, H. (2013). The CIO's chance of a lifetime: Using big data and analytics as the ticket to strategic relevance. *IDG White Paper* (pp. 1–13).

Wang, K. W. (2010, Winter). Creating competitive advantage with IT architecture. *McKinsey on Business Technology*, (18), 18–21.

Westby, J. R. (2012). How boards and senior executives are managing cyber risks. *Governance of enterprise security: CyLab 2012 report*, 1–28. Carnegie Mellon University CyLab.

Wixom, B. H., Ross, J. W., & Beath, C. M. (2013, November). comScore, Inc.: Making Analytics Count. *Working Paper* (pp. 1–9). Center for Information Systems Research, Sloan School of Management, MIT.

Wixom, B. H., & Beath, C. M. (2014, March). Winning the data race. *Research Briefing* (Vol. XIV, 3, pp. 1–3). Center for Information Systems Research, Sloan School of Management, MIT.

World Economic Forum. (2014a). *Insight report: Global risks 2014* (9th ed., pp. 1–59).

World Economic Forum. (2104b, April). *Delivering digital infrastructure: Advancing the Internet economy*, (pp. 1–51).

Xu, J., & Quaddus, M. (2009). *E-Business in the 21st century: Realities, challenges, and outlook.* Singapore: World Scientific Publishing.

Xu, J., & Quaddus, M. (2013). *Managing information systems: Ten essential topics.* Paris: Springer & Atlantis Press.

Chapter 3
Digital Enterprise Strategy Planning and Implementation

This chapter discusses digital transformation, looks at digital enterprise strategy framework, reviews some success factors of digital enterprise, and introduces a model of sustainable digital business.

3.1 Digital Transformation

The IBM 2010 Global CEO study (reported in Berman and Bell 2011, p. 1) identified that technology was second only to market factors as a force for change. It has been argued that evolution of digital transformation has so far gone through three stages (Berman and Bell 2011, p. 2):

- Stage-1 (from late 1990s): digital products (e.g., music, entertainment) and infrastructure (i.e., telecommunications, software, information systems)
- Stage-2 (around 2000s): digital distribution and web strategy (e.g., e-commerce, online services)
- Stage-3 (around 2010s): mobile revolution, social media, hyper digitization, and power of analytics.

They also suggest nowadays people are using mobile devices and interactive tools to decide who to trust, where to go and what to buy. They have been increasingly empowered by the capability and convenience of accessing information anytime and anywhere, their expectations have risen dramatically, and they have now become the primary force behind digital transformation across different industries.

3.1.1 Organization's Readiness for Digital Transformation

How do you assess your organization's readiness for digital transformation? Berman and Bell (2011, p. 10) suggest the following questions from two perspectives of reshaping customer value proposition and optimizing operation to be looked at:

J. Xu, *Managing Digital Enterprise*, DOI 10.2991/978-94-6239-094-2_3

- How are you engaging with customers to understand their needs and expectations? How are customers changing in the digital environment?
- How will you drive the digital agenda in your industry rather than having it imposed on you by competitors?
- How do you integrate various touch points and information from multiple channels and different sources across the enterprise?
- What are you doing to make sure you are putting the customer at the center of your supply chain planning and execution every time?
- How are you realizing the benefits of open collaboration within your enterprise, with customers and with partners?
- How are you optimizing your digital and physical (non-digital) components across all aspects of your operating model?
- Meanwhile according to a recent study of 1,559 executives and managers from a wide range of industries by MIT Sloan Management Review and Capgemini Consulting (reported in Fitzgerald et al. 2014):
- Seventy eight percentage of the participants believed achieving digital transformation will become critical to their organizations with next 2 years.
- Sixty three percentage suggested that the pace of technology change in their organizations is too slow.
- Seventy five percentage indicated that their companies lack experience with emerging digital technologies.
- While 93 % agreed that employees in their company have a shared vision of digital transformation, only 36 % agreed that their senior executives have a shared vision of digital transformation (for such reason as the difficulty or the lack of management skills to pick the right direction of digital transformation or to create a road map towards digital transformation).
- Fifteen percentage of most digital mature participating companies of the study, which have executives who share a strong version for digital transformation and who commit to digital technologies, gain the most value from digital transformation.
- More than 50 % reckoned that their companies failed to set right key performance indicators (KPIs) for digital transformation (for reasons such as the difficulty of defining the right KPIs, the lack of management skills to carry through KPIs, and the need of changing culture to make KPIs work) and link incentives to digital transformation.
- Some identified top digital transformation barriers in the organization include (in order): no sense of urgency (39 % of the participants), not enough funding (33 %), limitations of IT systems (30 %), not clear roles and responsibilities (28 %), lack of vision (28 %), unclear business case (27 %), silo approach implementation by business units (24 %), culture not amenable to change (19 %), lack of leadership skills (16 %), and regulatory concerns (9 %).
- Some unveiled culture and attitude issues of digital transformation include (in order): competing priorities (i.e., we don't have time for digital transformation right now) (53 % of the respondents), lack of familiarity with digitization (e.g., we don't know what to do digital transformation) (52 %), resistance to new

approaches (i.e., this is the way we always do things) (40 %), digital transformation threatening current power structure (i.e., losing influence in the organization) (23 %), internal politics (i.e., the lack of the right political power) (21 %), and risk aversion (i.e., digital transformation is not worth the risk) (18 %).

The results of a recent study of more than 4,000 global C-suite executives by IBM Institute of Business Value (2013) indicate that some top barriers to unite their business and digital strategy include (in order): lack of a cohesive social media plan (63 % of the respondents), competing priorities or initiatives, difficulty measuring investment returns, legal and security concerns, and lack of appropriate technology.

3.1.2 Digital Transformation Capabilities

IBM Institute for Business Value suggests six capabilities of digital transformation (Berman and Bell 2011, p. 11):

- Business model innovation: building customer value as a core competency.
- Customer and community collaboration: engaging with customers fully via various channels and touch points.
- Cross-channel integration: integrating digital and non-digital channels.
- Insights from analytics: taking advantage of the predicative power of Big Data and advanced analytics.
- Digitally enabled supply chain: optimizing and integrating all components of supply chain.
- Networked workforce: getting the right skills around the right business opportunities.

A very good example of digital transformation/evolution in the organization is P&G-a consumer goods giant. As reported in Chui and Fleming (2011), its CEO Robert McDonald believes that digitization is a source of competitive advantage and aims at making the company the world's most technologically enabled company. Through actively pursuing digitization across the organization, P&G has achieved better relationships with customers and suppliers, better innovation, higher productivity, lower costs, and future growth prospects. They have:

- Developed "consumer plus" application, which scans and analyses customers' comments, to better understand and engage with customers in real time.
- Implemented the system using iPads to communicate production data in real time and worked on a system which could capture and disseminate the details and associated costs information of any product going through P&G's manufacturing line in real time.
- Developed digital applications such as Control Power (for monitoring all the transportation activities, maximizing the performance of the tracks, and reducing the chance of "deadhead" movements (trucks with no or not optimal load) and

Distribute Connect (for linking directly with distributors to improve the efficiency of the supply chain, reduce the costs of the supply chain (e.g., transportation, warehousing, and inventory costs) and enhance relationships with its partners).
- Implemented Global Data Synchronization Network (GDSN), which is a common data warehouse, to digitally connect with retailers and reduce the order errors, which happen very often (e.g., as high as 70 % as per a study by GS1 reported in Chui and Fleming 2011).
- Developed mobile applications for retailers to make orders and to get guidance from P&G regarding how to best display products on the shelf and in the store.
- Applied digital tools such as data modelling and simulation (e.g., digital prototype and virtual wall) to speed up the innovation and lower the cost (e.g., reducing the need for setting up consumer panels for testing the product concept since there is so much collected data about customers).
- Utilized digital tools (e.g., data mining and QR Code) to identify new service components which could be difficult to spell out in the past and provide value-added services (e.g., linking customers with production information concerning carbon emission, ingredients and bio-degradability).
- Developed digital conference room (called "Business Sphere") to allow management to make more effective decisions in real time.
- Implemented data governance policies to ensure the quality of the data and the protection and appropriate handling of the firm's data.
- Ensured digital leadership in the organization (e.g., senior leaders understand the importance of digitization, lead the development of digital business strategies, and establish pro-digitization culture, structure, business processes, and policies).
- Ensured the ideas for innovation are always informed by the data and arising from data analytics.
- Nurtured digital skills and digital workforce by recruiting and developing required digital skills and digital workforce.

Another important perspective of digital transformation for organizations is the digitization of business processes to meet with customers' demands of faster delivery of products and services, with a seamless user experience comparable to such firms as Apple, Zappo, and Amazon; to achieve such objective, a start-up approach coupled with the establishment a cross-functional team should be adopted to accelerate the process of digitizing business processes (Markovitch and Willmott 2014). Curt Gartner, CIO of Starbucks (reported in Fitzgerald 2014) has the similar view and he believes firms embarking on digital transformation should view themselves as a consumer technology company, which typically needs to have quick release cycles of products with great agility and flexibility and services, have market-relevant products and services with thorough understanding of the needs of the customers, and have an open-learning attitude and the willingness to cooperate internally and externally without boundaries.

3.2 Digital Enterprise Strategy Framework

One of the most difficult aspects of digital enterprise is translating innovative ideas into a framework of specific projects. Digital enterprise can be discussed at a high level, but actual implementation in the day-to-day organisation is a major challenge. The process is long and complex and is generally not well understood; there is no clear model for turning identified digital enterprise opportunities into a fully operational digital enterprise organisation.

The literature on digital business strategy lacks the clarity and certainty, and it reports a confused mix of tools and techniques. Such phenomenon reflects the new and relatively immature nature of digital enterprise/e-business strategy. The reasons for such phenomenon could be (1) the Internet is still quite new even though it has been commercially around for more than 20 years; (2) there is a lack of well-established business models/strategies and clearly demonstrable understanding of how to do business on the Internet; (3) there is a lack of clear and well developed standards and regulations designated for Internet businesses; and (4) the Internet and digital technologies have been changing faster and faster (Do you think Moore's law still holds today?). In addition, it should be noted that there is no magic formula and nor a one-size-fits-all solution for digital enterprise strategy planning and implementation. On the other hand, there exist some strategy frameworks and lessons learned.

An approach suggested by Turban et al. (2012, p. 623) is a good one and could be applied to planning and implementation of any digital initiative. Turban et al.'s approach consists of four steps of (1) initiation, (2) formulation, (3) implementation, and (4) assessment.

Tables 3.1, 3.2, 3.3 and 3.4 present the activities and issues of each of four steps of digital enterprise strategy planning and implementation suggested by Turban et al. (2012).

At the same time, the digital enterprise strategic planning process should have two-way communication and take advantages of both top-down approach (e.g., longer term view and more consistence) and bottom up approach (e.g., better understanding of environment, business and customers from people in the front line) (Xu and Quaddus 2009, p. 17).

3.3 Success Factors of Digital Enterprise

According to a recent study of 850 senior executives representing the full range of industries and regions, and firm sizes (reported in Brown et al. 2013), some success factors of the organization's digital initiatives include (in order): senior management interest or desire to change practices related to initiative (32 % of the participants), internal leadership (30 %), alignment between organizational structure and initiative's goals, good management of and sufficient organizational support for

Table 3.1 Key activities and issues of initiation stage

Key activities	Analysing the internal environment and external environment of an enterprise via such tools as SWOT analysis, Porter's five forces models, and systems dynamics
	After knowing its external operating environment and internal conditions, an enterprise needs to develop a list of potential digital initiatives, which support business strategy and strategic objectives of the organization, exploit opportunities, and deal with external threats in light of its strengths and weaknesses
Key issues	(1) Companies need to have good understanding of internal and external environments and take into consideration of emerging trends and future directions
	Five digital forces of globalization, millenialization, prosumerization, business virtualization, and platformization suggested by Gimpel and Westerman (2012)
	Other trends such as rapid growth of world population, aging population in the developed world, fasters pace of technological innovation, more globalized and integrated economy, the greatly increased importance of managing knowledge assets, the greatly enlarged role of technology in economy and society, the greatly increased control by the government, the great importance of education, the greatly increased power of consumers, the greatly increased value and scarcity of time, the greater emphasis on issues of climate change and renewable and new energy, the greater interest on space and the life outside of the earth, and the race between humans and automation)
	(2) Some broad strategic issues and initiatives the firm may look at include:
	Answering high level questions concerning digital business enterprise strategy and digital initiatives, including What is the relationship between our business strategy, IS/IT (also called ICT) strategy, and digital enterprise/digital business strategy? Could our digital business strategy replace our IS/IT strategy or even our business strategy? Why do we need digital strategy and initiatives? For whom are such digital strategy and initiatives? What kinds of digital strategy and initiatives do we need? How are we going to deliver such digital strategy and initiatives? Who is going to do the execution? What is the scope of our digital business strategy (e.g., internally only or external only or both internal and external? or certain functions only? or cross-functional approach? certain products and markets only or many products and many markets?)? What is the scale of our digital business strategy (e.g., how effective is our technical infrastructure to support strategic dynamic capability? How can we be effective in building up the scale and taking advantages of the network effects?)? What is the speed of our digital business strategy (e.g., speed of product launches, speed of decision making, speed of supply chains, speed of network formation and adaptation)? What are our sources of value creation and capture of our digital business strategy (e.g., value creation from collected information, multisided business models, coordinated business models in the networks, and the control of the firm's digital infrastructure)?
	Should our digital strategy focus on customers and capabilities or competition?
	How have digital technologies and networks changed the basis of competition in our industry?
	What are digital solutions for meeting and/or exceeding the expectations of our customers?
	Have we taken into consideration of exploring the full potential of digitization in our (3–5 years) corporate strategic plans?

(continued)

Table 3.1 (continued)

	Do we have required digital capabilities (e.g., unified digital platforms, analytics capabilities, business and IT integration, and solution delivery) and talent/expertise for our digital transformation efforts and digital initiatives?
	Do we need both short-term strategies and long-term strategies?
	How will digital initiatives add value to our business? Who the target customers of our digital initiatives? What is the value proposition for those target customers? What are the required capabilities? Can we target all the segments and all the areas at the same time? Can we quickly gain the volume and reach the scale to realize network effects?
	Should we keep the current status (no digital enterprise/e-business at all or no digital enterprise/e-business improvement)?
	Should we be a first-mover or a follower?
	Should we choose born-on-the-net or move-to-the-net approach?
	Should we have a separate/new digital business? Should we have a separate brand for our digital business?
	Should we lead our customers or follow them?
	Should we outsource or own our digital initiatives?
	Which role(s) and function(s) should be responsible for our digital initiatives?
	Which digital business model should we pursue (such as, innovator (e.g., apple), premium player (e.g., nordstrom), customizer (e.g., avon), differentiated green (e.g., general electric), aggregator (e.g., amazon), value player (e.g., ikea) suggested by Kauffeld et al. 2011)? Or what are our Content (e.g., what is consumed?), Customer Experience (i.e., how is it packaged), and Platform (e.g., how is it delivered) elements of our digital business model suggested by Weill and Woerner (2013b)? Or are we looking at creating new business models for or from our digital initiatives?
	Are our digital initiatives looking at enhancing customer experience and/or improving our collaboration with suppliers and partners and supply chains and/or bettering our internal operations?
	Are we looking at digitizing our physical/tangible assets (e.g., automation of manual processes) or/and our intangible assets (e.g., business processes, data, customer relations)?
	What is the focus of our digital initiatives (e.g., cost leadership, differentiation, innovation, growth, creating or entering new markets, diversification, disrupting existing markets, setting new technology standards, mergers and acquisitions, and strategic alliance)?
	Can our digital initiatives have sustainable advantages (e.g., they are valuable, rare, inimitable, and non-substitutable)?
	Can we develop digital initiatives via new technologies or their combinations (e.g., the Internet of Things, digital platforms, social and mobile computing, Big Data and Data Analytics, embedded devices, 3D/4D printing, robotics, virtual reality, and digital biology)?

Source Turban et al. (2012), pp. 623–627, 634–645; Xu and Quaddus (2013), p. 28–29; Xu and Quaddus (2009), pp. 21, 410–413; Gimpel and Westerman (2012); Favaro (2013), (2014); Manyika (2013); Downes and Nunes (2013); MIT Center for Digital Business and Capgemini Consulting (2011); Callahan et al. (2014); Fitzgerald et al. (2014); Huy and Vuori (2014); Hirt and Willmott (2014); Lopez et al. (2014); Kauffeld et al. (2011); Bharadwaj et al. (2013); Willmott (2013a, b); Willmott (2014); IBM Institute of Business Value (2013); Weill and Woerner (2013b); Brynjolfsson et al. (2013); Brown et al. (2013); the author's own knowledge

Table 3.2 Key activities and issues of formulation stage

Key activities	Identifying specific digital enterprise strategy: some techniques that can be used to help identify specific digital enterprise/e-business strategy include critical success factors, value chain analysis, scenario planning, and systems thinking
	Evaluating identified strategic options and conducting cost-benefit and risk analyses associated with those opportunities
	Choosing specific strategy as per the outcomes of the evaluation
	Developing roadmap and/or detailed action plan and/or more detailed project plan for chosen strategy
	Establishing dedicated senior position (e.g., chief digital officer) or dedicated senior executive to lead chosen digital initiative and cross-functional team to execute chosen digital initiative
	Developing programs for building up digital skills and strategies for hiring and retaining digital talent
Key issues	(1) Companies will look at digital enterprise opportunities when:
	Digital enterprise can provide a solution for its internal problems or enable it to exploit market opportunities (e.g., an additional distribution channel, a global operation)
	Digital enterprise can enhance its operations and business performance (e.g., enhancing customer relationships, improving supply chains, streamlining business processes, and optimising internal communication)
	Certain internet technologies and digital enterprise applications have become industry standard or have been adopted by the competitors, industry leaders, and have become a strategic necessity—in this case, a business may face the choice of either participating in digital enterprise or going out of the business
	Firms already possess advanced internet technologies which will be wasted if they are not utilised
	There are requirements of compliance imposed by the government and/or industry associations, so businesses have no option but to invest in digital enterprise
	When the existing systems cannot cope with the demands and challenges of the market
	(2) To properly evaluate an digital enterprise investment, a multiple-perspective and balanced approach should be adopted, which should look at:
	Both tangible and non-tangible costs and benefits
	Both qualitative and quantitative dimensions
	Both financial and non-financial perspectives
	Strategic, tactical, operational and other factors
	(3) Risk analysis
	Risk is inherent in all business activities (especially for entering new territory), and there is no exception for digital enterprise projects. Managing digital enterprise/e-business risk is a process of identifying the potential risks, analysing the potential impact of the identified risks, and taking appropriate actions to deal with identified risks
	(4) When a firm is deciding on its digital business strategy, a number of factors (e.g., industry, firm, customer, technology development, society, economy) need to be considered as well. Furthermore, there are other issues involved in the digital enterprise strategy formulation stage, including pricing strategy, channel conflicts, and others

Source Refer to Table 3.1

Table 3.3 Key activities and issues of implementation stage

Key activities	Some activities involve in the implementation stage include:
	Allocating/securing sufficient capital and resources to the digital enterprise project
	Establishing a project team and assigning responsibilities
	Developing effective project plan, change management action plan, and risk mitigation measures
	Deciding a development approach (i.e., in-house development or out-sourcing?)
	Addressing security and privacy issues: appropriate levels of security measures and privacy policies should be put in the place
	Preparing the organization for the digital initiatives and working on integration issues (e.g., both internal and external integrations)
Key issues	(1) A pilot project can quickly identify whether a new digital initiative is likely to be successful or not. There are several advantages of a pilot approach:
	A pilot does not cost as much as a fully-fledged implementation
	A pilot can be adjusted and modified before any official final roll-out
	A pilot can be abandoned if it turns out to be unsuccessful
	(2) Some pitfalls identified to be avoided include:
	Redesigning all business processes at once: this is tempting, but dangerous. It is better to choose tactical projects and implement them slowly and successfully. It is suggested that firms implement their digitization road map in stages. In doing so, learning from earlier phases can be applied in later phases
	Suspending traditional rules of good project management: projects (whether digital or not) fail for the same reasons-poor planning, insufficient staff, staff with wrong skills, lack of management support, lack of buy-in from stakeholders. Digital projects have the same prerequisites as any other project
	Making technology the master, not the servant: Technology is meant to serve business needs. The Internet can provide benefits to business, but it can also be misapplied and become a drain on a firm's resources. All digital initiatives should have a sound business goal and technologies should be selected to fit the purpose
	Focusing on existing customers: if organizations do this, they are likely to miss opportunities for new customers
	Assuming you know your competitors: new enterprises are agile and aggressive and come out of nowhere. Focusing on known competitors means that the firm has not understood the way that new Internet businesses in their industry can emerge at any time
	These common pitfalls can easily be avoided by an astute digital enterprise strategy team
	(3) Focusing on execution and people in the implementation
	Strategy is very much about execution, and execution is very much about people
	Average strategy with top execution is better than top strategy with average execution
	(4) Dealing with some common hurdles to digital programs identified by a recent McKinsey Global Survey of senior executives [reported in Josh and Willmott (2014)]:
	Difficulty finding talent (both functional and technical)
	Organizational structure not designed appropriately for digital initiatives
	Inflexible business processes to take advantage of new digital opportunities
	Lack of quality data to inform business decision
	Inability to adopt an experimentation mind-set that is the key for best practices

Source Refer to Table 3.1

Table 3.4 Key activities and issues of assessment stage

Key activities	Evaluating project performance to ensure the projects are delivering expected outcomes
	Examining whether digital enterprise strategy and the projects arising from the strategy are still viable in the current environment and if not actions need to be taken
	Identifying success factors and/or lessons learned from the projects
Key issues	As for any project, post-implementation evaluation of the digital enterprise project is important. It can help identify problems in the planning and implementation process so that these problems may be avoided in the future. It can also help confirm projected costs and benefits or identify new costs and benefits. Strategy assessment includes both the continual assessment of digital enterprise metrics and the periodic formal evaluation of progress toward the organization's strategic goals

Source Refer to Table 3.1

initiative (21 %), the ability to adopt experimentation mind-set that allows for certain practices (e.g., rapid test-and-learn cycles to quickly refine approaches used in initiative) (18 %), available technical talent (e.g., IT or technology staff) (18 %), quality data (16 %), business processes reworked to take advantage of the initiative's potential value opportunity (16 %), available functional talent (e.g., data scientists, data marketing experts) (15 %), technology infrastructure and IT systems (14 %), ability to influence or follow shifting customer expectations related to the initiative (11 %), and the ability to keep pace with rapid changes in activities required to meet the initiative's goals (10 %).

Weill and Woerner (2013a) suggest some best practices around value creation from digitization:

- Having transparent costs and performance metrics for each unit, whose costs, and performance will be reviewed centrally.
- Developing an enterprise-wide strategy process including digital spending plans.
- Establishing an enterprise-wide business case and capital allocation process.
- Implementing a multiparty approval process for new digital investments [e.g., separating the approval of business budget (approved by CFO) from the approval of technological issues (approved by IT)].

By reviewing success (as well as failure) factors of digital initiatives, better understanding of digital enterprise best practices could be achieved, and such understanding could better prepare organizations for future digital endeavors, put them in a better position to predict the impact and the potential of digital opportunities, and realize better outcomes by avoiding reinventing the wheel. In this section, a few of selected success (and failure) factors are discussed. On a related note, success factors that are more specific to certain digital enterprise models and applications will be discussed in subsequent chapters of the book.

3.3.1 Selection of Products and Services

Organization may need to have both short-term plans (e.g., providing attractive prices and carefully selected products and services as well as maximum flexibility and convenience, creating switching costs via loyalty programs and service contracts, applying Big Data and advanced analytics to better understand customers) and long-term strategies (e.g., developing exclusive products and unique features (ideally for each channel), developing innovative product and service packages, using data analytics to guide product design, product choices, channel decisions, and new product and service introduction by working with customers, manufacturers, suppliers and business partners) for its e-tailing operations (Brynjolfsson et al. 2013).

Meanwhile smartly bundling your products and services could be attractive to your customers as well. For example, Apple's product-focused strategy, which combined hardware, software, and services and presents them in a bundle for customers, has been effective for Apple to win customer satisfaction and then their loyalty (Palmguist 2014).

3.3.2 Sound Business Model and Business Practices

Digital business is just another kind of business. When it comes to achieving sustainability and viability of a digital business, the emphasis should be more on Business and less on Digital. On a related note, by many years' studies of the business activities and performance of top 5,000 enterprises in Australia, the leading market information and market research firm IBISWorld has identified 12 best practices (success factors) of best enterprises in Australia (cited in Ruthven 2014):

- Sticking to one business at a time and do not diversify.
- Aiming to dominate some segment(s) of their market.
- Being forever innovative, values the business intellectual property.
- Outsourcing non-core activities to enable growth.
- Not owning "hard" assets (especially for certain industries such as education, agriculture).
- Having good and professional financial management.
- Planning from the outside-in not the inside-out.
- Anticipating any new industry lifecycle changes.
- Following relevant world best practice in the industry.
- Developing strategic alliances.
- Developing unique organizational cultures.
- Valuing leadership first and management second.

On a related note, any start-up needs to go through a process of (1) examining your idea and identifying the consumer or business needs in the marketplace (many businesses simply begin with a good idea about an innovative way to meet a need, even needs that are not yet recognised by customers) as well as looking at other factors (e.g., competition, potential customer base, relevant experience and ability, and market conditions and regulatory environments); (2) investigating the opportunity (to see whether it is real) and see whether your business is profitable by understanding the total cost and the quantified demand for your products and services; and (3) determining the business owner's ability to meet the need (assuming that a realistic business opportunity exists, does the prospective business owner have the ability to convert the opportunity into success?) and his/her execution skills (Turban et al. 2010, pp. 669–671; Brownee 2014).

3.3.3 Being a Global Player

Globalization provides the opportunity for digital enterprise organizations to serve not only their traditional geographic markets, but potentially the global market. To be a global player, organizations need to think Glocally (global plus local), have a detailed and repeatable regional rollout plan, ensure the website accommodates local languages and customs, develop a pricing and tax-compliance strategy, employ a scalable technical infrastructure, and have strategies in place to ensure robust logistics and support capabilities (Brooks 2014; the author's own knowledge). A combined approach of having both centralization and decentralization should also be looked at. A centralization approach focuses on organizations' strategic objectives and on gaining more control while a decentralization approach works on localizing their products and services, complying with local regulations, and meet local expectations (e.g., local buyers will expect the international provider to use local practices in terms of warranty, money-back guarantee, and refund policies).

3.3.4 Being the Best Player in Your Field

When the first mover strategy can give organizations advantages of establishing their brands and building strong user base before competition comes in, such advantages cannot guarantee them the sustainable success. In the long run, best-mover advantage not first-mover advantage determines the market leader. Organizations need to be the best in the areas/industries they are competing in and constantly generate new/better products and services to win and retain their customers. Some organizations that so far have been very successful in this strategy include: Alibaba, Amazon, Google, Apple, Microsoft, Netflix, to name a few.

3.3.5 Being Small Could Be Beautiful

Is being small is beautiful or not so beautiful when it comes to digital business? The answer is Yes. According to a recent research of 400 U.S. Internet consumers by AYTM Market Research (reported in eMarketer 2014), reasons for their preference for small businesses and not large companies include: supporting the local economy (56.2 % of the respondents), personal service (52.7 %), high quality items (29.5 %), and lower prices (27 %). Meanwhile it can be said that the main reason that consumers favour small businesses is their customer focus. For example, the results of a recent study of U.S. consumers by Web.com and market research firm Toluna (reported in eMarketer 2014), indicate some key considerations when consumers are choosing small businesses. These are: customer service and customer focus (86 % of the participants); personal, intimate, human, face-to-face interaction (84 %); knowing customers and their needs (84 %); being easy to do business with (84 %); being local, close by, and convenient (83 %); having a website and using social media (83 %); being reliable, consistent, and available when you need them (82 %); and being owner-occupied, committed, and accountable (81 %).

3.3.6 Establishing a Data-Driven Decision-Making Culture in the Organization

Even though it is true that Big Data and Data Analytics could not make decision for us, it can definitely assist us making decision more effectively and more efficiently (e.g., via knowing more and deeper and with some previously unknown and unexpected patters and previously too expensive or impossible to get). For the purpose of maximizing the value and the potential of digital capital and digital technologies, organizations need to establish a data-driven decision-making culture in which decisions about customers and meeting their needs is built on the collected data about them, even though the hypotheses/decisions about customers and meeting their needs) and the testing of the hypotheses are done by us not the data and analytics applications/systems (Olanrewaju et al. 2014; Laseter 2014).

3.3.7 Working on Having a Good Understanding of the Impact of Digital Capital

Even though accounting for digital capital in the balance sheet has not been a really mature or widely accepted practice, it does have a big impact (or potential big impact) on the economy and on the business performance. In order to have a good understanding of the impact of digital capital, organizations need to develop effective measures and accounting systems for digital capital, especially for intangible assets (e.g., relationships, patents, business processes, Big Data and analytics capabilities, business models, knowledge and skills, unique designs, innovativeness, brand values, trade secrets, copyrights, trademarks) (Bughin and Manyika 2013). Two good examples of intangible digital assets/capital are innovativeness and brand values. For example, in a recent study by Booz and Company (reported in Acker et al. 2013), top ten most innovative companies are (in order): Apple, Google, 3M, Samsung, GE, Microsoft, Toyota, Procter and Gamble, IBM, and Amazon; and according to branding and brand management consulting firm Interbrand (2014), the top 5 most valued global brands in 2013 are (in order): Apple, Google, Coca Cola, IBM, and Microsoft. On a related note, according to the consulting firm Deloitte (reported in Hagel et al. 2011, p. 2), digital infrastructure (also called Digital Resources by Bharadwaj et al. 2013) is "more than just bits and bytes, the digital infrastructure consists of institutions, practices, and protocols that together organize and deliver the increasing power of digital technology to business and society".

3.3.8 *Keeping in Mind of Developing a Digital Ecosystem*

Organizations (whether they are small or big) need to look at developing a digital ecosystem for their digital initiatives since it can be argued that ultimately in the future companies are competing on the global supply chains and their business ecosystems. For digital enterprises, the global digital supply chains and digital ecosystems are the keys for the firm's long term growth and success. Some good examples are Amazon, Google, and Apple; each of them has ventured many areas in addition to its core business and has leveraged the advantages of hardware, software, networks, and the large user base (the network effects) and the collected large amount of data from the large user base (e.g., Amazon, the largest digital retailer, has ventured into digital services, software services, cloud-computing, mobile phones, e-readers, tablets, payments, television, media, entertainment, and other areas). Simply put, to stay in the competition, organizations need to develop a range of products and services that businesses need. For example, in the ICT sector, leading firms have been continuing in providing a distinctive set of products and services across areas of hardware, software, IT services, and telecommunication/networks (Acker et al. 2013).

3.3.9 *Demonstrating Digital Leadership*

It can be said that leadership is the most decisive and important factor for the success (or failure) of a digital program (Brown et al. 2013). More and more senior executives have been supporting and getting involved with their organizations' digital initiatives since they have realized the importance of the digitization to the corporate performance and competitive advantages. For example, in a recent study of 850 senior executives representing the full range of industries and regions, and firm sizes (reported in Brown et al. 2013), 31 % of CEOs of the participants' organizations personally sponsored their digital initiatives in 2013 while the figure in 2012 was 23 %. In the same study, 30 % of the participants indicated that the Chief Digital Officer (CDO) is a member of their firms' executive teams. Senior executives in the organization are in the position to lead required cross-functional changes across the organization and mandate the digital agendas. The results of a recent study of interviewing 157 executives n the various industries from 50 large companies (with at least US$1 billion annual sales revenue) of 15 countries by MIT Center for Digital Business and Capgemini Consulting (2011) suggest that successful digital transformation must be driven by the senior executives, and it doesn't happen bottom up. Another related matter is digital governance (i.e., governance for digital transformation and initiatives), successful digital initiatives will most likely adopt a top-down ambition setting approach for the directions and outcomes of their digital initiatives, have a central coordination mechanism for their digital initiatives (i.e., defining digital strategy and investment at the enterprise level but leaving the responsibilities of developing and managing digital operations to business units), and closely monitor the progress and the performance of their digital initiative through a transparent set of metrics and KPIs (MIT Center for Digital Business and Capgemini Consulting 2011).

3.3.10 Making Required Organizational Adjustments

Preparing the organization for the chosen digital initiative is also very critical to the success of a digital project. According to a recent study of 850 senior executives representing the full range of industries and regions, and firm sizes (reported in Brown et al. 2013), the top four success factors of the organization's digital initiatives are (in order): senior management interest or desire to change practices related to initiative (32 % of the participants), internal leadership (30 %), alignment between organizational structure and initiative's goals, and good management of and sufficient organizational support for initiative (21 %). These identified key success factors suggest that in addition to leadership, organizational issues are another key factor, which could hinder the firms' efforts to realize the real and full impact of digital initiatives. One particular organizational issue is having an organizational culture fostering digital initiatives, which supports such mindsets as data driven decision-making and pro-entrepreneurship in the organization [e.g., putting product failure as an essential part of the employee's performance evaluation as suggested by Silicon Valley entrepreneur and author Eric Ries (reported in Chui 2014)]. Meanwhile even though digital technologies are essential and are enabling organizations' digitization efforts and digital transformation, more important factors for the success (or failure) for their digital initiatives are non-technological factors, such as leadership, organizational issues, digital business strategy, cultural challenges, governance, performance measures, and talent and skills management.

3.3.11 Digital Talent Management and Digital Skills Development

There are wide concerns among many organizations about finding the required digital talent and skills (Brown et al. 2013; MIT Center for Digital Business and Capgemini Consulting 2011). While locating and recruiting digital talent is important, equally important is the development and retention of the hired digital talent. The more detailed discussion on digital talent management was presented in Chap. 2.

3.3.12 Open Innovation and Organizational Learning Strategy

Open innovation emphasizes an organization's efforts to engage and collaborate with external sources and its partners in its innovation process (Lichtenthaler et al. 2011). The telecommunications networks and Internet technologies have made the open innovation more appealing to organizations. Open innovation strategy has been adopted by many innovative companies in the world. For example, 3 M has been very successful in developing smart products via its open innovation approach involving 10,000 research and development people in 73 locations from 63 full-scale operating businesses across dozens of industries working together as well as working with large number of external partners via 300 joint programs and customers via 30 customer technology centers around the world (Jaruzelski et al. 2011).

While established brands do help organizations in the marketplace, it is the continuous innovation efforts that have provided them with sustainable growth and competitive advantage. It is particularly true in some industries (such as media and publishing) providing many examples of failed traditional news and referencing material publishers as a result of emerging digital content providers (i.e., Wikipedia, Google, Youtube and many others online players). Meanwhile when we are talking about innovation, we are referring not only to R&D for new products but also to changes and new things in the various parts of the business, such as business processes, customer services, marketing and sales, training and learning, talent management, knowledge management, data collection and decision-making, design of organizational structure, intra-organizational and inter-organizational communications, procurement, payment systems, and logistics management.

Furthermore organizational learning (especially open learning) could be viewed as an important element of innovation, without effective and continuous learning and quick responses to market changes, organizations won't be able to have the skills and knowledge for creative ideas. It can be said that even though the success or failure of a business is a result of multiple factors including management issues (such as leadership, management experiences and skills, decision making process, investment strategies), organizational factors (such as culture, structure, processes, people's skills), changes in the industry and in the marketplace, and economic conditions, the ability and commitment to continuous innovation are definitely critical to the sustainable competitive advantage and long-term growth of the organization.

In fact, innovation is the source of the added-values and profits. For example Chinese manufacturers working on OEM orders typically make very slim margin while the owner of the intellectual property does much better. If an organization is able to make its innovation accepted as industry standard, then competitive advantages and good financial outcomes will follow-just look at the competition between Google's Android operation system and Apple's iOS (iPhone operating system) for mobile devices.

Furthermore when we are talking about using technology for innovation, technology alone won't be enough for successful innovation, and it is a joint effort of IS/IT and business (users), which needs a top-down push to deal with silo problems and foster cooperation (Roberts and Sikes 2011). On a related note, Kleiner (2012) argues that only a few firms (i.e., Amazon, Apple) have successfully locked down their intellectual capital (technological information), and most companies hope that the speed of innovation beats the risk of leaking information to competitors. Continuous innovation could be used for dealing with intellectual property issues.

3.3.13 Justification and Evaluation of Digital Investments

There is an increased demand for financial justification of investing in technology projects. Through effectively managing technology investment benefits, organizations can achieve such benefits as: (1) better planning; (2) improved relationship between technology and business; (3) better technology investment decisions; and (4) increased realized benefits from technology investments (Peppard et al. 2007).

It can be argued that so far an unclear business case and justification for digital initiatives is quite common among the organizations; however more efforts have been put into perspective. The results of a recent study of interviewing 157 executives in the various industries from 50 large companies (with at least US$1 billion annual sales revenue) of 15 countries by MIT Center for Digital Business and Capgemini Consulting (2011) indicate that the firms are using one or the combination (at least 2 methods) of the following four methods to justify digital investments:

- Economic business case (i.e., traditional quantified approach of cost and benefit analysis).
- Burning platform (i.e., do-or-die/survival issue or the digital initiative mandated by the regulations or caused by the policy changes, without a strict financial business case).
- Low-risk experiment (i.e., investments with limited size and risk to learn about technologies, customers, or potential capabilities via experiments, trials, and pilot studies).
- Strategic foundation investment (i.e., investment for building infrastructure and important organizational capabilities, usually without a quantified financial business case).

At the same time, it should be pointed out that whether an initial digital investment is financially justified or not, the true value of digital transformation and digital initiative comes from building some foundational digital infrastructure and capabilities, which enable organizations to continuously better themselves (e.g., increasing revenue, cutting costs, being more innovative) and have a good understanding of their customers.

3.4 A Sustainable Digital Business Model

To achieve sustainable digital business, organizations could embark on a model of sustainable digital business, which consists of three parts of Adoption of (1) Step-1: Digital Business Adoption Decision Making Stage; (2) Step-2: Achieving Digital Business Success Stage; and (3) Step-3: Achieving Sustainable Digital Business Success Stage (see Fig. 3.1). Meanwhile, the model is not a static model, and a constant feedback process through closely monitoring and evaluating a digital business initiative is built into the model (see Fig. 3.2). Such feedback process allows going back on and re-working on previously completed steps. In the adoption decision making stage (step-1), the model suggests that internal factors (such as organizational factors, knowledge management, learning and innovation), external factors (such as external environment, external influences), and digital business factors (such as digital business strategy planning, expected trust, expected benefits, expected characteristics of Digital business systems) will have direct influence on the adoption decision of e-business. In the achieving success stage (step-2), it suggests that factors related to the organization's efforts in embracing Digital business including organizational adjustments and ongoing knowledge management, learning, and implementation and factors concerning the performance of digital business systems and evaluation of digital business activities including realized characteristics of digital business systems, realized benefits, gained trust, digital business strategy implementation will have direct impact on the digital success. In achieving the sustainable success stage (step-3), it postulates that by successfully repeating activities of step-1 for reviewing and embarking new digital

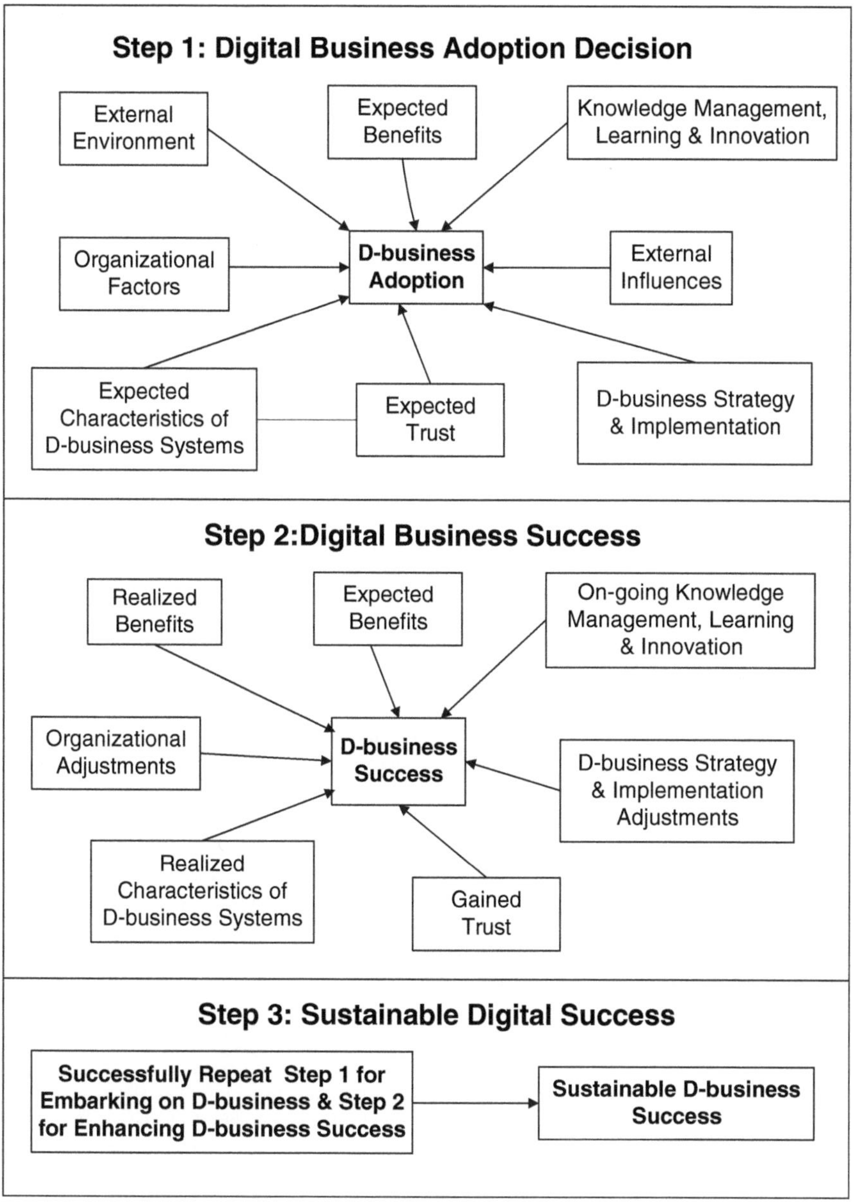

Fig. 3.1 A model of sustainable success of digital business. *Source* Adapted from Xu and Quaddus (2009), p. 418

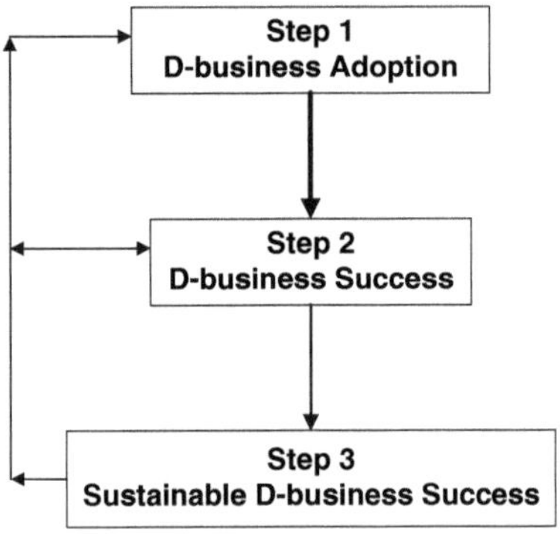

Fig. 3.2 Sustainable digital business cycle. *Source* Adapted from Xu and Quaddus (2009), p. 419

Table 3.5 Factors of the Sustainable Digital Business Model

Factors	Description
External environment factors	Include dimensions of competitive pressure/competition, regulations and policies, opportunities arising from development of information technology infrastructure and advances of Internet technologies, economic conditions, and social environment
External influences	Are represented by such factors as following the trend/fashion and/or the lead by industry's leaders, influence from external consultants and experts, customer expectation and demand, market opportunities, and peer business influence
Knowledge management, learning and innovation factors	Consist of creation of knowledge, capture of knowledge, storage and organization of knowledge, dissemination and sharing of knowledge, application of knowledge, existence of culture for knowledge management, existence of structure for knowledge management, existence of processes for managing knowledge, existence of tools for managing knowledge, existence of strategies for managing knowledge, co-creation attitude, learning desire and activities, learning ability and knowledge building, research and development investments, innovation efforts, innovation environment, innovativeness and talent management
Organizational factors	Are made of dimensions of nature of business, established brand and reputation, size of business, business growth/strategic direction, age of business, top management support, people's support, the need for problem solving, strategic alliance and supply chain improvement, business processes, organizational structure, organizational culture, information technology infrastructure and expertise for developing digital business applications, management's experience and knowledge of digital business, and people's experience and knowledge of digital business

(continued)

Table 3.5 (continued)

Factors	Description
D-business/digital business strategy planning	Cover perspectives of digital business strategy, digital strategic planning process, digital model, sufficient analysis and planning, implementation plan, and post-implementation maintenance and evaluation
Expected characteristics of digital business systems	Focus on the expectations of digital business systems' user-friendliness and performance, including such dimensions as ease of use, cheap to learn and use, speed, accessibility, availability, regular maintenance and updates, and systems integration
Expected benefits of digital business	Look at potential benefits arising from adopting digital business in the organization and is represented by following dimensions: better/new products and services, efficiency, effectiveness, time and cost reduction, net benefits, relationships with customers, relationships with suppliers and business partners, relationships with government agencies, relationships with competitors, enlarging market share, achieving market leader position, increasing revenue, improving profit, better image, responsiveness to changes in the market
Trust of digital business	Can be expected from such dimensions of security, quality of products and services, provision of third party assurance services, privacy policy, intellectual property management, terms and conditions, online communities, online feedback/reputation systems, providing opportunities to talk to human beings, and providing information of the organization
Digital business adoption	Can be reflected in organizational uses of digital business for internal operations and communications, interaction with suppliers and business partners, interaction with customers, interaction with government agencies, interaction with competitors, using the internet-based channel as a new business channels, and channel integration
Realized benefits of digital business	Look at realized benefits arising from adopting digital business in the organization and is represented by following dimensions: better/new products and services, efficiency, effectiveness, time and cost reduction, net benefits, relationships with customers, relationships with suppliers and business partners, relationships with government agencies, relationships with competitors, enlarging market share, achieving market leader position, increasing revenue, improving profit, better image, and responsiveness to changes in the market
Ongoing knowledge management, learning and innovation	Look at ongoing efforts of creation of knowledge, capture of knowledge, storage and organization of knowledge, dissemination and sharing of knowledge, application of knowledge, existence of culture for knowledge management, existence of structure for knowledge management, existence of processes for

(continued)

Table 3.5 (continued)

Factors	Description
	managing knowledge, existence of tools for managing knowledge, existence of strategies for managing knowledge, co-creation attitude, learning desire and activities, learning ability and knowledge building, research and development investments, innovation efforts, innovation environment, innovativeness, and talent management
Organizational adjustments	Represented by organizations' adjustments to various parts of the organization for the purpose of embracing their e-business initiatives, including enhanced top management support, better organizational culture, adjusted organizational structure, improved business processes, updated information technology infrastructure and expertise, updated management's knowledge and skills of digital business, updated people's knowledge and skills of digital business, refined portfolio of products and services, refined pricing strategies, and refined brand portfolio
Digital business implementation	Looks at the organization's implementation of developed digital business strategy and post-implementation evaluation
Realized characteristics of digital business systems	Look at the realization of digital business systems' user-friendliness and performance, including such dimensions as ease of use, cheap to learn and use, speed, accessibility, availability, regular maintenance and updates, and systems integration
Gained trust of digital business	Look at gained trust from such dimensions as security, quality of products and services, provision of third party assurance services, privacy policy, intellectual property management, terms and conditions, online communities, online feedback/reputation systems, providing opportunities to talk to human beings, and providing information of the organization
Digital business success	Measure the success of digital business by looking at such areas as internal operations and communication, interaction with suppliers and partners, interaction with government agencies, interaction with competitors, dealing with channel conflict, integration, achieving expected benefits, making organizational adjustments, achieving digital business user-friendliness and performance, achieving expected trust, implementation of digital business strategy, and achieving on-going knowledge management, learning, and innovation
Sustainable digital business success	Measure the sustainable success of digital business by looking at such areas as internal operations and communication, interaction with suppliers and partners, interaction with government agencies, interaction with competitors, dealing with channel conflict, integration, achieving expected benefits, making organizational

(continued)

Table 3.5 (continued)

Factors	Description
	adjustments, achieving digital business user-friendliness and performance, achieving expected trust, implementation of digital business strategy, and achieving on-going knowledge management, learning, and innovation

Source Developed from Xu and Quaddus (2009), pp. 419–438

business initiatives and activities of step-2 for enhancing gained digital business success, organizations will be able to achieve sustainable digital success. Table 3.5 presents the description of factors of the model.

References

Acker, O., Geerdes, H., Gröne, F., & Schröder, G. (2013). Builders of the digital ecosystem: The 2013 Booz and Company global ICT 50 study, 1–17. *Research Report*, Booz & Company.

Berman, S. J., & Bell, R. (2011). Digital transformation: creating new business models where digital meets physical. *IBM Global Business Service Executive Report*, 1–17. IBM Institute for Business Value.

Bharadwaj, A., El Sawy, O. A., Pavlou, P. A., & Venkatraman, N. (2013). Digital business strategy: Toward a next generation of insights. *MIS Quarterly*, *37*(2), 471–482.

Brooks, C., (2014, February 19). 6 Tips for taking your e-commerce business global. Businessnewsdaily.com. Retrieved March 10, 2014 from http://www.businessnewsdaily.com/5948-how-to-make-your-e-commerce-business-an-overseas-success.html.

Brown, B., Sikes, J., & Willmott, P. (2013, August). Bullish on digital: McKinsey global survey results. *Insights & Publications*. McKinsey & Company. Retrieved December 10, 2013 from http://www.mckinsey.com/insights/business_technology/bullish_on_digital_mckinsey_global_survey_results.

Brownee, D. (2014, March 13). Answer these 3 questions before jumping into entrepreneurship. Entrepreneur.com. Retrieved April 20, 2014, from http://www.entrepreneur.com/article/232127.

Brynjolfsson, E., Jeffrey, Y., & Rahman, M. S. (2013). Competing in the age of omnichannel retailing. *MIT Sloan Management Review, 54*(4), 23–29.

Bughin, J., & Manyika, J. (2013, July). Measuring the full impact of digital capital. *McKinsey Quarterly*, 1–8.

Callahan, T., Kutcher, E., & Manyika, J. (2014). Breaking through the start-up stall zone. *McKinsey Quarterly, 24*(1), 20–21.

Chui, M., & Fleming, T. (2011). Insight P&G's digital revolution. *McKinsey Quarterly*, November 2013, 1–11.

Chui, M. (2014, May). Disruptive entrepreneurs: An interview with Eric Ries. *Insights & Publications*. McKinsey & Company. Retrieved June 12, 2014, from http://www.mckinsey.com/insights/high_tech_telecoms_internet/disruptive_entrepreneurs_an_interview_with_eric_ries.

Downes, L., & Nunes, P. F. (2013, March). Big-bang disruption: A new kind of innovator can wipe out incumbents in a flash. *Harvard Business Review*, 1–12.

eMarketer. (2014, April 21). Consumers favour small businesses because of their customer focus. eMarketer.com. Retrieved May 8, 2014, from http://www.emarketer.com/Article/Consumers-Favor-Small-Businesses-of-Their-Customer-Focus/1010771.

Favaro, K. (2013, December 2). Introducing s + b's Strategy of the year. *Blog of Business + Strategy*. Retrieved January 12, 2014, from http://www.strategy-business.com/blog/Introducing-sb-Strategy-of-the-Year?gko=d1f90.

Favaro, K. (2014, April 28). Strategy is not about the competition. *Blog of Business + Strategy*. Retrieved May 15, 2014, from http://www.strategy-business.com/blog/Strategy-Is-Not-about-the-Competition?gko=e564a.

Fitzgerald, M. (2014). How Starbucks has gone digital: Interview with Adam Brotman and Curt Garner (Starbucks). *MIT Sloan Management Review*, April 2013, pp. 1–5.

Fitzgerald, M., Kruschwitz, N., Bonnet, D., & Welch, M. (2014). Embracing digital technology: A new strategic imperative. Findings from the 2013 Digital Transformation Global Executive Study and Research Project by MIT Sloan Management Review & Capgemini Consulting, Research Report 2013. *MIT Sloan Management Review*, 1–12.

Gimpel, G., & Westerman, G. (2012, October). Shaping the future: Seven enduring principles for fast-changing industries. *Working Paper*, 1–24. The MIT Center for Digital Business.

Hagel III, J., Brown, J. S., & Kulasooriya, D. (2011). The 2011 shift index: Measuring the impact of long-term change. *Deloitt Center for the Edge Report*, 1–232. Deloitt Development LLC.

Hirt, M., & Willmott, P. (2014). Strategic principles for competing in the digital age. *Insights & Publications*, May 2013, McKinsey & Company. http://www.mckinsey.com/insights/strategy/strategic_principles_for_competing_in_the_digital_age.

Huy, Q., & Vuori, T. (2014, March 13). What could have saved Nokia, and what can other companies can learn?. *INSEAD Knowledge*. Retrieved May 8, 2014, from http://knowledge.insead.edu/strategy/what-could-have-saved-nokia-and-what-can-other-companies-learn-3220.

IBM Institute of Business Value. (2013, October). The customer-activated enterprise: The insights from the global c-suite study. *IBM Global Business Services Paper*, 1–24.

Interbrand. (2014). Best global brands 2013. *Internbrand.com*. Retrieved June 26, 2014, from http://www.interbrand.com/en/best-global-brands/2013/top-100-list-view.aspx.

Jaruzelski, B., Holman, R., & Baker, E. (2011, May 30). 3 M's open innovation. *Strategy + Business*. Retrieved July 12, 2012, from http://www.strategy-business.com/article/00078?gko=121c3.

Josh, G., & Willmott, P. (2014). *The digital tipping point* (pp. 1–8). McKinsey Global Survey Results, McKinsey & Company.

Kauffeld, R., Mueller, C., & Michaels, A. (2011). The capable supply chain linked with strategy for superior performance. *Perspective*, pp. 1–13. Booz & Company.

Kleiner, A. (2012, June 25). Brand transformation on the internet. *Strategy + Business*. Retrieved July 20, 2012, from http://www.strategy-business.com/article/00117?pg=all.

Laseter, T. (2014, Summer 2014). Management in the second machine age. *Strategy + Business*, (75), 1–5.

Lichtenthaler, U., Hoegl, M., & Muethel, M. (2011). Is your company ready for open innovation. *MIT Sloan Management Review, 53*(1), 45–48.

Lopez, J., Burkett, M., Meehan, P., Scheibenreif, D., & Tully, J. (2014, March 24). Agenda overview for digital business, 2014, *Free Preview of Gartner Research*, G00260349.

Manyika, J. (2013, May). The impact of disruptive technology: A conversation with Eric Schmidt. *Insights & Publications*. McKinsey & Company. Retrieved January 10, 2014 from http://www.mckinsey.com/insights/high_tech_telecoms_internet/the_impact_of_disruptive_technology_a_conversation_with_eric_schmidt.

MIT Center for Digital Business and Capgemini Consulting. (2011). Digital transformation: A roadmap for billion-dollar organizations. *Massachusetts Institute of Technology and Capgemini Consulting Report*, pp. 1–67.

Palmguist, M. (2014). Why the Steve Jobs approach pays off. *Strategy + Business*, September 27, 2013. Retrieved March 20, 2014, from http://www.strategy-business.com/article/re00253?gko=1615d.

Peppard, J., Ward, J., & Daniel, E. (2007). Managing the realization of benefits from IT investment. *MIS Quarterly Executive, 6*(1), 1–11.

Roberts, R., & Sikes, J. (2011, Spring). How IT is managing new demands: McKinsey Global Survey results. *McKinsey on Business Technology, 22*, 24–33.

Ruthven, P. (2014, May 7). *What businesses need from MBAs in the future*. Dinner Address by Phil Ruthven, Chairman, IBISWorld, 8th Annual Australia & New Zealand MBA Directors Forum at Hotel Windsor, Melbourne, Australia.

Turban, E., Lee, J. K., King, D., Liang, T. P., & Turban, D. (2010). *Electronic Commerce: A Managerial Perspective 2010* (International ed.). Upper Saddle River: Prentice Hall.

Turban, E., King, D., Liang, T. P., & Turban, D. (2012). *Electronic commerce: A managerial and social networks perspective* (Global, 7 ed.). U.K: Pearson Education.

Weill, P., & Woerner, S. L. (2013a, October). The new digital divide: Emerging trump developed economies. MIT sloan center for information systems research. *Research Briefing, 13*(10) 1–4.

Weill, P., & Woerner, S. L. (2013b). Optimizing your digital business model. *MIT Sloan Management Review, 54*(3), 71–78.

Willmott, P. (2013a, June). The do-or-die questions boards should ask about technology. *Insights & Publications*. McKinsey & Company. Retrieved December 8, 2013, from http://www.mckinsey.com/insights/business_technology/the_do-or-die_questions_boards_should_ask_about_technology.

Willmott, P. (2013b, November). The digital enterprise. *Insights & Publications*. McKinsey & Company. Retrieved December 8, 2013, from http://www.mckinsey.com/insights/business_technology/the_digital_enterprise.

Willmott, P. (2014, May). Digital strategy. *Insights & Publications*. McKinsey & Company. Retrieved June 6, 2014, from http://www.mckinsey.com/insights/business_technology/digital_strategy.

Xu, J., & Quaddus, M. (2009). *E-business in the 21st century: Realities, challenges, and outlook*. Singapore: World Scientific Publishing.

Xu. J., & Quaddus, M. (2013). *Managing information systems: Ten essential topics*. Amsterdam: Atlantis Press & Springer.

Chapter 4
B2C Digital Enterprise: E-Tailing

This chapter provides an overview of e-tailing, discusses issues of e-tailing, reviews success factors of e-tailing, and presents some emerging trends and future directions of e-tailing.

4.1 Overview of E-Tailing

This chapter focuses on electronic retailing (e-tailing). E-tailing (also called B2C digital enterprise/e-business/e-commerce) is the selling of retail goods and services online, over the Internet (or digitally). This book treat the words of Internet-based, Online, Electronic, and Digital as equivalent terms and used interchangeably and they all refer to both wired/cabled and wireless/mobile businesses, applications/ systems, and networks. This type of digital enterprise/e-business is highly visible and has received much attention by the popular press. The Internet has provided opportunities for new, fully online retail businesses. The Internet is making many existing, brick-and-mortar retailers wonder to what extent they ought to put their own operations online/digitally. The B2C e-tailing market will grow substantially in the coming years. It is reported that by 2016, the web will influence more than 50 % of all retail transactions, representing a potential sales opportunities of almost US $2 trillion (Bommel et al. 2014).

Online retailers could enjoy such benefits as wider product selection (there is no limitation of physical space for product display), 24/7/365 availability, convenience, cheaper prices, easier comparison of prices and vendors, better personalization, the capability of mass customization, update-to-date information, and global reach. Meanwhile the notion that not every product or service is appropriate for online retailing has been challenged in recent years when more and more products and services become available online. The argument could be whether you can get the products/services digitally (e.g., If you order a dish from a restaurant, the dish has to be delivered to you physically but not digitally/electronically).

J. Xu, *Managing Digital Enterprise*, DOI 10.2991/978-94-6239-094-2_4

4.2 Issues of E-Tailing

Some commonly discussed e-tailing issues include channel conflict, pricing, and personalization.

4.2.1 Channel Conflict

Channel conflict can occur when an upstream member of the supply chain begins to sell directly to customers. It can also happen where online and offline departments/ channels in one company compete with each other—organizations need to balance resources and support for them. One frequently asked question associated with channel conflict is: Should we offer the same or different products and/or services for online and offline channels? There are no universal answers to this question since each retailer could have its own unique circumstances. In principle, they should examine certain products and/or services (if not all products and/or services) which are either exclusive or unique to them; and in order to achieve that they need to use data analytics to understand their customer better and to guide product design, product line choices, channel decisions, and new product decision, and they also need to closely work with the manufactures and/or their suppliers to create uniqueness in their products and service (Brynjolfsson et al. 2013).

4.2.2 Pricing

Pricing is another frequently discussed question associated with channel conflict. Pricing a product or service on the Internet, especially by a click-and-mortar company, is complicated. On the one hand, prices need to be competitive. Today's online comparison engines will show the consumer the prices at many stores for almost all commodity products, at almost no cost to the consumer. However balanced against this is the fact that for some items, transaction costs will decrease, choices/options will increase, the cost of distribution will decrease, and supply chains will become more efficient and shorter (i.e., changing from linear to hub structure), meaning that e-tailers might be able to compete in the aggressive online market space against larger traditional players. On the other hand, pricing strategy should be in line with the corporate policy on profitability and, in a click-and-mortar company, online pricing strategy should be also in line with the offline channel's pricing strategy. To avoid channel and price conflicts between online and offline channels, some companies have established independent online operations or have adopted the strategy of selling/offering different products/services via online and offline channels respectively. E-tailing organizations could also charge extra fees for rapid delivery and additional value-added services, and ask for premium prices for exclusive and unique products and services. In addition, they should avoid direct pricing competition with their competitors by working on differentiation efforts (i.e., different product features, retailer's own brands, overseas products (especially those not available locally), product bundles and product-service bundles which make it difficult to do a direct price comparison), however for the common/non-exclusive products and services, cost and efficiency are the key aspects for winning the competition (Brynjolfsson et al. 2013).

In the future, dynamic pricing should be applied to multi-channels of retailing, it could be done via technologies such as electronic shelf labelling (ESL) and smart algorithms for dynamic pricing (Desai et al. 2012; Gandhi et al. 2014) and real-time and personalized discounts/incentives via mobile phones to customers while they are shopping in the store.

4.2.3 Personalization

Online businesses have the ability to create an element of personalization (tailoring products and services) for each individual consumer, which could be very expensive in the offline world. An e-tailer can use cookie files and other technologies to track consumers' online behavior. By using information collected online, the online retailer is able to provide personalized and more targeted products and services. The Internet also gives consumers increased interaction with the online retailer and can clearly express what he/she wants without face-to-face contact. Many e-tailers allow customers to customize products and services online. Furthermore, the Internet also makes the retailers' dream of mass customization (providing personalized services to everyone) a reality. And it has been proven that personalized websites do lead to higher conversation rates, and some good examples are Facebook, Twitter, Pinterest (Ferguson 2013). Personalized services are also important in the store. While the customer walks into the store, the in-store systems should immediately check his/her profile in the database and provide relevant information to the sales staff (through mobile devices) on the floor, so they can approach the customer in a more personalized and better informed way.

4.3 Success Factors of E-Tailing

In this section, some selected success factors of e-tailing are discussed, including the multiple-channel strategy, developing effective supply chains for multi-channel services, addressing people's needs, excellent customer services, effective and dynamic e-tailing site, and education and trust building.

4.3.1 The Multi-channel Strategy

Retailers should leverage the multi-channels/multiple screens (e.g., mobile phones, tablets, smart TVs, PCs, laptops) by offering the advantages of each marketing channel to customers from all channels (e.g. returning items purchased online to physical stores). In order to provide seamless and quality services to the customers via all channels and touch points (e.g., telephones, TVs, kiosks, faxes, the Internet, mobile phones, in-store, agents and partners), retailers need to develop cross-function and cross-channel capabilities, along with required organizational structure and culture. On a related note, as Walker (2013) points out it is true that there could be differences in targeting segments for different channels (e.g., young customers could be more for digital channels while older customers could be more for physical channels), the philosophy and the approach of cross-channel/cross-function and speaking with one voice is accurate and effective, in terms of providing seamless and same quality service and experience.

According to Google's retail industry leader Ross McDonald (reported in Redrup 2013), Google's research suggests 80–90 % of purchases still happen in-store, and the challenge for retailers is to integrate digital technologies with the in-store experience and achieve total alignment of digital and physical solutions with a seamless presence across all digital medium and all channels (e.g., in-store touchscreen kiosks which allow customers to choose and customize products and email/send to their friends and family members for comments before their purchase in the store, thus significantly improve the conversion rate in the store. Without them, the customers may need to come back next time with their friends or family members or their suggestions, but very often they walk away and never come back). Retailers also need to recognize both web-influenced in-store sales (e.g., doing research online and then purchasing offline) and showrooming-approach of online sales (i.e., browsing in the store and then purchasing online). According to a recent research of 6,000 online shoppers from 6 countries of the USA, the UK, France, Germany, Italy, and Australia by LivePerson (2013):

- 78 % of respondents researched online before shopping in store.
- 25 % researched on their mobile phones while in store.
- 39 % spent the same time online as they did in store.
- Impulse buying is happening online as well-50 % bought more online than planned.

However for many of them, driving traffic to the physical store via different methods and digital technologies is a way forward in the foreseeable future. For example, according to a recent research of 3,000 social media users in North America and the UK by Sevitt and Samuel (2013), 41 % of the respondents indicated that they used "reverse showrooming" (i.e., browsing online and then purchasing in stores).

The multi-channel strategy is really about delivering the same customer experience via any channel the customer choose; and in order to make that happen, the support and commitment by senior executive is critical, and the relentless and seamless delivery by joint and cross-functional efforts from marketing, sales, technology, and operations is a must (Sealey 2014). In addition, multi-device optimization of customer experience (e.g., quality experience across mobile phones, tablets, PCs, laptops) is also very important for the success of multi-channel strategy.

4.3.2 Developing Effective Supply Chains for Multiple-Channel Services

In many retailing organizations, their supply chains are primarily built for a single-channel retailing business, which is obviously obsolete in the era of digital retailing (e.g., not enough distribution centers covering orders cost-effectively for a large geographic area, lack of integration between supply chains for the stores and for digital channels, and the high costs for serving multi-channel customers with the traditional supply chains); and the increasing expectations of multi-channel consumers for speed and convenience have forced retailers to revamp their supply chains (Chaturvedi et al. 2013). Retailers have to develop integrated, transparent, collaborative, networked, agile and global supply chains to win and retain multi-channel consumers. Benefits of such supply chains include: higher distribution center throughput and capacity from enhanced peak responsiveness, optimal layout, and processes; reduction of lead time to customers from reconfiguring the distribution footprint and improving supply chain speed; lower distribution center cost and handling/labor cost from lean and efficient distribution centers, processes in the store, and shifting work upstream; reduction in the likelihood of markdown by moving stocks across channels and reducing the reliance on online discount intermediaries such as www.Groupon.com which often have conflicting objectives and actually erode the profitability of e-tailers (Girotra and Wachter 2013); lower working capital from achieving better efficiency along the supply chains; and higher revenue from reduced out-of-stocks and improved customer experience. A good example is Amazon's supply chains (cited in Chaturvedi et al. 2013):

- Collecting 90 % of items from suppliers using Amazon freight networks, thus saving shipping charges.
- Keeping top 20 % items in all distribution centers and distributing the items unevenly.
- Tracking and trace through Advanced Shipping Notices.
- Establishing 20 distribution centers within 95 % of all U.S. metropolitan areas/regions, which could ensure most orders to be shipped within one shipping zone.
- Having favorable contracts with delivery service providers.
- Putting in place advanced order-management systems to maximize the shipping capacity.

Meanwhile, for retailers embarking on transforming their supply chains for serving multi-channel consumers, some suggestions include (Chaturvedi et al. 2013):

- Designing multi-channel business supply chains for the future (i.e., at least for the next 3–5 years).
- Identifying and addressing the gaps between the existing supply chains with the expected ones (e.g., looking at additional distribution space, automation, and new store processes to manage returns).
- Closely overhauling the existing supply chains and working on supply chain configurations (ideally 3 or 4 configurations) with making maximum use of the current network and capabilities (e.g., looking at such questions as the number and location of distribution centers needed, whether (and how) to deal with online order fulfilment from stores, and how much to integrate online and offline inventories).
- Thinking end to end supply chain costs (or total costs of the supply chain), working capital, capabilities, and resources requirements, which should include qualitative and quantitative measures as well as tangible and intangible dimensions.
- Planning for uncertainty by allowing for agility and flexibility.

One important consideration associated with multi-channel strategy is to decide the speed of delivery (e.g., asking such questions as which product categories are most sensitive to delivery speed? how long are customers willing to wait? how much are they willing to pay for rapid delivery? what is the cost and required capabilities for us (retailers)?). While some leading e-tailers and traditional retailers have been pushing or testing their rapid delivery services (e.g., the same day delivery services by Amazon, eBay, Google, Nordstorm), such initiatives are expensive and difficult to expand beyond narrow geographies (Muller et al. 2013). According to a recent survey of 1,000 online shoppers in the U.S. conducted by the consulting firm Booz & Company (reported in Chaturvedi et al. 2013), most of online shoppers don't necessarily need same-day delivery, and the next day delivery (or overnight delivery) was viewed by them almost as good as the same-day delivery (only 5 % less valuable to them than same day delivery). In another recent study of 6,000 online shoppers from six countries of the USA, the UK., France, Germany, Italy, and Australia by LivePerson (2013), the top reason for abandoning online purchases is unexpected delivery costs (70 % of the respondents). For e-tailing organizations this is a piece of good news since the cost of next-day delivery will be significantly less than that of the same day delivery. To be able to provide low-cost (if not free next-day delivery to shoppers which is preferred by them) next-day delivery services, e-tailing organizations need to pay attention to the following issues suggested by Muller et al. (2013):

- Effectively coordinating across channels (e.g., using the store's inventory and proximity to fulfil online orders).
- Achieving real-time, transparent and detailed inventory management of all channels.

- Optimizing order fulfilment systems (e.g., making better decision of fulfilling the orders by balancing factors such as proximity to the customers, inventory level, and staff capacity to deal with fulfilling the order).
- Establishing a flexible workforce (e.g., providing training to the sales staff in the store so they can fulfil the online orders (especially at their idle times), and examining sales personnel commission and compensation schemes to support multi-channel strategy).
- Developing robust logistic partnerships.
- Actively promoting the next-day delivery as well as the concept of "store to home" by taking advantage of the store's proximity to the customers and leveraging idle sales capacities (especially for out-of-season stock).

4.3.3 Addressing People's Needs

Retailers, whether digital or physical, are there to fulfil consumers' fundamental needs. The Internet has not changed that, and it simply provides them with more tools, more information, easier search and comparison, and convenience for looking at options and making purchase decision even though it could influence buyer choices via activities such as searching online before buying in-store, in-store search via mobile devices, and location-based promotion through mobile devices (Redrup 2013). The leading online auction site of eBay's recent initiative of Bub's Concern in Australia (reported in Waters 2014), a dedicated section of baby essentials for time-poor new parents, is a good example of identifying and addressing people's needs (in this case, parents' needs). Through its research, eBay found that 70 % of surveyed new parents who were woken during the night often used the time to do online shopping and nearly 90 % of those parents had baby essentials (e.g., nappies, wipes and formula) as their top shopping priorities. Some other examples include Amazon's initiative of using 3D-modelling technology, via its recently acquired 3D Modelling company PhiSix, to enable customers to find the right sizes of clothes more easily online (reported in McFarland 2014); Virutal Designer function on the retailers' mobile application (Bommel et al. 2014); 3D Scanners in the stores or shopping malls. Big W Australia's online layby and click and collect (i.e., purchasing online and collecting in the chosen store around 2–3 business days) initiatives are also good examples.

4.3.4 Excellent Customer Services

E-tailers need to empower the customers with high quality services, such as 24/7 channel for service; secure and smooth online purchases, extensive information on products and services, assistance in purchasing decision, flexible order fulfilment methods (e.g., common carrier, overnight to same day delivery, and pickup in the nearby store), and personalized services. They also need to speak with one voice by providing consistent information and service to customers from both physical and digital channels. In addition, loyalty programs and service contracts could create switching costs for retailers and help them retain their customers (Brynjolfsson et al. 2013).

According to Tony Heish (reported in Heish 2010), CEO, www.Zappos.com, which is a leading e-tailer of shoes and was acquired by Amazon in 2009, exceptional customer service is critical to the success of e-tailing; and some of their customer service practices include:

- Making customer service a company-wide priority.
- Empowering your customer representatives.
- Firing customers who are insatiable or abuse employees.
- Not measuring call times, No upselling, and Not using scripts.
- Never hiding your phone number-You want to talk to your customers.
- Viewing the cost of handling customers' calls as an investment in marketing, not an expense.
- Celebrating great service by telling exceptional stories to the entire company.

Customer service is very important to the success and long term growth of e-tailers, especially in the digital environment where there is no physical (or face-to-face) interaction. Providing excellent services and keeping on bettering and innovating your services is essential. Some common practices are: establishing call centers or customer hotlines, responding to customer online quires and emails quickly (definitely no longer than 24 h), real-time online chatting, quick, non-expensive and accurate delivery with multiple options, and fair and transparent dispute resolution process. Some firms are providing more to their customers via such initiatives as free return (e.g., Theiconic.com.au's free 100 days return policy), free shipping (e.g., www.Amazon.com's free shipping for certain products and/or for certain amount and/or for certain regions/places), free shipping and free return (e.g., www.Zappos.com' free shipping and free 365 days return policy), and free trial at home (e.g., Jeansonline.nl's Easy Fit and Return initiative-you can try clothes delivered to your home for free and if you don't like them you can return them to the courier who will be waiting for 15 min at your door step while you are trying them on).

E-tailing organizations should engage their customers throughout their journey with the organization (i.e., from pre-purchase activities until post-purchase activities) via multiple channels and touch points (e.g., contact centers, email, live chat, click to call, social media); and the focus should be on speed of response and providing an easy and simple resolution to issues. According to a recent research of 6,000 online shoppers from six countries of the USA, the UK, France, Germany, Italy, and Australia by LivePerson (2013), some perspectives of excellent customer services include:

- The three identified elements of a great online customer service experience include: getting issues resolved quickly (82 % of the respondents), getting an issue resolved in a single transaction (56 %), and dealing with a friendly customer service representative (45 %).

- 59 % indicated that they would like to have more choices in how they contact the e-tailing organization whether it is via a call center (61 %), email (60 %), or Live Chat (57 %).
- 93 % suggested that real-time help is helpful during their whole online journey with the e-tailing organization.
- 73 % were satisfied with Live Chat while 60 % were happy with both email and telephone support.
- 51 % would be more likely to buy again if they could answers via Live Chat while 48 % would be more likely to return to the e-tailing website and 41 % would be more likely to trust a brand if Live Chat is available.
- 83 % needed some form of support during their online shopping journey.
- 51 % either tried once or gave up immediately when seeking help before an online purchase.
- 71 % expected to be able to access help when purchasing online within 5 min while 31 % expected immediate access to help. And if a response is not delivered in the expected timeframe, 48 % will either go elsewhere or abandon the online purchase altogether.

In the same study, some identified top reasons for abandoning online purchases include: unexpected delivery costs, lack of information about product/service/delivery, navigation difficulties, issues with online customer service/support (such as wanting to ask a question or not finding the answer and difficulty in getting any help on the website). Collier and Beinstock (2006) suggest that customers would judge quality of an e-tailer from three perspectives:

- Interaction with the website (e.g. ease of use, privacy, simple design, consistency, reliability, flexibility, good information of the site).
- Delivery of the product (e.g., the timeliness of fulfilling the order, the accuracy of fulfilling the order, and the undamaged condition of the delivered product).
- Addressing problems when they occur (e.g., the opportunity to talk to a person, fairness of policies and procedures, and offering compensation and apologies).

Providing customers with a consistent experience and communication across multiple channels and various touch points throughout their journey with the retailing organization is critical to the success and performance of the retailer. According to a recent study of 27,000 American consumers across 14 different industries (reported in Pulido et al. 2014), focusing on customer journey could deliver 35 % more predictive of customer satisfaction and 32 % more predictive of customer churn than performance on individual touch points; and maximizing customer satisfaction with the journey could potentially increase revenue by up to 15 % and reduce the cost of serving customers by up to 20 %. Consistent communication plays a very important role in achieving consistent customer experience; organizations need to fulfil their promises and then actively highlight the delivery of the made promises to reinforce their commitments and promote the successes of providing consistent customer experience.

Providing the customers with the option of speaking to human assistants is very critical as well. It is reported that 70 % of mobile searchers use Google's click-to-call to contact suppliers; 54 % of customers want to speak to a real person; 74 % of UK adults would change supplier as a result of poor contact center customer experience; 63 % of UK. consumers prefer to call a firm with customer service queries; 70 % of customer complaints on social media (e.g., Facebook and Twitter) are ignored; and only 11 % of people expect to receive customer service via social media as opposed to 71 % via telephone (Bell 2013).

Effectively managing customers' online public complaints is also critical. A popular example is the incident of musician Dave Carrol's US$3,500 guitar damage caused by United Airlines baggage services (Tripp and Grégoire 2011). Dave had been trying to get an answer from the company for 9 months without success; he then wrote a song and created a music video about this incident and posted the music video in Youtube, the video brought very bad publicity in a very short timeframe (e.g., 150,000 views within one day, over 5 million views 1 month later) to United Airlines and United Airlines finally offered Dave compensation for the damage to his Guitar and promised to re-examine its policies. When there are online public complaints which typically happen after they have tried other (traditional) channels and/or attempted a series of failed resolutions, e-tailing organizations need to offer responses with fair and transparent processes and sincere apology quickly (within 24 h however after 4 weeks, any post-complaint recovery will likely be ineffective), and the best way to deal with online public complains is to prevent them and put them off before they become uncontrollable.

4.3.5 Effective and Dynamic E-Tailing Site

The e-tailing site must be effective with superior technical performance and functionalities; and the site must be kept updated, dynamic and interesting, with current and accurate content and the interactions with customers. Navigation difficulty is unveiled as one of the top reasons for abandoning online purchases in a recent research of 6,000 online shoppers from six countries of the USA, the UK, France, Germany, Italy, and Australia by LivePerson (2013). According to a recent study by the consulting firm Booz & Company (reported in Hölbling et al. 2012), some top digital commerce(e-commerce website) functionalities include (in order): ratings and reviews (65 % of the respondents), search and filter (58 %), check-out (58 %), my account (57 %), shopping cart (57 %), recognition (54 %), product comparison (54 %), offers and promotions (54 %), shopping experience (50 %), advisor (46 %), cross and up-selling (45 %), support (45 %), consistency (40 %), payment options (36 %), and order management and delivery (36 %). Generally speaking digital commerce capabilities could be categorized into three groups: (1) foundation capabilities (including data management, analytics and testing, content management systems, user tools and application programming interfaces, workflow and processes), (2) design capabilities (including user interface and navigation, segmentation and targeting, multi-channel, search engine optimization), and (3) purchase funnel capabilities (including exploration capabilities of showroom, account management, marketing channels and shop links; shopping and order fulfilment capabilities of offers and promotions, order management, post-order management; and interaction and support capabilities of user engagement and support).

Meanwhile to ensure the effectiveness of the e-tailing site, a set of KPIs (key performance indicators) should be established, including the number of unique visitors, the average time a visitor spent on the site which could range from a few seconds to 20 min for many online retailing sites, the average amount spent per order, number of sales per number of site visits (conversation rate, which could range from less than 1–30 % for many e-tailing sites), and the monthly return visitors (ratio between total visits and unique visits) (Hölbling et al. 2012). In addition, the speed of site is also very important. According to Econsultancy (reported in Parker 2013), 40 % of customers will abandon a web page if it takes more than three seconds to load. And customers' attention spans are getting shorter. A recent study by Associated Press (cited in Parker 2013) suggests that American adults have an eight second attention span (dropping 20 % from 2000), and 20 % of them spend fewer than 4 s on a site. The e-tailing site also needs to be reliable and available all the time, especially during the peak period. The recent glitch of the e-commerce site of Myer (one of leading department stores in Australia) during critical post-Christmas sales period definitely caused some financial losses and frustration among its customers.

While digital technologies and applications, such as blogs and microblogs (e.g., Twitter), wikis, mobile Apps, social media, have been gaining in popularity, the importance of the e-tailing website should not be undermined. SMEs may believe that there is little they can do with digital technologies and they don't have Big Data to play with; however they actually have not really grasped what is happening and what is coming. For example, the whole digital retailing industry has been getting bigger and will become much bigger in the future, and their future customers will be very digital ones. So digital commerce is a must-do thing for them, and they need to think big otherwise they will not be able to stay in the competition in the future (Stafford 2014).

According to a recent report by MYOB Business Monitor (reported in Reardon 2013), around 20 % of Australian SMEs who had a website previously have abandoned their websites while we are seeing a upward trend of e-tailing in terms of online sales, sales influenced by websites, Google search, time spent online. In the foreseeable future, the e-tailing site is still and will be playing a critical role even though other digital technologies and applications could no doubt complement and enhance the e-tailing site. The results of a recent study of automotive dealers in the U.K. and Germany suggest a very similar notion; and indicate that the digital technologies and applications they adopted include (in order): own website (41 % of the participants), online markets and platforms (33 %), e-mail/newsletters (23 %), and Apps and social networks (18 %).

4.3.6 Education and Trust Building

While factors such as security, not comfortable with using credit online, the lack of opportunities of physically touching and trying the product, not being able to get the product at the time of purchasing, and not being able to speak face-to-face to shop assistants, could prevent people from participating online shopping but the more experience people have online, the more likely they are to buy online. And people now even have more confidence in buying costly items online (e.g., jewelries). For e-tailers, they need to focus on engaging customers as human beings (rather than focusing on products and devices of which customers are the buyers and users) and connect with them emotionally (e.g., sharing Apple's vision with iPhone users about innovation and creativity) and then demonstrate the professionalism and trustworthiness of the organization (Powell 2013).

On a related note, educating the customers has been and will be largely on the shoulders of the sales staff (in-store or online), so they need to have good a understanding of multi-channel strategy and the capabilities and roles of the technology in the shopping experience of the customers. Meanwhile for the senior management of the e-tailing organization, the more important skills could be providing retail services and experience in a fast changing product lifecycle environment than having a technology background, even for a technology-oriented retailer (Moore 2013). For example, Apple's newly created role of Senior Vice President of Retail and Online Store, which looks after Apple's retail sales, its own Apple stores, its re-seller network, and its online channel, has been filled by a candidate (former CEO of fashion brand Burberry) with a strong background in fashion retailing and track record of working with fashion icons but not with any technology firms previously.

As an extension of this, Xuan et al. (2007) studied e-tailing in one of the largest retail group in China and Asia and suggest that e-tailing success in China is influenced by a number of internal and external factors:

- External factors (e.g., policies and regulations, competition, cost of computing devices and access to the Internet, payment systems and banking services, the presence of advanced retail networks in China, national culture, and credit/reputation system).
- Organizational factors (e.g., IS/IT infrastructure, IS/IT expertise, organizational structure, organizational culture, mission, vision and strategic directions of the organization, business processes, brand and reputation, profit objectives, and organizational size).
- Senior management factors (e.g., senior management's commitment, allocating sufficient resources for e-tailing initiatives, and senior management's knowledge of e-commerce).
- E-commerce strategy (e.g., e-commerce investment cost and benefit considerations, integration issues, strategic alliances, product selection, pricing strategies, marketing and advertising, and leveraging first-mover advantages).

- Consumer factors (e.g., age, gender, education, income, experience of e-commerce, innovativeness, work and life style, in-store shopping experience, and existing relations with the retailer).
- E-commerce system measures (e.g., system quality, content quality, trust, and support services).

4.4 Emerging Trends and Future Directions

The future of e-tailing is bright since it has huge growth potential. At the moment, e-tailing is only accounted for less than 10 % of the retail market (for example, according to McKinsey Global Institute (reported in Dobbs et al. 2013), e-tailing accounts for around 5 % of the retail market in both China and the U.S., who are the two largest retail markets in the world). Whether we are going to be still using the word of "Omni-channel" emphasized by Rigby (2011) or something else, the future retailing will take advantage of both digital (e.g., much wider product ranges, 24/7 availability, convenience, anytime, anything and anywhere access, rich product information, easy comparison of products and prices, customer reviews and tips, social engagement and interaction, and mass personalization) and physical (e.g., edited assortment, convenient returns and repairs, instant access to products and instant gratification, services provided by shop staff or/and automation, in-store personal experience, the feeling and experience of physical shopping, being able to touch and try different products, more easier to establish trust than digital channels, and shopping as social activities with friends and family members) channels. In fact, shoppers are actually creating the best shopping experience by complementing online, mobile and in-store channels; and the use of mobile channel actually complements the in-store channel rather than threatens it (Brandweiner 2013). According to a recent survey of 13,000 consumers across 20 countries by BuzzCity (reported in Brandweiner 2013), 59 % of surveyed consumers shopped both online and in-store; 32 % left a store because what they wanted was not available or discounted; while in store, 29 % of them used mobiles to ask their family and friends' advices when making final selection; 20 % preferred to use their mobile phones to find information rather than asking the sales assistance while visiting a store; and 16 % indicated that they had a better shopping experience in-store when shop assistants used the latest technology to interact with them. In the same study, some top factors influencing consumers' buying decision are: the product variety available (33 %), display of product and being easy to find (32 %), and discounts (24 % in-store; 14 % shopping online).

In the future, the physical store will be more for experience, brand exposure, and creating moments for impulse buying; and staff in the store will be focusing more on providing more value-added services and knowledge to the customers (Stafford 2014). And the future shopping experience is a combination of technology and traditional shopping; an excellent example is Hointer Jeans shop in the U.S.: instead of going through a pile of jeans to look for your size and taking the jeans to the change room, you can simply scan the QR Codes of jeans with your mobile phones, then select the size on your phone screen, then a allocated change room will be informed (e.g., fitting room 3), and when you walk into the allocated change room your selected jeans with your size will be there waiting for you (GeekWire 2012). On a related note, there are concerns that the growth of pure e-tailers may have already started slowing down as traditional retailers are catching up in selling digitally. According to a recent analysis of 1.3 billion credit card transactions by Commonwealth Bank of Australia (reported in Robin 2014), it was unveiled that online sales for retailers with both online and offline operations grew 22 % in the year to January 2014, while online sales at online-only retailers grew only 13 %; and for the first time, more than 50 % of the online spending analyzed by the Commonwealth Bank of Australia was being done by multi-channel retailers after an extended period of their catch-up in e-commerce.

One of the most interesting topics (if not the most interesting topic) in the retail sector is the competition between Walmart (the largest retailer in the U.S. and in the world with annual revenue around US$500 billion in 2013) and Amazon (the largest e-tailer (the digital everything store) in the U.S. with annual revenue around US$74 billion in 2013), and they both are competing in the market where consumers want stuff cheap and fast (Knowledge@Wharton 2013). For Walmart it has been struggling with weakening store traffic in recent years and it has been seriously challenged by Amazon (it could be the only major competitor to Walmart in the U.S. market in the foreseeable future); Walmart has been responding by actively engaging with e-tailing and investing heavily in integrating its online, offline and mobile channels, and increasing its development of smaller stores to reduce the price further and drive down the cost, but so far e-tailing has only made a small contribution (for example, approximately US$10 billion revenue (around 2 % of total revenue) in 2013) and without doubt more needs to be done to catch up with Amazon's US$74 billion e-tailing revenue (Zillman 2013; Schafer 2014). So who will win the race in the long run? I am not sure. Even though Amazon has been leading the way in online sales (e.g., Amazon's 200 million items and US$74 billion sales revenue versus Walmart's 5 million items and US$10 billion in revenue in 2013), the question is how long Amazon can keep the lead and its growth? On the other hand, Walmart has more than 4,100 stores within 5 miles of two-thirds of the US population (Banker 2013) as well as its well established supply networks and logistics systems in the U.S. and its extensive global supply chains and its large international coverage; it can definitely leverage those things for its multi-channel retailing strategy.

Another emerging trend is shopping from social networks (e.g., From May 2014, Twitter's more than 250 million users can now shop directly on Amazon by clicking on the #AmazonCart); and the potential market for social commence is huge, for example, the expected social commerce revenue in the US by 2015 will be US$30 billion (Hölbling et al. 2012). Furthermore, social media and mobile applications should look at driving traffic to both digital channels and physical stores (Honigman 2014). Social media could also affect people's purchase decision;

for example Pinterest was found to have impacted on customers' purchase decisions by providing additional information, introducing/exposing the product to customers, reminding customers that they intended to buy the product or service, referral (in terms of pinning something) from someone trusted or respected, showing customers where to get the product or service, altering customers to a sale or a deal, and providing the coupon (Sevitt and Samuel 2013).

Mobile retailing (including location-based initiatives) is another emerging trend. According to McKinsey Global Institute (reported in Brennan et al. 2013), by 2025, 50 % of retail purchases will be made on a mobile device. However that estimation could be conservative, for example, there are more and more product categories that are quickly migrating from physical stores to online. Digital technologies are shaping all markets and product categories; categories such as pet supply, household products and grocery are still being primarily bought from the (physical) stores, categories such as electronics, computer hardware and software, video games, books, DVD/Video, and music have gone digital, and categories such as large appliances, furniture, sporting goods, health and beauty, do-it-yourself, office suppliers, home décor, footwear, toys, clothing and jewelry are the digital battlefield (i.e., still buying in-store or online but moving more to online) (Brennan et al. 2013). Cloud commerce (i.e., individuals selling goods from a personal cloud) could be the next big thing in the near future (Hölbling et al. 2012).

Platform-based retailing, which is based on multi-sided markets and involves various stakeholders and value-added partners, could be another emerging trend (Hill 2014). Platform-based retailers could provide a much larger range of products and services to large numbers of customers; and could disrupt the single-sided market of the majority of e-tailers, for example, Safeway, Vodafone, Dell are being disrupted by platform-based firms such as Google Facebook, and Apple (Hill 2014). In addition, the Internet of Things and Big Data and Data Analytics definitely have a big impact on retailers (e.g., better understanding of customers thus better products and services to customers, more targeted and effective larger scale marketing and advertising, and better communications with suppliers and business partners). According to a recent research by consulting firm McKinsey & Company (reported in Bommel et al. 2014), grocers and big-box retailers (very large retailers) could achieve better financial performance by focusing on consumer analytics (e.g., 11 % vs. 3 % of the growth rate of earnings before interest, tax, depreciation, and amortization for grocers; 10 % vs. 2 % for very large retailers). These aspects have been discussed previously (e.g., in Chap. 2) and more discussion will be presented in subsequent chapters of this book (e.g., in Chap. 8).

The trend of global e-tailing has been going on for some time, and generally speaking some progress has been made but more efforts are required. The markets of the future will be China, India, Brazil, and Russia as well as Africa (after the growth opportunities in these four countries). For example, according to The Economist Intelligence Unit (2012), in 2012, the six largest retail markets (in order) are: United States of America (US$3,389,633 million), China (US$2,311,226 million), Japan (US$1,691,548 million), India (US$845,676 million), Russia (US $658,991 million), and Brazil (US$500,338 million). But in 2016, the top six retail markets will be (in the order): China (US$4,207,729 million), United States of America (US$3,961,146 million), India (US$1,877,429 million), Japan (US $1,496,789 million), Russia (US$932,014 million), and Brazil (US$768,459 million); and in 2022, the top six retail markets will be (in order): China (US $8,345,813 million), United States of America (US$4,470,376 million), India (US $3,822,770 million), Japan (US$1,628,421 million), Russia (US$1,482,362 million), and Brazil (US$1,155,286 million). From the above figures, it can be seen that emerging markets of China, India, Russia and Brazil are and will be having much faster growth than the advanced markets of United States of America and Japan. For example, by 2022, the size of China's retail market will be twice as much as that of the U.S. while in 2012 it was only around 68 % of the U.S. market.

One of the key challenges is to deal with different cultures in different markets. For example, through their studies of online auction sites in China, Quaddus and Xu (2006) found that subject norm (the influence of friends, family, and media) has the most significant impact on buyer behavior of users of online auction sites (both domestic and foreign ones) in China. This is in line with the notion that for Chinese consumers, referral is the most powerful way of opening the market for new products and services (Yang 2004). At the same time, while trust is an important issue and can have an impact on forming positive attitudes toward online auction sites (especially foreign ones) in China, Chinese consumers will not use an online auction portal just because they trust it (Bin et al. 2003). In addition, Chinese consumers may not buy into "western honor system" and/or "trust the system or the people's honor" (Efendioglu and Yip 2004, p. 59). Chinese people believe such notion of never letting out your hawk until you see the hare (Bin et al. 2003). On a related note, the younger generation in China tends to be more open to the new ideas and new things; one reason could be the China's opening up to the rest of the world since 1979 and the global connectedness resulting from the Internet. Some initiative for persuading Chinese consumers to use online auction sites include: (1) creating the image that buying via online auction is a prestige and/or a fashion that everyone should follow. This differs from the Western model where more of an emphasis is put on the idea of getting cheap products via online auction, as Chinese people believe that "cheap products are never good"; (2) having strategic alliances with famous local and international firms will help to boost Chinese consumers' trust and acceptance of online auction sites; (3) providing free trials to let Chinese consumers see how online auction sites work and experience the benefits; (4) targeting market segments where people are willing to take a risk and try new products and services, especially young and educated consumers, but also high earners, and the very busy; (5) encouraging the word-of-mouth effect and providing incentives for introducing peer customers, relatives, friends, and colleagues to use online auction; (6) customizing the auction site to appeal to Chinese consumers is also vital, and (7) allowing people to bid online while completing the transaction offline. The strategy of 'order online and pay offline' has been proven to be very effective in China and will be so for the foreseeable future. Li (2014) shares a very similar view by looking at Amazon's progress in China; and he suggest that Amazon has not progressed well so far in China for such reasons as: not paying enough attention to Chinese market, the constraints by Chinese policies and regulations (e.g., the required licenses by Chinese government), the slow progress of localization (e.g., customizing for local culture and needs), and the fierce competition from successful local Chinese competitors (e.g., www.jd.com, www.taobao.com, www.dangdang.com.cn, www.yhd.com). Furthermore, country differences also have the influence on the operations and the strategy of e-tailing organizations. For example, in China the most popular e-business/e-commerce model is consumer-to-consumer (via marketplaces) e-tailing and the most popular online product category is Apparel while in the U.S., business-to-consumer e-tailing and travel are the most popular e-tailing model and product category respectively; and compared with the U.S., fewer e-tailers in China has offline roots (i.e., having offline operations first before moving online) (Dobbs et al. 2013).

References

Banker, S. (2013, October 4). Amazon vs. walmart: E-commerce vs. omni-channel logistics. *Forbes.com*. Retrieved December 6, 2013, from http://www.forbes.com/sites/stevebanker/2013/10/04/amazon-vs-walmart-e-commerce-vs-omni-channel-logistics/.

Bell, D. (2013, November 22). Infographic: Social customer service via traditional service. *Mycustomer.com*. Retrieved January 10, 2014, from http://www.mycustomer.com/news/infographic-social-customer-serice-explained?qt-most_read_commented=0.

Bin, Q., Chen, S. J., & Sun, S. Q. (2003). Cultural differences in e-commerce: A comparison between the U.S. and China. *Journal of Global Information Management, 11*(2), 48–55.

Bommel, E. V., Edelman, D., & Ungerman, K. (2014, June). Digitizing the consumer decision journey. *Insights & Publications*. McKinsey & Company. Retrieved July 8, 2014, from http://www.mckinsey.com/insights/marketing_sales/digitizing_the_consumer_decision_journey.

Brandweiner, N. (2013, November 25). Omnichannel consumers blending online and in-store shopping. *Mycustomer.com*. Retrieved January 10, 2014, from http://www.mycustomer.com/news/omnichnanel-shoppers-blend-online-and-store-ultimate-experience.

Brennan, J., Kelly, G., & Martinez, A. (December, 2013). Tough choice for consumer goods companies. *Insights & Publications*. McKinsey & Company. Retrieved January 20, 2014, from http://www.mckinsey.com/insights/consumer_and_retail/tough_choices_for_consumer_goods_companies.

Brynjolfsson, E., Hu, Y. J., & Rahman, M. (2013). Competing in the age of omnichannel retailing. *MIT Sloan Management Review, 54*(4), 23–29.

Chaturvedi, N., Martich, M., Ruwadi, B., & Ulker, N. (2013, February). The future of retail supply chains. *Operations as a Competitive Advantage in Retail*, 59–67. McKinsey & Company.

Collier, J. E., & Beinstock, C. C. (2006). How do customers judge quality in an e-tailer? *MIT Sloan Management Review, 48*(1), 35–40.

Desai, P., Potia, A., & Salsberg, B. (2012, December). Retail 4.0: The future of retail grocery in a digital world. *Asia Consumer and Retail Practice.*, 1–67. McKinsey & Company.

Dobbs, R., Chen, Y. A., Orr, G., Chui, M., & Chang, E. (2013, March). China's e-tail revolution: Online shopping as a catalyst for growth. *McKinsey Global Institute Report*, 1–64.

Efendioglu, A. M., & Yip, V. F. (2004). Chinese culture and e-commerce: An exploratory study. *Integrating with Computers, 16*, 45–62.

Ferguson, R. B. (2013, September). How analytics is giving fashion a makeover. *MIT Sloan Management Review*, 1–5.

Gandhi, A., Magar, C., & Roberts, R. (2014, February). How technology can drive the next wave of mass customization. *Business Technology Office.*, 1–8. McKinsey & Company.

GeekWire. (2012, November 29). The hointer shopping experience: Buying jeans from a robot-powered apparel startup. *Youtube video clip*. Retrieved June 10, 2014, from http://www.youtube.com/watch?v=2ZjWwlzRYBM.

Girotra, K., & Wachter, S. (2013, November 26). The dark side of online discounts. *INSEAD Knowledge*. Retrieved February 20, 2014, from http://knowledge.insead.edu/strategy/the-dark-side-of-online-discounts-3012.

Heish, T. (2010, July–August). Zappo's CEO on going to extremes for customers. *Harvard Business Review*, 41–45.

Hill, G. (2014, February 18). Customer-centric confusion: Why customer focus is not enough to succeed. *Mycustomers.com*. Retrieved April 10, 2014, from http://www.mycustomer.com/feature/experience/customer-centric-confusion-why-customer-focus-not-enough-succeed/166515.

Hölbling, K., Gröne, F., Seelbach, F., & Maekelburger, B. (2012). Advantaging digital commerce capabilities to drive financial value: Perspective and benchmarking framework. *Leading Research*, 1–14. Booz & Company.

Honigman, B. (2014). How to sync your e-commerce store with your offline business. *Sumall.com*. Retrieved June 20, 2014, from http://blog.sumall.com/journal/sync-e-commerce-store-initiatives-brick-mortar-store-better-results-2.html.

Knowledge@Wharton. (2013, November 13). In amazon and walmart's battle for dominance, who loses out? *Knowledge.wharton.upenn.edu*. Retrieved January 12, 2014, from https://knowledge.wharton.upenn.edu/article/amazon-walmarts-battle-dominance-future-retail-stake/.

Krings, J., Bakker, J., Koster, A., & Densborn, R. (2013). Unlocking the value of digitization in automotive sales and distribution. *Perspective*, 1–9. Booz & Company.

Li, H. G. (2014, June 21). Magic amazon is destined to fail in China (in Chinese). *Topchinesenews.com*. Retrieved June 28, 2014, from http://www.topchinesenews.com/viewheadlinenews.aspx?topic_id=1000&msg_id=149258.

LivePerson. (2013, January). The connecting with customers report: A global in-depth study of the online customer experience. *LivePerson Inc*, 1–23.

McFarland, M. (2014, March 29). Returns plague fashion e-commerce: Can technology fix the problem. *Washingtonpost.com*. Retrieved April 20, 2014, from http://www.washingtonpost.com/blogs/innovations/wp/2014/03/28/returns-plague-fashion-e-commerce-can-technology-fix-the-problem/.

Moore, K. (2013, November 3). Think out of the box for retail skills and experience. *Smartcompany.com.au*. Retrieved January 12, 2014, from http://www.smartcompany.com.au/growth/34402-think-out-of-the-box-for-retail-skills-and-experience.html.

Muller, C., Schmahl, A., & Tipping, A. (2013, Winter, August 19, Issue 73). Same-day delivery? Not so fast. *Strategy + Business*. Retrieved December 10, 2013, from http://www.strategy-business.com/article/00213?pg=all.

Parker, R. (2013, August 14). Four key stats to help optimise website design. *Smartcompany.com.au*. Smartcompany.com.au. Retrieved December 10, 2013, from http://www.smartcompany.com.au/technology/33168-four-key-stats-to-help-optimise-website-design.html#.

Powell, R. (2013, October 25). The key to successful selling are emotional and irrational: Why being a small business is your secret weapon. *Smartcompany.com.au*. Retrieved December 12, 2014, from http://www.smartcompany.com.au/finance/34296-the-general-store-partner-matt-newell-explains-keys-to-successful-selling-are-emotional-and-irrational.html#

Pulido, A., Stone, D., & Strevel, J. (2014, March). The three Cs of customer satisfaction: Consistency, consistency, consistency. *Insights & Publications*. McKinsey & Company. Retrieved April 20, 2014, from http://www.mckinsey.com/insights/consumer_and_retail/the_three_cs_of_customer_satisfaction_consistency_consistency_consistency.

Quaddus, M., & Xu, J. (2006). Success factors for online auction. *Business Forum China, 3*, 46–47.

Reardon, C. (2013, August 13). Desperate measures as Australian SMEs abandon their websites. *Smartcompany.com.au*. Retrieved December 8, 2013, from http://www.smartcompany.com.au/technology/online/33141-desperate-measures-as-australian-smes-abandon-their-websites.html.

Redrup, Y. (2013, June 27). The new customer: Targeting new-age consumers in an e-commerce environment. *Smartcompany.com.au*. Retrieved December 8, 2013, from http://www.smartcompany.com.au/growth/economy/32384-the-new-customer-targeting-new-age-consumers-in-an-ecommerce-environment.html.

Rigby, D. (2011, December). The future of shopping. *Harvard Business Review*, 65–76.

Robin, M. (2014, April 2). Pure-play sales growth dramatically slows as the majors catch up: Why the online retail honeymoon is over. *Smartcompany.com.au*. Retrieved May 6, 2014, from http://www.smartcompany.com.au/marketing/sales/41362-pure-play-sales-growth-dramatically-slows-as-the-majors-catch-up-why-the-online-retail-honeymoon-is-over.html.

Schafer, L. (2014, February 28). Big retail challenges not confined to a target-walmart has them too. *Startribune.com*. Retrieved March 28, 2014, from http://www.startribune.com/blogs/247905771.html.

Sealey, D. (2014, February 11). Omnichannel: How Domino's delivers a highly integrated customer experience. *Mycustomer.com*. Retrieved April 10, 2014, from http://www.mycustomer.com/feature/experience/how-dominos-delivers-highly-integrated-customer-experience/166466.

Sevitt, D., & Samuel, A. (2013). How Pinterest puts people in stores. *Harvard Business Review, 2013*, 26–27. July–August.

Strafford, P. (2014, January 6). 10 key ways the retail store is changing. *Smartcompany.com.au*. Retrieved January 28, 2014, from http://www.smartcompany.com.au/marketing/sales/35030-10-key-ways-the-retail-store-is-changing.html#.

The Economist Intelligence Unit. (2012). Retail 2022: How the economist intelligence unit sees the retail landscape changing over the next decade. *A Report from The Economist Intelligence Unit Limited*, 1–14.

Trip, T. M., & Grégoire, Y. (2011). When unhappy customers strike back on the internet. *MIT Sloan Management Review, 52*(3), 37–44.

Turban, E., King, D., Liang, T. P., & Turban, D. (2012). *Electronic Commerce: A Managerial and Social Networks Perspective* (7th ed.). UK: Pearson Education. Global Edition.

Walker, B. (2013, August 13). Myth-busting: The top three omni-channel retail myths. *Smartcompany.com.au*. Retrieved December 2, 2013, from http://www.smartcompany.com.au/growth/economy/33143-myth-busting—the-top-three-omni-channel-retail-myths.html.

Waters, C. (2014, April 24). eBay launches Bub's corner site to target time-poor parents. *Smartcompany.com.au*. Retrieved May 8, 2014, from http://www.smartcompany.com.au/marketing/796-online-sales/41664-ebay-launches-bubs-corner-site-to-target-time-poor-parents.html#.

Watson, R. T., Berthon, P., Pitt, L. F., & Zinkhan, G. M. (2000). *Electronic Commerce*. Fort Worth, TX: The Dryden Press.

Xuan, W. B., Xu, J., & Quaddus, M. (2007). *A manager's guide to e-tailing success in China's retail industry: Proceedings of the 13th Asia Pacific Management Conference* (pp. 179–184). Melbourne, Australia.

Yang, R. (2004). To reach China's consumers: adapt to Guo Qing. *Harvard Business Review on Doing Business in China* (pp. 123–140). USA: Harvard Business School Publishing Corporation.

Zillman, C. (2013, November 25). 5 headwinds walmart's new CEO will face. *Fortune.com*. Retrieved January 12, 2014, from http://fortune.com/2013/11/25/5-headwinds-wal-marts-new-ceo-will-face/.

Chapter 5
E-Services

This chapter provides an overview of e-services, then discusses e-learning, e-government, digital publishing and e-health respectively, and concludes with 3D-design and 3D-printing.

5.1 Overview of Providing Services Online

Digital enterprise/e-business is not purely the domain of organizations which have a product to sell. In fact, the service industries (in particular, the financial industry) were among the very first to embrace electronic transactions among business partners.

Generally speaking, providing services electronically/online/digitally is the ideal candidate for many services provision sectors and content/information supply businesses, such as:

- Travel, tourism, and event services (e.g., Tripadvisor, Priceline, Qantas Australia, Expedia, Lonelyplanet, Tickmaster, Eventbrite, Fangando).
- Employment services (e.g., Monster, LinkedIn, Seek Australia, Freelancer, oDesk, Elance).
- Real estate services, home renovation, and home automation (e.g., Zillow, Realtor, Realestate Australia, Airbnb, Houzz, Nest).
- Banking, finance, and funding services (e.g., ETrade, Square, Lending Club, PayPal, VeriSign, Wealthfront, Indiegogo, Kickstarter).
- Education (e.g., Open University Australia, EdX, Coursera, Udacity, Universitas 21, Chegg, Moodle, Blackboard, Khan Academy).
- Learning tools (e.g., Youtube, Dropbox, Google, Wikipedia, Slideshare).
- Communication, messaging and monitoring services (e.g., Skype, WhatsApp, QQ, WeChat, Twitter, Facebook, Dropcam).
- Government services (e.g., digital government initiatives by South Korea, Holland, the U.K., Australia, Hong Kong, and Singapore).
- Marketing and advertising (e.g., Glam Media, DoubleClick, Google, Groupon).
- Computing services (e.g., Salesforce, Akamai, Amazon, GitHub).

J. Xu, *Managing Digital Enterprise*, DOI 10.2991/978-94-6239-094-2_5

- E-health services (e.g., e-health initiatives by the government of Australia, Denmark, the U.S.; Jawbone, Dred, Patientslikeme, ZocDoc, Digital Autopsy, Fitbit, Myfitnesspal, Zephyr Health Inc.).
- Entertainment (e.g., Twitch, WWE, Hulu, Netflix, Youtube, Spotify, SBS On-demand Australia, ABC iView Australia).
- Online dating services (e.g., Match, eHarmoney, Lavalife, Baihe, POF, DatingDirect).
- Restaurant booking services (e.g., OpenTable, Book a Restaurant, GrubHub).
- Traffic intelligence and Car rental and sales services (e.g., Waze, Automatic, Zipcar, Uber, Carsales Australia).
- Product development, 3D modelling, scanning, design, and printing (e.g., Minted, Quirky, 99designs, 3d-a-porter, Sketchup, Autodesk, MakerBot, Shapeways, Styku, Constrvct).
- Digital publishing (e.g., Pearson Education, Wall Street Journal Online, Twitter, Blog, Pinterest, Imgur).
- Classifieds, directories and guides (e.g., Yelp, Craigslist, Google Maps, Foursquare).
- Deal makers, information brokers and marketplaces (e.g., Alibaba, Global-sourcing, eBay, Taobao, Etsy).
- Information portals, references and knowledge centers (e.g., Google, Yahoo, Live, Baidu, Wikipedia, Naver Corporation, Yandex).
- Communities and networks (e.g., Facebook, Tencent, WhatsApp, LinkedIn, Waze, Gotinder), among many others.

In fact, in July 2014, 18 of the top 20 websites (based on web traffic) are in the services domain, including www.google.com (information search engine), www.facebook.com (online communities), www.youtube.com (online entertainment), www.yahoo.com (Internet information portal), www.baidu.com (information search engine), www.wikipedia.org (online references), www.twitter.com (online microblogs), www.qq.com (Internet service portal), www.taobao.com (e-marketplace), www.linkedin.com (online communities), www.live.com (online search engine), www.google.co.in (information search engine), www.sina.com.cn (Internet information portal), www.weibo.com (microblogs), www.hao123.com (Internet information portal), www.blogspot.com (blogs), www.sohu.com (Internet information portal), and www.google.co.jp (information search engine); and the remaining two websites in the top 20 list are Amazon.com (B2C e-tailing) and T-mall (B2C e-tailing) (Alexa.com 2014). It is noted from the top 20 list that 12 of them are American firms and the remaining 8 are Chinese firms (including www.baidu.com, www.qq.com, www.taobao.com, www.sina.com.cn, www.weibo.com, www.hao123.com, www.sohu.com, www.t-mall.com). Meanwhile these top 20 sites are actually owned by only a few companies, for example:

- Google owns www.google.com, www.youtube.com, www.google.co.in, www.google.co.jp, and www.blogspot.com.
- Tencent owns www.qq.com and www.weibo.com.
- Baidu owns www.baidu.com and www.hao123.com.

- Alibaba owns www.taobao.com and www.t-mall.com.
- Many success factors of e-tailing that were discussed in the Chap. 4 are relevant to digital services/e-services/online services. The key difference is the emphasis on providing customers with the opportunities of interacting and communicating with real people (not machines), and it is much greater for digital services as a result of their lack of physical presence or/and tangibility of the product.

5.2 E-Learning

E-learning, such as online corporate training, distance learning via the Internet, and online universities, can provide learning at a lower cost with greater flexibility. E-learning has been quickly becoming more accepted, for example, according to Meeker and Wu (2013), in 2011, 32 % of students in degree-granting postsecondary institutions in the U.S. took at least one online course; and in 2012, 77 % of academic leaders at 2,800 U.S. colleges viewed e-learning/online education as the same as or better than traditional face-to-face education. Meeker (2014) mentions that there are more than 4,300 million views on Khan Academy Youtube Channel, more than 65 million courses have been downloaded from iTunes U Open University, and more than 7 million students are enrolled in Coursera courses. In the future, digital technologies and e-learning will be a more natural and essential thing for born digital generations, and in fact many schools around the world have adopted digital technologies in the classroom. A recent survey of over 500 Cambridge schools around the world (reported in IDG Connect 2014a) unveiled that more than 50 % of participating teachers had a strategy for using technology in the classroom and 90 % of participating teachers believe all lessons will be supported by some form of technology in the future; meanwhile two-thirds of students had individual access to laptops and PCs, and there is an increasing trend of bringing your own devices to school. In addition, mobile learning has becoming popular in rural areas of developing countries as a result of the lack of schools, the lack of technological infrastructure, and the difficulty to access the Internet.

While e-learning tools do offer some benefits (such as convenience, flexibility, self-paced learning, individualized/personalized learning, 24/7 availability, access to much more learning material, more course and unit options, cost reduction, capacity of teaching large numbers of students without the constraint of space limitation, being cheaper and easier to update and store content, access to global expertise, democratization of knowledge, contribution to education equality via providing people in the less developed regions with access to global teaching and learning resources), they also have a number of challenges and drawbacks, which include the need for instructor retraining for e-learning (digital teaching and learning has different pedagogical perspectives and issues, simply digitizing student materials and having online activities are not e-learning), dedicated resources for e-learning (including required digital platforms, telecommunication networks, and more critically support to students), the lack of face-to-face interaction and campus life, limited group work and peer feedback opportunities, assessment issues (e.g., difficulties in ensuring who actually completed the assessment items), quality control issues, difficulties in ensuring appropriate and adequate student learning experience (especially learning-by-doing opportunities), challenges of keeping study materials up-to-date (e.g., could be time-consuming and expensive to ensure the currency of the study materials), difficulties in developing higher-level cognitive skills to function as university qualified professionals or scientists by watching online sessions and doing online activities; protection of intellectual property (e.g., difficulties in controlling the transmission of copyrighted works downloaded from the e-learning site/platform), access equality issue (e-learning could not reach to people who don't have the access to the Internet and don't have certain skills of using computing devices; even though mobile learning could offer some help in this regard, it still in the early stage of development, and mobile devices and mobile networks have the technical limitations (such as mobile devices' small screens and small keyboards, mobile networks' smaller bandwidth and bigger security concerns), and learning outcomes and satisfaction issues (e.g., as a result of the lack of face-to-face interaction and campus life, students could find hard to keep mentally engaged and motivated about e-learning, and thus achieve poor learning outcomes and dislike their e-learning experiences (Turban et al. 2012, p. 243; Maiolo 2014; Cusumano et al. 2013; the author's own knowledge).

Some factors of e-learning failures include (Turban et al. 2012, p. 352; the Author's Own Knowledge):

- Under-estimating the cost of e-learning, especially when the student numbers are not sufficient to justify the capital investment and high-fixed cost associated with e-learning.
- Over-estimating the achievement of e-learning: e-learning has its limitation and may only be suitable for certain segments, especially in the early stage.
- Overlooking the difficulties of self-study: some people are not capable of doing or are not willing to do self-study.
- Failing to engage with students, not providing timely and adequate feedback, and not providing enough opportunities for team work.
- Failing to apply appropriate pedagogy to e-learning: traditional teaching and learning approach has to be adjusted for online delivery.
- Treating content/study material as a commodity could lead to a lack of attention to quality and delivery to individual students.
- Placing too much emphasis on technology or not full utilizing available tools: A balanced approach should be adopted.
- Assuming learned knowledge will be applied: Learned knowledge needs to be applied in real-life actions, which could be difficult to control and measure in the digital learning environment.
- Confusing with adoption and diffusion issues: even though people have adopted e-learning systems, they may not use them or use them properly. So the assumption of once e-learning system is developed, people will use it is not true.

Massive Open Online Course (MOOC), which is a recent development in distance learning and e-learning and is Internet-based and college level classes typically offered free of charge or lower fees (than traditional face-to-face courses) for credit by colleges and universities, has been gaining publicity in recent years, especially after the announcement of a non-profit open-sourced joint online learning platform called EdX (Cusumano et al. 2013), which includes "self-paced learning, online discussion groups, wiki-based collaborative learning, assessment of learning as a student progresses through a course, and online laboratories" (Gannes 2012). On top of traditional course materials (e.g., videos, readings, and problem sets), MOOC provides interactive user forums and facilitate the building of teaching and learning communities among students, instructors and professors (www.wikipedia.org 2014). The popularity and more recognition of Massive Open Online Courses (MOOCs) will pose significant threat to pure online private universities and lower-tier universities who charge moderate fees but deliver poor quality teaching or learning outcomes since students can access better professors and instructors and gain better teaching or learning outcomes through MOOCs with lower fees (Cusumano et al. 2013).

Some best practices of e-learning include (Epignosis LCC 2014; Henry et al. 2014; Cusumano et al. 2013; the author's own knowledge):

- Developing a strategic plan (or a roadmap) for e-learning.
- Allocating sufficient resources and making necessary adjustments to organizational culture and structure to facilitate the implementation of e-learning strategy and strategy initiatives.
- Providing sufficient training to teachers and instructors (including online teaching pedagogy, effective use of digital technologies for teaching, developing high quality digital content, and the blended teaching and learning approach).
- Keep monitoring the experiences of e-learning and making necessary changes.
- Having clear expectations and communication them effectively to students.
- Developing quality content and maintaining its currency.
- Planning and executing the online course delivery well.
- Including both asynchronous and synchronous teaching and learning activities.
- Ensuring the usefulness and ease of use of the digital platforms.
- Providing reliable and responsive support to students (including actively participating online discussions with students and providing feedback to their inquiries in a timely manner).
- Facilitating the development of supportive communities and study groups and providing peer networks.
- Providing opportunities and channels for face-to-face interactions (e.g., contact offices, meeting places).
- Making both explicit knowledge (e.g., study material and digital content) and tacit knowledge (e.g., professors' expertise) available to students.
- Leveraging advantages of both online and offline channels (e.g., online sessions coupling with personal instruction or one-to-one tutoring, using collected data to better understand students' learning patterns and outcomes).

- On top of offering online courses to existing markets, using online channel to tap into new segments and markets (both domestic and international) (e.g., domestic and international students are not able to do on-campus studies) should be heavily emphasized.
- Using online learning to complement and enhance traditional teaching and learning but not to replace traditional teaching and learning.

The combined (also called hybrid or blended) teaching and learning approach is very critical to the knowledge-intensive business like education. The tacit dimension of our knowledge cannot be managed by the technology even though it may provide some facilitating roles (e.g., connecting people who need knowledge (such as students) with people have the required knowledge (such as teachers, instructors, professors). In fact, traditional education providers could benefit greatly from such approach by offering both online and offline courses and delivering courses in both online and offline channels. In addition, the completion rates of MOOCs (pure online courses) have been low (if not very low with less than 10 % completion rates) (Pertz 2014) even though it could be argued that some people may only want to gain knowledge but not the completion certificate and there is no mechanism or intention at this stage to control the quality of the learners of MOCCs (Cusumano et al. 2013). Furthermore the results of a recent federal study in the U.S. suggested blended learning models can produce learning outcomes that are equal to or better than face-to-face or pure online learning (Henry et al. 2014).

5.3 E-Government

Digital government/E-government is the use of digital tools to provide access to government information and delivery of public services to citizens and business partners. Digitization could assist governments in aggregating their capabilities across agency boundaries, developing the most cost-effective services to meet the needs of their citizens and users, enabling them to enhance their services, improving operational efficiency, reducing cost, increasing transparency of government operations, enhancing data sharing and interoperability across government entities, boosting economic growth, and eliminating bureaucracy and red tape (Hovenden and Bartlett 2013; Shehadi et al. 2012). Some world e-government leaders are: Republic of Korea, Australia, Singapore, France, Netherlands, Japan, United States of America, New Zealand, and Finland (United Nations 2014, p. 5); these countries have very high E-Government Development Index points measured by three perspectives of telecommunication infrastructure (e.g., online population, personal computer (PC) users, fixed-telephone subscriptions, mobile-cellular subscriptions), human capital index (e.g., adult literacy, gross enrolment (including primary, secondary, and tertiary) ratio, expected years of schooling, and mean years of schooling), and online service index (e.g., whole-of-government, multichannel service delivery, bridging the digital divide, increasing usage, open government, and e-participation) (United Nations 2014, pp. 187–192).

Some major e-government initiatives include government-to-citizens, government-to-business, government-to-government, and government-to-employees (Turban et al. 2012, p. 233). The ultimate goal of e-government is to present A-Whole-Government or One-Government to its citizens and users and provide them with access to personalized and secure services based on their specific circumstances, needs and preferences. In order to achieve this goal, governments need to invest in a number of enablers and facilitating factors of digital transformation (Hovenden and Bartlett 2013; Kappos 2014; Shehadi et al. 2012, 2013a, b; Thompson 2013; United Nations 2014, p. 80; the author's own knowledge):

- Embracing the digital shifts by strengthening collaborative leadership capacities and fostering a service-oriented and customer centric culture, having cross-agency/function and streamlined business processes, and deploying change management strategy.
- Deploying institutional framework for effective coordination, cooperation, and accountability.
- Designing innovative integrated processes and mechanisms for service delivery and citizen engagement and empowerment.
- Establishing a flexible workplace (e.g., addressing such perspectives as organizational learning, knowledge management, teleworking, and e-learning).
- Taking advantage of the large volume of government data and achieving better understanding of the needs of citizens and businesses thus providing better services to them.
- Actively seeking input from the citizens and users as well as other relevant stakeholders for the development of digital government systems and applications and harnessing the power of social media for such purposes.
- Developing digital government systems and solutions with the citizens and the users in mind (e.g., taking an agile approach to systems development, measuring the success in terms of user acceptance).
- Developing digital government employees (e.g., providing them with appropriate training, providing incentives for their achievements of digital government, aligning their performance plan with digital government strategy, extensively getting them involved in the beginning, and engaging them as partners of digital government initiatives).
- Establishing policies, platforms, and clear objectives for social government and mobile government, dedicating resources (including human resources) to them, and tracking and measure the performance of them.
- Embarking on social government (e.g., using social networks to communicate the messages) and mobile government (e.g., developing digital government apps) initiatives.
- Working on strategic sourcing and partnerships (e.g., having strategic partnerships with private sector, using cloud-based applications, and leveraging open source software development).
- Establishing IT management strategies for enhanced collaboration.

- Developing common and sustainable IT infrastructure (e.g., consolidating IT hardware, digital platforms, and data centers).
- Adopting open standards and architecture for digital government applications,
- Applying shared software and digital platforms (e.g., consolidating applications and systems across agencies).
- Utilizing shared telecommunication infrastructure (e.g., eliminating duplication, avoiding agency specific investments and maximizing the existing telecommunication infrastructure).
- Addressing security and privacy concerns.

The transformation to e-government will not be done overnight. A systematic process will definitely make the transformation more successful. Turban et al. (2010, pp. 344–345) introduce a seven-stage e-government transformation process, considered across two dimensions: the eminence of Internet-based application and the degree of enterprise transformation (i.e., the lowest level of eminence of Internet-based application and the lowest degree of enterprise transformation in Stage-1 to the highest level of eminence of Internet-based application and the highest degree of enterprise transformation in Stage-7):

- Stage-1: Publishing and disseminating information (mainly one-way transaction and communication from the government).
- Stage-2: Having "official" two way transactions/communications (e.g., citizens could submit information online and conduct transactions with the government, normally starting with single government departments).
- Stage-3: Establishing multipurpose portals (e.g., providing a single portal for various government services).
- Stage-4: Providing portal personalization (e.g., giving users more personalized portals and allowing them to customize their personal portals with their desired features)
- Stage-5: Clustering common services (e.g., allowing users to pay bills from different government departments at one time in one place).
- Stage-6: Implementing full enterprise transformation and collaboration (e.g., putting cross-department business processes and platforms in place).
- Stage-7: Working on transition to social government (i.e., providing government services via social media) and mobile government (i.e., providing government services via mobile channel).

One emerging trend in digital government is the government's initiative of open data, which looks at making more government data public and making government data more useful for people and organizations. According to United Nations (2014, p. 11), 46 Countries have established dedicated data portals for data sharing while many other countries are utilizing government websites for such purpose. According to consulting firm McKinsey (reported in Chui et al. 2014), open data could generate more than US$3 trillion in global economic value annually; and governments could play an important role in unleashing the economic potential of open data via (1) providing its captured data to citizens, businesses and non-governmental organizations; (2) serving as a catalyst for the use of open data by leading the open data campaign, developing an ecosystem of open data, and creating an open-data culture; (3) investing in required systems and talent for open data and actively taking advantages of Big Data and Data Analytics; and (4) establishing pro-open data policies and developing standards for data quality and format. A good example of the government's open data initiatives is the establishment of the online portal of data.gov.au and the publication of the Principles on Open Public Section Information (PSI) by the Australian Government (Sadauskas 2014). In addition, many governments and international organizations have promoted open government data initiatives by hosting competitions (e.g., German Government's Open Data Challenge, Australian Government's GovHack, Dutch Government's Apps for the Netherlands, Singaporean Government's Ideas 4 Apps Challenge, World Bank's Water Hackathon, among many others) (United Nations 2014, p. 174).

5.4 Digital Publishing

Online/Digital publishing is the electronic delivery of newspapers, magazines, books, news, music, videos and other digitizable information over the Internet. Online publishing is generally more flexible than print publishing because it is easier to modify content and create personalization. Online blogs (for publishing personal views and comments online) and wikis (for creating online publications together with many people voluntarily and sharing knowledge online) can also be considered as e-publishing applications.

E-book is one of the most discussed topics of digital publishing. It can be said that e-books have made the book industry more dynamic and helped transform the book industry; and it is no doubt that e-books will become more popular in the future. According to IDG Connect (2014b) e-books sales have increased a total of 4,456 % since 2008 even though the printed books still outnumber their digital counterparts. On the other hand, e-books will not replace books, but will coexist with books and books will still dominate the book market for the foreseeable future (at least). For certain areas such as textbooks or special interest subjects or books we don't need to use very often, e-books could be more attractive and useful, especially interactive e-books (e.g., ePUB files). According to a recent survey of 251 global tech-professionals by IDG Connect (2014b):

- 69 % of respondents agreed that e-books will be the most popular book format in the future.
- 59 % of the respondents reckoned that e-books hold the most potential in Education sector.
- 83 % believed interactive e-books will catch on in the future, and the two largest stumbling blocks to interactive eBooks catching on are: publishers (47 % of respondents suggested) and readers (42 %).

Some advantages of e-books include: portability, ability to store many books on a small mobile device with affordable prices (e.g., for US$9.99 per month, users can access over 600,000 titles via Amazon's Kindle Unlimited service), light weight (i.e., only the weight of an e-reader or a mobile phone for many books), convenience, frequent updates, current information, ease of searching, lower costs, instant delivery, ease of reproduction and distribution, media-rich (e.g., video and audio could be easily embedded into e-books and such interactive features are very useful for early childhood education), longer durability than traditional books, ability to change the format and font size of the text, and easy integration of content (Turban et al. 2012, pp. 251–252; the author's own knowledge). On the other hand, some disadvantages and issues of e-books include: adoption issue (e.g., reading books on the computing device is not everyone's cup of tea), copyright issues (e.g., how to control the copyright of e-books by avoiding illegal distribution?), comfort and relaxation issues (e.g., reading a printed book is a kind of comfort and relaxation for many people. Can reading e-book provide the same level of comfort and relaxation to readers?), cost concerns (e.g., need to purchase e-book reading devices and/or software), the lack of common standards and platforms (e.g., different and competing standards, software and devices by various providers), and navigation issues (e.g., some people just simply enjoy flipping back and forth while reading a printed book, can e-books provide the same experience to readers?). In addition, book publishers need to pay attention to other issues such as taxation issues (e.g., at the moment, varied taxation policies on e-books exist in different countries), channel conflict issues (e.g., production, distribution and sales of printed copies versus eBooks), pricing strategies (e.g., different prices for e-copy and printed copy of the book or the same price?), product and service selection issues (e.g., only publishing certain books digitally, only providing on-demand printing services to some books), digital transformation issues (e.g., in responding to the competition from www.wikipedia.org and the declining demand for printed copies, Britannica's decision to stop producing printed sets of the iconic Britannica Encyclopedia and focusing on offering the Encyclopedia online and online education and competing with its competitive advantage of editorial quality (Cauz 2013)).

Another popular topic of digital publishing is digital news. News publishers have been hurt quite badly by the free news on the Internet. For example, according to a survey of 523 self-described news readers in the Gulf Cooperation Council regions (reported in Chahine et al. 2011): 76 % of the respondents with broadband access had either decreased or stopped reading print newspapers or planned to do in the next two years, 40 % of the respondents with broadband access still chose to read print newspapers, and 23 % of the respondents would only read the digital version of their favorite print newspapers they had stopped reading or read less often when they were reading news online. Consequently moving towards digital news has been a trend in the news publishing industry, but so far there is a lack of well-established strategies and best practices for winning the competition of news publishing in the digital era. Of course, one of the main reasons is charging news online is still quite new for news publishing industry. Some suggestions for news publishers facing digital challenges include (Xu and Wong 2012; El-Darwiche et al. 2013; Chahine et al. 2011; the author's own knowledge):

- Working on a multi-channel strategy and taking advantages of both online and offline channels.
- Effectively dealing with channel conflicts.
- Establishing effective and cross-channel pricing strategies.
- Clearly identifying and addressing needs of different market segments.
- Emphasizing the quality content and maximize the value of such content which need specific knowledge and exclusive offerings.
- Optimizing the use of social media and crowd-sourcing for co-developing content but with an effective quality control process in place.
- Developing flexible, user-friendly and secure digital payment systems (such systems should be able to deal with micropayments in the range of 1–99 cents. Ideally news publishers should only charge a few cents per past article.)
- Developing business ecosystems and creating win-win solutions with various stakeholders (e.g., news readers, advertising agencies and networks, content suppliers, strategic partners).
- Having learner organization to reduce the operational costs and help absorb loss arising from print revenue.
- Avoiding relying on the advertising revenue from digital channel, which alone is not likely to support the costs of generating content, but working on generating revenue from quality content, advertising, bundling and packaging, innovative products and services and value-added services (e.g., ESPN Insider site offers exclusive content (e.g., articles, videos), gaming tools, and partner offerings (e.g., tickets to professional sporting events). Users pay a monthly or yearly subscription, which includes a free subscription to ESPN's print magazine).
- Looking at alternative and/or complementary strategies for business growth (e.g., being a pure content player by only supplying the content and letting the others taking care of the user interface, hardware, and connectivity; being an application player by only supplying content and interface and letting others supply the rest; being a digital retail player by supplying the content, the user interface, and the store where the content is sold; and being an integrated player by integrating different services and offerings).
- Optimizing the core operations (including editorial, circulation and distribution, printing and Ad sales and supporting functions of news publishing with the principles of shared services, common platforms, customer-centric culture and structure, cross-functional business processes, and co-creation and co-development with internal and external knowledge and resources).

Table 5.1 presents a multi-channel and multi-perspective business model for news publishers.

Table 5.1 A multi-channel and multi-perspective business model for news publishers

Target segment	Required/provided products and services	Revenue sources
User who are currently only interested in print newspapers or primarily print newspapers (e.g., digital outsiders who are over 51 years old)	Providing them with both print newspapers and digital access (i.e., online and mobile)	Normal charges for print newspapers with free access to digital content
	Promoting advantages of digital delivery, such as online communities, readers' comments, archive of past issues, individual accounts (ideally one account for all digital content), personalized and customized content (such content could be in various formats and could from within and outside news publishers), and the opportunities to create and/or co-create content	Generating revenue by viewing past issues (single articles or whole issues), premium and local content, and exclusive stories, and other personalized, customized and value added services from the news publisher and/or its suppliers and strategic partners
	The main purpose is to educate them and make them buy into the trend of digital content	Implementing flexible, user friendly and secure micropayment systems, which could be able to handle micropayments in the range of 1 cent to 99 cents-Ideally news publishers should only charge a few cents per past article
Users who are currently only interested in online/digital delivery (e.g., digital natives who are 15–35 years old)	Providing them with both print newspapers (some sample issues for promotion) and digital content	Charging standard fees for online delivery (cheaper than subscription of print newspapers)
	Promoting print copies to them, such as via the above mentioned sample issues and a compact edition of selected past newspapers	Creating revenue by subscribing print newspapers (the total costs should be no more than print copy subscription)
	Providing them with mobile platforms with embedded social media and location-based applications	Generating revenue by viewing past issues (single articles or whole issues), premium and local content, and exclusive stories, and other personalized, customized and value added services from the news publisher and/or its suppliers and strategic partners

(continued)

Table 5.1 (continued)

Target segment	Required/provided products and services	Revenue sources
	Providing them with free innovative e-readers or mobile phones as a part of their subscriptions to digital content	Generating revenue by working with app developers, mobile device suppliers, search engines, advertising networks, television networks, utility firms, and telecom operators
	Bundling their subscriptions with their mobile services contracts, telephone bills, television bills, utility fees by working with relevant stakeholders	
	Supplying them with cross-platform/device functions and interactive features	
Users who are currently interested in both digital content and print newspapers (e.g., digital immigrants who are 36–50 years old)	Providing them with both print newspapers and digital content	Generating revenue from standard packages (including both print newspapers and digital access) and bundled products and services
	Promoting the benefits of both print newspapers and digital content	Generating revenue by viewing past issues (single articles or whole issues), premium and local content, and exclusive stories, and other personalized, customized and value added services from the news publisher and/or its suppliers and strategic partners
	Providing them with mobile platforms with embedded social media and location-based applications	Generating revenue by working with app developers, mobile device suppliers, search engines, advertising networks, television networks, utility firms, and telecom operators
	Informing them of the opportunities of their subscription with their mobile services contracts, telephone bills,, telephone bills, utility fees by working with relevant stakeholders	

(continued)

Table 5.1 (continued)

Target segment	Required/provided products and services	Revenue sources
	Providing them with new services that combine print, online, interactivity, and mobility	
	Supplying them with cross-platform/device functions and interactive features	
Users currently have no interest and Ad hoc visitors/users	Providing them with sample print newspapers and guest access to digital content	Generating revenue by print newspapers and online subscriptions
	Promoting the benefits of both print newspapers and digital content	Generating revenue by viewing past issues (single articles or whole issues), premium and local content, and exclusive stories, and other personalized, customized and value added services from the news publisher and/or its suppliers and strategic partners
	Providing them with guess access to mobile platforms with embedded social media and location-based applications	Generating revenue by working with app developers, mobile device suppliers, search engines, advertising networks, television networks, utility firms, and telecom operators
	Providing them with guess access to new services that combine print, online, interactivity, and mobility	Customers/visitors/users should be allowed to read a part of the story before they decide to purchase
	Informing them of the opportunities of bundling their subscription with their mobile services contracts, television bills, phone bills, and utility fees by working with relevant stakeholders and of the relevant deals (e.g., free innovative e-readers or mobile phones as a part of their subscriptions)	Some content should be made free to public, such as national and international news, weather forecast, and financial news
	Providing them with guess access to cross-platform/device functions and interactive features	Free access to certain amount of digital content within certain period should be offered to potential users of news sites to let them have some feeling about digital content

(continued)

Table 5.1 (continued)

Target segment	Required/provided products and services	Revenue sources
People who have firmly refused to pay for digital content-they are either believers of free-lunch and/ or those who believe they have paid their fees for digital content via their Broadband (Internet) access fees and their spending on Internet-related expenditures	Provide them with guest account to digital content	Generating revenue from online subscriptions
	Providing them with guess access to mobile platforms with embedded social media and location-based applications	Generating revenue by viewing past issues (single articles or whole issues), premium and local content, and exclusive stories, and other personalized, customized and value added services from the news publisher and/or its suppliers and strategic partners
	Providing them with guess access to new services that combine print, online, interactivity, and mobility	Generating revenue by working with app developers, mobile device suppliers, search engines, advertising networks, and telecom operators
	Informing them of the opportunities of bundling their subscription with their mobile services contracts by working with relevant stakeholders and of the relevant deals (e.g., free innovative e-readers or mobile phones as a part of their subscription)	Customers/visitors/users should be allowed to read a part of the story before they decide to purchase
	Providing them with guess access to cross-platform/ device functions and interactive features	Some contents should be made free to public, such as, national and international news, weather forecast, and financial news
		Free access to certain amount of digital content within certain period should be offered to potential users of news sites to let them have some feeling about digital content

Source developed from Xu and Wong (2012), EI-Darwiche et al. (2013), Chahine et al. (2011), the author's own knowledge

5.5 E-Health

With expected benefits of reducing medical errors, enhancing healthcare quality, minimizing healthcare costs, and empowering consumers to understand their healthcare needs and make informed decisions on their healthcare, e-health initiatives, such as practice management (e.g., practice scheduling, prescribing and billing), information sourcing and sharing (e.g., active input or passive collection of patient information via such smart devices as wireless blood pressure monitors, passive and active tracking devices, activity and sleep wristband trackers, recommendation engines), service delivery (e.g., chronic disease support tools and telehealth applications), remote care management (e.g., via smart devices, video conferencing technologies, and other tele-health applications), clinical decision support (e.g., aid collaborative diagnosis, treatment and care processes), electronic health records, and public health intelligence), have been introduced and accepted as an essential and important element in healthcare systems (Xu et al. 2013; Department of Health and Aging, Australia 2011; Gupta et al. 2013). On a related note, m-health has been useful in registering and monitoring patients, gathering data, and tracking and analyzing health-related surveys; some good examples of m-health include: mTrac (a rapid SMS-based disease surveillance and medicine supply tracking system with 10 million users in Uganda), "text4baby" service in the U.S., Mobile Alliance for Maternal Action (MAMA) in Bangladesh, and Mwana (a m-health project using SMS to deliver early infant HIV test results to Malawi and Zambia) (United Nations 2014, pp. 154–155). In addition, social networks and online communities have been using for sharing ideas, discussing symptoms, and debating treatment options (Gaganayake et al. 2011). In the future, more efforts could be put into exploring creative solutions for accessing health information via social networks and online communities (Xu et al. 2013); on the other hand, ensuring the security and privacy of the personal health information in social media arising from the nature of social media (e.g., the lack of subsequent control of expose of personal health information) definitely presents a challenge to policy makers and health practitioners (United Nations 2014, p. 156).

Even though it can be argued that the current environment of e-health is disjointed and is not functioning as planned or expected, digital tools have been gaining more acceptance among health consumers/patients and health services providers; and in the future, various stakeholders in the digital healthcare ecosystems (e.g., consumers, hospitals, physicians, clinics, specialists, allied health professionals, pharmaceutical firms, and governments) will be expected to embark on e-health systems to develop better and more effective medicines or healthcare to health consumers (Strategy + Business 2014). According to a recent McKinsey survey of 1,000 patients in Germany, Singapore, and the U.K. (reported in Biesdorf and Niedermann 2014):

- More than 75 % of respondents would like to use digital health services, as long as those services meet their needs and provide quality services. Meanwhile digital channels will be used along with non-digital channels, so a multichannel health services strategy needs to be deployed.

- More than 70 % of all age groups of participating patients want to use digital health services. Older patients (those over 50) would prefer to use e-mail and websites while younger patients are open to social media and smartphone apps.
- While there is certainly demand for mobile health applications, it is strongest among young people. Accordingly, mobile health applications, such as prenatal health and lifestyle apps, could be developed to target this segment. On the other hand, certain mobile applications targeted at older patients (e.g., for managing chronic conditions typically found in older people) should be deployed even though this segment has not shown their interest in or has not been aware of mobile health.
- The key expected benefits of e-health applications are addressing people's basic health care needs and looking at efficiency, better access to information, integration with other channels, and the availability of a real person if the digital services don't give them what they want; on the other hand, highly innovative services, better mobile apps, and more social media are far less important to them.
- The commonly demanded e-health services are basic services and assistance with routine tasks such as finding and scheduling physician appointments, helping select the right specialist, providing support for repetitive administrative tasks (e.g., prescription refills).
- As a result, health services providers need to have a thorough understanding of the needs of their patients, assess the demand in the market carefully, decide their strategy and investment, and develop and implement best solutions to address their needs and the market demand. They also need to continually add new digital health services to keep patient attention and engagement (e.g., providing integrated care companion apps, and developing mobile-based personal health record systems).

Meanwhile as a health information source, electronic health records (EHRs) underpin all other e-health initiatives (Xu et al. 2013). E-health records include such information as the patient's prescribed medications, test results, care plans, immunization records, health alerts, event summaries, discharge summaries, Medicare data, and personal data. Real-time and convenient access to such information will improve the quality of healthcare, especially in emergency situations and special conditions (Townsend 2012). Many countries have embarked on personal e-health record systems (e.g., Australia, Canada, China, Germany, Netherlands, New Zealand, Singapore, U.K., U.S.), but the success of such initiatives has been low (if not very low). Through studying e-health in seven countries namely U.S., Canada, U.K., Germany, Netherlands, Australia, and New Zealand, Jha et al. (2008) suggest that only those countries, which are willing to put in significant investments and take up the challenges of developing standards and interchanges will realize the benefits of e-heath records. In addition, even though large-scale government IS/IT projects (such as personal e-health record systems) typically have large budgets and longer timeframes, unfortunately they often failed (e.g., cost overruns, time slippage, technical shortfalls impairing performance, and failure to obtain anticipated benefits (Laudon and Laudon 2014, p. 560)). Some commonly discussed issues are: poor planning, poor project management, poor change management, no benefit realization strategy, poor risk management, insufficient user engagement and consultation, lack of commitment from senior management, lack of transparency and communication, silo mentality (i.e., protecting own data and not sharing with others), insufficient testing, large bureaucracies (including the courage to admit mistakes and make corrections), trying to do too much and solve very complex problems in one go, inappropriate methodologies, approaches and architectures, and treating the project as a political agenda (e.g., releasing the systems that are not ready with many bugs and errors to fulfil certain political purposes or agendas).

One emerging area in electronic health records is cross-border electronic health record sharing, which is really useful for the increasing trend of global mobility. However at the moment sharing health information electronically is very much in its infancy even though there are some efforts (Vest 2012; Xu et al. 2012, 2013). One main reason is the uneven development of electronic health record systems (especially national-wide systems) in different countries arising from country differences (i.e., in the economic, social, technological, and political dimensions). The Author (Jun Xu) and other researchers recently completed a research project looking at sharing electronic health records between Australia and China. Some key findings of the research projects are (Xu et al. 2012, 2013; Gao et al. 2012, 2013; e-healthsys.org.au 2014):

- Generally speaking, Australia is in a more advanced stage (i.e., Australia has a national-wide system of personally controlled electronic health records (PCEHR) system) while there is no established national-wide system in China and there still coexist two systems of electronic health records (mainly used in community health service centers) and electronic medical records (mainly used in hospitals).
- China has been doing some things more effectively than Australia (e.g., the approach of acquiring information for the electronic health record system and the link between personal identification and electronic health records) while Australia has been struggling with the adoption issues and the choices of 'opt-in' and 'opt-out'.
- The exchange and sharing of electronic health records between Australia and China could start with sharing the health information of Australian travelers and Australians living and working in China with some metropolitan cities in China (especially Beijing, Guangzhou, Shanghai, and Shenzhen-these four cities are the most advanced cities in China (called tier-one cities). These cities have all hosted international events in recent years and have established some international health care facilities and systems).

5.6 3D-Design and 3D-Printing

On top of taking advantage of Big Data and advanced analytics (e.g., data visualizations, correlation analyzes, significance testing, artificial neural networks) (Auschitzky et al. 2014) and advanced robotics (Cohen et al. 2014), companies (especially manufacturers) could embark on 3D-design and 3D-printing to reduce process flaws, improve productivity, provide better personalized and customized products and services, optimize supply chains, develop new capabilities and more innovation opportunities, and save time and money. 3D design and 3D printing utilize computer-aided design tools, leverage the Internet to provide people with access to design tools that are increasingly inexpensive (i.e., democratization of design), and make use of the increasingly improved 3D-printing technology (i.e., from could only printing plastic parts to printing jewelry, furniture, dental products, parts for nuclear facilities, food, even artificial skin, tissue, and body organs, and many other materials) (Waters 2014; Solman 2014).

3D printing (also called additive manufacturing) is different from traditional manufacturing techniques (e.g., molding or subtractive techniques) by building objects layer by layer (Cohen et al. 2014). According to McKinsey Global Institute (reported in Cohen et al. 2014), 3D printing could have an economic impact of up to US$550 billion a year by 2025. So far, the adoption of 3D printing and 3D printers among consumers has been slow, but could have good future potential if the price of 3D printers becomes more affordable (e.g., in the range of US$ 100–200 or lower), consumers have more understanding and capabilities of 3D printing, and there are more killer applications and content available to drive personalized printing of everyday projects at home (Lomas 2014, the author's own knowledge). According to Juniper Research (2014), the sales of consumer 3D printers will exceed 1 million in 2018 from only 44,000 in 2014 and will have significant growth after 2018.

On a related note, 4D-Printing (a term coined by MIT's Skylar Tibbits) could be the future trend; and it adds the ability for things to change and transform over time to 3D-printing and explores the opportunities of material-based Internet of Things and smart material (e.g., components with sensors, electronics, motor and intelligence could assemble themselves) (Wallbank 2014).

References

Alexa.com. (2014). *The top 500 sites on the web*. Retrieved July 26, 2014, from http://www.alexa.com/topsites.

Auschitzky, E., Hammer, M., & Rajagopaul, A. (2014, July). How big data can improve manufacturing. *Insights & Publications*. McKinsey & Company. Retrieved July 22, 2014, from http://www.mckinsey.com/insights/operations/how_big_data_can_improve_manufacturing.

Biesdorf, S., & Niedermann, F. (2014, July). Healthcare's digital future. *Insights & Publications*. McKinsey & Company. Retrieved July 24, 2014, from http://www.mckinsey.com/insights/health_systems_and_services/healthcares_digital_future.

Chui, M., Farrell, D., & Jackson, K. (2014, April). How government can promote open data. *Insights & Publications*. McKinsey & Quarterly. Retrieved May 10, 2014, from http://www.mckinsey.com/insights/public_sector/how_government_can_promote_open_data.

Cauz, J. (2013). How I did it … Encyclopedia Britannica's president on killing off a 244-year-old product. *Harvard Business Review*, *91*(3), 39–42.

Chahine, G., Vollmer, C., Bhargava, J., & Lahham, A. (2011). The advent of digital news in the GCC newspaper publishers' path to winning. *Perspective*, 1–25. Booz & Company. Retrieved July 20, 2014, from http://www.strategyand.pwc.com/media/file/Strategyand-Digital-News-GCC.pdf.

Cohen, D., Sargeant, M., & Somers, K. (2014). 3D printing takes shape. *McKinsey Quarterly, 24* (1), 40–45.

Cusumano, M., Page, G., Sahai, E., & Zarate, A. (2013, May). MOOCs: Contexts and Consequences. *Working paper*, 1–17. The MIT Center for Digital Business, Retrieved July 10, 2014, from http://ebusiness.mit.edu/research/papers/2013.05_Cusumano_MOOCs%20Contexts%20and%20Consequences.pdf.

Department of Health and Aging, Australia. (2011, May). *The eHealth readiness of Australia's medical specialists*. Department of Health and Aging, Retrieved September 20, 2012, from http://www.health.gov.au/internet/publications/publishing.nsf/Content/CA2578620005D57ACA25790900158A0A/$File/Medical%20Specialist%20ehealth%20readiness%20survey%20report.pdf.

e-healthsys.org.au. (2014). *Sharing e-health records between Australia and China*. Retrieved July 20, 2014, from http://www.e-healthsys.org.au/sharing-e-health-records-between-australia-and-china/.

El-Darwiche, B., Bhargava, J., & Jamous, S. A. (2013). Value retention by newsprint publisher in the MENA region: A three-pronged strategy-Optimized performance, digital transformation, revenue diversification. *Perspective*, 1–21. Booz & Company, Retrieved Aug 2, 2014, from http://www.strategyand.pwc.com/media/file/Strategyand_Value-Retention-by-Newsprint-Publishers-in-the-MENA-Region.pdf.

Epignosis LCC. (2014, January) *E-learning: Concepts, trends, applications*, Version 1.1. Retrieved March 20, 2014, from http://www.talentlms.com/elearning/e-learning_Concepts_Trends_Applications.pdf.

Gaganayake, R., Iannella, R., & Sahama, T. (2011). Sharing with care: An information accountability perspective. *IEEE Internet Computing, 15*, 31–38.

Gannes, L. (2012, May 2). Harvard and MIT launch $60 million non-profit online EdX platform. *Allthingsd.com*. Retrieved December 10, 2013, from http://allthingsd.com/20120502/harvard-and-mit-launch-60m-non-profit-online-edx-platform/.

Gao, X. Z., Xu, J. Sorwar, G., & Croll, P. (2012). Current status, challenges, and outlook of e-health record systems in China. *7th International Conference on Intelligence Systems and Knowledge Engineering*. December 15–17, 2012, Beijing, China.

Gao, X. J., Xu, J., Sorwar, G., & Croll, P. (2013). Implementation of e-health record systems and e-medical records systems in China. *International Technology Management Review, 3*(2), 127–139.

Gupta, A., Schumacher, J., & Sinha, S. (2013). Digital health: A way for Pharmacy companies to be more relevant in healthcare. *Briefing, 213*, 1–9. Booz & Company, Retrieved May 20, 2014, from http://www.strategyand.pwc.com/global/home/what-we-think/reports-white-papers/article-display/digital-health-pharma-companies.

Henry, T., Pagano, E., Puckett, J., & Wilson, J. (2104, April 10). Five trends to watch in higher education. *BGG Perspective*. The Boston Consulting Group. Retrieved April 20, 2014, from https://www.bcgperspectives.com/content/articles/education_public_sector_five_trends_watch_higher_education/.

Hovenden, D. & Bartlett, C. (2013, Spring). The digital government. *Strategy + Business*, *70*, 1–3.

IDG Connect. (2014a, May 15). *eLearning: How global schools keep pace with digitization*. Retrieved May 20, 2014, from http://www.idgconnect.com/abstract/8241/elearning-how-global-schools-keep-pace-with-digitisation.

IDG Connect. (2014b, May 13). *Infographic: The future of eBooks*. Retrieved May 20, 2014, from http://www.idgconnect.com/abstract/8177/infographic-the-future-ebooks.

Jha, A. K., Doolan, D., Grandt, D., Scott, T., & Bates, D. W. (2008). The use of health information technology in seven nations. *International Journal of Medical Informatics, 77*, 848–854.

Juniper Research. (2014, April 22). Press release: 3D printers for home-use to exceed 1 million unit sales globally by 2018, finds Juniper Research. *Juniperresearch.com*. Retrieved May 18, 2014, from http://www.juniperresearch.com/viewpressrelease.php?pr=439.

Kappos, D. J. (2014, April). Building a service-oriented agency: Lessons from the USPTO. *Insights & Publications*. McKinsey Center for Government. Retrieved July 20, 2014, from http://www.mckinsey.com/insights/public_sector/building_a_service-oriented_agency_lessons_from_the_uspto.

Laudon, K. C., & Laudon, J. P. (2014). *Management information systems: managing the digital firm* (13th ed.). UK: Global Edition, Pearson.

Lomas N. (2014, April 22). Mainstream 3D printer ownership to build slowly. *Techcrunch.com*. Retrieved May 15, 2014, from http://techcrunch.com/2014/04/22/one-million-consumer-3d-printers-by-2018/.

Meeker, M., & Wu, L. (2013, May 29). 2013 internet trends. *2013 D11 conference presentation*. Kleiner, Perkins, Caufield and Byers. Retrieved April 2, 2014, from http://www.kpcb.com/insights/2013-internet-trends.

Meeker, M. (2014, May 28). 2014 internet trends. *2014 CODE conference presentation*. Kleiner, Perkins, Caufield and Byers. Retrieved July 10, 2014, from http://www.kpcb.com/internet-trends.

Maiolo, A. (2014, March 31). Online study debate rages. *Campusreview.com.au*. Retrieved April 20, 2014, from http://www.campusreview.com.au/2014/03/online-study-debate-rages/.

Pertz, K. (2014, February 3). Low completion rates for MOOCs. *IEEE roundup*. Retrieved March 8, 2014, from http://theinstitute.ieee.org/ieee-roundup/opinions/ieee-roundup/low-completion-rates-for-moocs.

Sadauskas, A. (2014, April 14). Malcolm Turnbull commits to opening up more government data to app developers. *Smartcompany.com.au*. Retrieved May 8, 2014, from http://www.smartcompany.com.au/technology/41530-malcolm-turnbull-commits-to-opening-up-more-government-data-to-app-developers.html.

Shehadi, R. T., Kassatly, F., Karam, D., & Cherfan, M. (2012). Digital spring: MENA governments must speak the language of social media. *Perspective*, 1–3. Booz & Company Ltd. Retrieved April 10, 2014, from http://www.strategyand.pwc.com/global/home/what-we-think/reports-white-papers/article-display/digital-spring-mena-governments-must.

Shehadi, R. T., Khoury, R., Kassatly, F., & Lamaa, A. (2013a). Winning the mobile government game mechanisms for better customer engagement. *Perspective*, 1–9. Booz & Company Ltd. Retrieved March 18, 2014, from http://www.strategyand.pwc.com/global/home/what-we-think/reports-white-papers/article-display/winning-mobile-government-game.

Shehadi, R. T., Khoury, R., Kassatly, F., & Lamaa, A. (2013b). Self-sustainable e-government: A road map to financial independence and value creation. *Perspective*, 1–3. Booz & Company Ltd. Retrieved March 20, 2014, from http://www.strategyand.pwc.com/global/home/what-we-think/reports-white-papers/article-display/self-sustainable-e-government.

Solman, P. (2014, June 25). Additive processes lays it on thick. *The Connected Business, FT Special Report*. p. 2.

Strategy + Business. (2014, May 12). s + b trend watch: the coming digital healthcare landscape. *Strategy + Business, 75*. Retrieved June 18, 2014, from http://www.strategy-business.com/article/14201?gko=f09ab.

Thompson, M. (2013, December). Don't politicise digital government-public platforms belong to no-one. *Computerweekly.com*. Retrieved January 10, 2014, from http://www.computerweekly.com/opinion/Dont-politicise-digital-government-public-platforms-belong-to-no-one.

Townsend R. (2012, July 5). Doctors and patients uneasy about new e-health record system. *The conversation*. Retrieved August 10, 2012, from http://theconversation.edu.au/doctors-and-patients-uneasy-about-new-e-health-records-system-7706.

Turban, E., Lee, J. K., King, D., Liang, T. P., & Turban, D. (2010). *Electronic commerce: A managerial perspective 2010*. Upper Saddle River, NJ: Prentice Hall. International Edition.

Turban, E., King, D., Liang, T. P., & Turban, D. (2012). *Electronic commerce: A managerial and social networks perspective* (Vol. 7). UK: Pearson Education. Global Edition.

United Nations. (2014). *E-government survey 2014: E-government for the future we want*. New York: Department of Economic and Social Affairs, United Nations

Vest, V. J. (2012). Health information exchange: National and international approaches. *Advances in Health Care Management, 12*, 3–24.

Wallbank, P. (2014, April 30). 4D printing and the quest for elegance. *Smartcompany.com.au*. Retrieved June 8, 2014, from http://www.smartcompany.com.au/technology/41733-4d-printing-and-the-quest-for-elegance.html.

Waters, R. (2014, June 25). Power to the people on product design. *The Connected Business, FT Special Report*. p. 1.

Wikipedia.org. (2014, July 24). Massive open online course. *Wikipedia.org*. Retrieved July 28, 2014, from http://en.wikipedia.org/wiki/Massive_open_online_course.

Xu, J., Gao, X. Z., Sorwar, G., & Croll, P. (2012, December 15–17). Current Status, Challenges, and outlook of e-health record systems in Australia. *7th International Conference on Intelligence Systems and Knowledge Engineering*. Beijing, China.

Xu, J., & Wong, P. (2012, February 26–28). Charging News online: Is it a strategic move for news publishers? *The Proceeding of the 2012 International Conference on Economics, Business and Marketing Management (CEBMM 2012)*. Singapore, pp. 235–239.

Xu, J., Gao, X. J., Sorwar, G., & Croll, P. (2013). Implementation of e-health record systems in Australia. *International Technology Management Review, 3*(2), 92–104.

Chapter 6
B2B Digital Enterprise and Supply Chain

This chapter explains B2B digital enterprise, discusses supply chains and B2B digital enterprise for supply chains, reviews issues and success factors of managing digital supply chains, and presents some emerging trends and future directions of digital supply chains.

6.1 B2B Digital Enterprise

This chapter focuses on B2B (business-to-business) digital enterprise, which refers to transactions between businesses conducted electronically over the Internet. In spite of all the hype about B2C e-tailing and consumers' participation in digital enterprise, the vast majority of digital enterprise concerns business-to-business transactions. Also, the size of the market for business-to-business digital enterprise is far greater than the market for business-to-consumer digital enterprise. According to World Trade Organization (2013, p. 3), Global B2B transaction contributes about 90 % of all e-commerce; and International Data Corporation suggests (reported in World Trade Organization 2013, p. 3), the value of Global B2B e-commerce reached US$12.4 trillion at the end of 2012 and by 2017, B2B and B2C e-commerce transactions will account for about 5 % of all inter-company transactions (B2B) and retail sales (B2C).

Four major B2B digital enterprise models include the company centric models [sell-side (one seller to many buyers model) and buy-side (one buyer from many sellers model)], exchange (many sellers to many buyers), and collaborative commerce (Turban et al. 2012, p. 181). The company centric models (e.g., selling from the sell-side marketplaces or buying from buy-side marketplaces) are the most common models. The major types of B2B sell-side transactions include selling from electronic catalogues, selling via intermediaries, and selling through forward auctions. Searching for quality suppliers and comparing prices can be very slow and costly. As a solution, organizations, especially large buyers, can set up their own marketplaces called buy-side e-marketplaces to invite suppliers to submit their bids and invite other buyers as well. A buy-side e-marketplace is a corporate-based acquisition site that typically uses reverse auctions, negotiations, group purchasing,

J. Xu, *Managing Digital Enterprise*, DOI 10.2991/978-94-6239-094-2_6

or any other e-procurement methods for the acquisition of goods and services for a business.

Many-to-many B2B digital enterprise is also known as B2B Exchange, Electronic Marketplace, Online Marketplace, Trading Community, Exchange Hub, B2B Portal, and Internet/Web Exchange. A B2B exchange is a many-to-many e-marketplace for business-to-business transactions. Private exchanges are e-marketplaces that are owned and operated by one company (very often a third party); and are also known as company-centric marketplaces, which have been discussed previously in this topic. Public exchanges are open to all interested parties (both buyers and sellers). Public exchanges face a number of challenges: transaction fees which keep the users away, companies' willingness to share information, realized cost savings (may not be as high as expected), difficulties in recruiting suppliers, and tough competition. At the same time, private exchanges and consortia could face the antitrust issue as a result of the private ownership and the dominance of a few industry major players. Collaborative commerce is 'the use of digital technologies that enable companies to collaboratively plan, design, develop, manage and research products, services and innovative e-commerce applications' (Turban et al. 2012, p. 260). Through collaborative commerce organizations can enhance communication within the organization and with business partners, achieve better information sharing, and have better forecasting and planning capabilities. It also improves supply chains by providing more accurate information about needs and trends which could stabilize the chain and reduce flow times. Another very similar concept is "The Collaborative Community of Firms Model" for organizing continuous product development and commercialization developed by Snow et al. (2011).

Heavy users of B2B digital enterprise are industries such as aerospace, defense, healthcare, utilities, computer and electronics which typically have significantly used electronic data interchange (EDI) and put in large investments in IT. So far supply chain management (especially e-procurement) has been a core focus of B2B digital enterprise activities.

6.2 Supply Chains

Many of the world's most successful companies have excellence in their supply chains, and some people even argue the competition between businesses is the competition between their supply chains or global supply chains. For example, the two largest supermarket chains being Woolworths and Coles in Australia are competing head-to-head with their global chains, in terms of high agility with great service and cost productivity. Another example is the iPad's supply chains: its semiconductors came from three countries, the assembly is done in a different country, the displays/screens come from another set of countries, whilst the design and branding is done in the U.S. where the Apple Inc. is headquartered (Manyika 2014). Turban et al. (2006, p. 279) define supply chain as 'the flow of materials, information, money, and services from raw material suppliers through factories and warehouses to the end customers'. Supply chains have existed for thousands of years. The ancient Silk Road from China to other parts of the world is a good example of a very old supply chain. Laudon and Laudon (2005, p. 347) suggest that supply chains can be viewed from a push-based or pull-based perspective. The push-based model is basically the traditional build-to-stock approach while pull-based model is the strategy of build-to-order approach (i.e., make what we sell not sell what we make). A good example of pull-based model is Dell Computer's online direct selling model.

A complete supply chain typically consists of three parts (Turban et al. 2006, p. 280; Haag et al. 2008, p. 118):

- Upstream supply chain: including activities of a manufacturing company with its suppliers. The major activity is procurement.
- Internal supply chain: including in-house processes for transforming the inputs from the suppliers into the outputs. Main concerns are production management, manufacturing, and inventory control.
- Downstream supply chain: including delivering the products to the final customers. Here the attention is on distribution, warehousing, transportation and after-sale services.

Some typical problems along the supply chain include (Turban et al. 2006, p. 283):

- Slow and prone to errors because of the length of the chain involving many internal and external partners.
- Large inventories without the ability to meet demand.
- Insufficient logistics infrastructure.
- Quality problem or difficulties in controlling quality.

Lacking an effective information sharing mechanism is a major cause of failures of supply chains, and minor inaccurate information in demand could be amplified to become a much big one while the information moves along the supply chain (bullwhip effect) (Laudon and Laudon 2005, p. 340).

6.3 B2B Digital Enterprise and Supply Chain

Business-to-business digital enterprise is generally used in existing supply chains to make them more efficient and effective. The four B2B digital enterprise models discussed previously in this chapter, namely sell-side (one-to-many), buy-side (many-to-one), exchange (many-to-many), and collaborative-commerce, can make significant contributions to organizational supply chains.

The roles of B2B digital enterprise and other digital technologies in supply chain management can be discussed as per the three parts of the supply chain (see Table 6.1).

Table 6.1 B2B digital enterprise and other digital technologies for supply chain management

Supply chain part	B2B digital enterprise and other digital technologies for supply chain management
Upstream activities	Using tool such as buy-side B2B (including reverse auctions and aggregation of vendors' online catalogues), purchasing via exchanges (independent and consortia), buying via e-auctions (reverse auctions), group purchasing, and electronic bartering for e-procurement; POS, RFID tags, Rubee, QR codes, and barcodes for capturing real-time information; and supply chain planning systems, Big Data and Data Analytics, and The Internet of Things for demand forecasting and planning
	Collaborative commerce (via tools such as extranets, corporate portals, Internet-based EDI, groupware, and e-mail) for information sharing and collaboration in demand forecasting and planning with suppliers and business partners
Intra-business activities	Purchasing from internal marketplaces; online services for self-services in the organization; automating processes; information sharing via intranets; business process management, lean management, and work flow systems for improving processes; and 3D/4D design and printing for improving the productivity
	Collaborative commerce (via tools such as corporate portals, e-mail, e-learning systems, internal wikis, predication markets, and groupware) for collaboration in learning, design, research, and product development
Downstream activities	Selling via sell-side marketplaces, e-auctions (forward auctions), B2B exchanges; Internet-based EDI for order taking; digital payment systems for processing and accepting payments; online self-services for customization and online tracking; and supply chain execution systems, inventory management systems, automated warehouses, RFID tags, Rubee, QR codes, and barcodes, location-based technologies, Big Data, and The Internet of Things for order fulfilment and logistics
	Collaborative commerce (via tools such as extranets, corporate portals, and groupware) for sharing information with business partners and suppliers

Source Developed from Turban et al. (2012), Laudon and Laudon (2014), the author's own knowledge

On a related note, according to a recent survey of 2,600 workers in the U.S., the U.K., and South Africa (reported in Gill 2013), e-mail was chosen by the respondents as the best tool they trust for collaboration even though the main uses of e-mail has changed from communication between individuals to such things as exchanging documents (76 % of the respondents), sending information to groups (69 %), improving communication across the zones (61 %), accountability (60 %), and searching for information (59 %). Some collaboration tools identified by the participants include (in order): e-mail to individuals (60 % of the respondents), e-mail to lists (34 %), e-mail to teams (23 %), teleconferencing (19 %), video/web conferencing (15 %), instant messaging (10 %), Facebook (8 %), Business collaboration tool (6 %), LinkedIn (4 %), and Twitter/Microblog (3 %).

6.4 Issues and Success Factors of Digital Supply Chain Management

Some identified challenges and issues of digital supply chain management include (Niemeyer 2014; Dhawan et al. 2014; Chaturvedi et al. 2013; Manyika 2014; Kirkland 2014; Ebel et al. 2013; Manyika 2014; Martin et al. 2013; Houston et al. 2012; Hinze et al. 2011; Glatzel et al. 2011; Kauffeld et al. 2011; Harper et al. 2009; Laudon and Laudon 2005, p. 349; O'Brien and Marakas 2011, p. 38; Cohen 2005):

- Lack of proper demand planning knowledge, tools, and guidelines.
- Inaccurate or over-optimistic demand forecasts and inaccurate production, inventory, and other business data.
- Lack of collaboration with external partners and input from internal functions.
- Firms' reluctance to share information.
- Firms' chase of a silver bullet (for example, firms believe such notions as 'we just do this and everything will be fine' or 'we just adopt this system and problem will be solved').
- Unpreparedness and lack of skills for dealing with the high volatility of supply chains.
- Lack of sufficient engagement and commitment from senior management.
- Complexity and size of supply chain networks.
- Lack of agility and flexibility of supply chain.
- Lack of an integrated view of digital and non-digital supply chains or the lack of One Supply Chain [i.e., many (if not most) businesses' supply chains are optimized for stores, with digital channels only treated as a 'bolt-on' separate business].
- Over-reliance on certain suppliers and in certain parts of the world (e.g., China).
- Challenges of managing suppliers and maintaining sustained relationships.
- Impacts of changing business trends such as those trends identified by a recent global supply management study by Booz & Company (in order and reported in Houston et al. 2012): globalization, demographic change, redistribution of wealth, lifestyle transformation, race for resources, educated individualism, shift of political powers, and migration.
- Lack of required supply chain management skills and training.
- Lack of clear visibility of various parts of the supply chain even though we might already have some information.
- Global supply chain issues (including geographic distances and time differences; additional costs for transportation, inventory, and local taxes; managing value creation in various parts of the global supply chain; foreign government regulations; cultural differences; varied performance standards; quality control issues; intellectual property concerns; and local talent recruitment and retention challenges).

So what are some solutions to various SCM system implementation challenges and problems? Some suggestions and industry best practices include (Niemeyer 2014; Manyika 2014; Dhawan et al. 2014; Philips and Coghlan 2013; Chaturvedi et al. 2013; Martin et al. 2013; Ebel et al. 2013; Schwarting et al. 2012; Houston et al. 2012; Hinze et al. 2011; Glatzel et al. 2011; Kauffeld et al. 2011; Harper et al. 2009; Haag et al. 2008, p. 123; Paulonis and Norton 2008; Cohen 2005; Lee 2004; Sheffi 2005; and Turban et al. 2006, pp. 284–285):

- Developing the trust among partners though it is not easy to achieve.
- Sharing information and having transparency along the supply chain, with appropriate confidentiality agreement and measures in place.
- Clearly specifying the roles, tasks, and responsibilities of all parties and ensuring that the terms of all agreements are clearly defined and agreed up front.
- Sharing risks, costs and rewards (e.g., engaging and cooperating with partners to manage supply chain risks, compensating for the loss to retailers as a result of new product development, and buying back the excess stocks) with chosen collaboration partners, and such partners should be chosen wisely (e.g., aligned strategic initiatives, well-established relationships, high value-creation for both sides, agreed benefit-sharing models, capabilities and willingness to act as a team, dedicated resources and leadership support for collaboration, jointly managing performance and impact assessment, and having long-term perspective while working on short-term perspective).
- Building relationships with your partners (especially long-term and important partners). Face-to-face communication is very important.
- Building an adaptable supply chain with the ability to spot trends and the capability to change supply chain (adaptability).
- Taking care to align the interest of all the firms in the supply chain with your own to create incentives for better performance and develop trust (alignment).
- Changing linear supply to hub structure (agility).
- Using intermediaries, who normally have access to a network of suppliers and customers, to develop new partners to complement existing ones.
- Evaluating needs of ultimate consumers not just immediate customers to avoid being a victim of the 'bullwhip effect'.
- Determining where your products stand in terms of technology cycles and product life cycles to decide approximate markets and supply chains for every product and service.
- Creating supply chains that respond to sudden and unexpected changes in markets.
- Establishing supply chain collaboration among partners [e.g., Collaborative Planning, Forecasting and Replenishment (CPFR) program; integrated product-development systems; integrated supply chain planning systems] and developing internal cross-functional as well as relevant stakeholders collaboration (e.g., integrated requirements planning, demand management, sourcing strategy development, supplier selection and negotiation, contract management, order process management, performance measurement and tracking, and ongoing value management).
- Considering outsourcing certain (even core) supply chain processes to specialist providers to focus on the core business of the organization, improve efficiency, and reduce the cost, especially for small and medium enterprises.

- Using inventories to solve problem: optimise and control inventories (e.g., only maintaining a stockpile of inexpensive but key components).
- Drawing up contingency plans and developing crisis management teams.
- Integrating IS/IT systems between suppliers and partners.
- Choosing right digital technologies and platforms for effective and efficient responses to face pace of change of the market and high volatility of the supply chain.
- Effective management (both recruitment and retention) of local talent.
- Monitoring economies all over the world to spot new supply bases and markets.
- Designing multiple and differentiated supply chains for different segments to be more responsive, improve service, reduce the cost, and generate better profitability (for example, having three supply chains for three segments of an apparel firm. Each of these is different with lead time, inventory size, cost, speed, and mode of business planning; one for the latest fashions needing much timely delivery but the highest price can be charged, one for seasonal styles typically updated four time a year, and one for basic items needed throughout the year and sent cheaply on slow freights); and building required internal capabilities (e.g., changes and adjustments in business processes, sourcing and procurement strategies, outsourcing and manufacturing processes, packaging, logistics and warehousing, distribution arrangements and networks, IT systems, culture, and structure).
- Creating unique supply chains suitable for your business models/types.
- Putting in place effective risk management process (including risk identification, evaluation, and mitigation) and looking at various tactics for managing risks (e.g., shifting risks to supplier, shifting risk to customer, physical heading, financial hedging, backward integration, co-investment, tolling, supplier redundancy, process redundancy, geographic diversification, and modifying specifications) and collaborating with partners on managing supply chain risks including their risks (e.g., risks in product quality, commodity fluctuations, capacity constraints, currency exchange rates, regulatory changes, supplier stability/solvency, and social/environmental attributes).
- Gaining sufficient engagement and commitment from top management (e.g., supply chain transformation is true cross-functional change management initiative, therefore needs the commitment and support (including required resources and organizational adjustments) from top management and letting senior management to drive supply chain strategy.
- Building the integration of digital and non-digital supply chains so a unified and whole view of inventory across the firm can be achieved.
- Creating win-win situations for the organization and its suppliers (e.g., collaboration for joint cost reduction); having long-term integrated and mutually benefited strategies (such as long-term incentives to work more closely and jointly develop new products and services and even new markets).
- Providing employees with required supply chain management skills [e.g., strong analytics, complex problem solving, product expertise, deep knowledge of the sourcing life cycle and processes, knowledge of commercial terms/business

acumen, project management, relationship management, and communication skills (oral and written)].
- Adopting advanced analytics (e.g., Big Data and Data Analytics) and analytics tools (e.g., Monte Carlo Simulation, Production and distribution planning, Capacity planning, Value-in-use modelling, Demand and pricing optimization, and Process parameter optimization) to gain better understanding and forecasting of the demand and solve previously unsolvable (and even unknown) problems along the supply chain.
- Utilizing the collected information to make better supply chain decision and leverage the capabilities of Big Data and Data Analytics and The Internet of Things to improve the performance of the supply chains.
- Adopting a single set of global standards that support data interchange, processes, and capabilities.
- Effectively identifying and managing value creation of various parts of the global supply chain.
- Designing alternative global supply chains that serve as supply backups and could provide much shorter and more secure supply chains (e.g., Mexico for the U.S. market).

Measuring the performance of digital supply chains is also very important (Ebel et al. 2013; Laudon and Laudon 2005, p. 343; Haag et al. 2008, p. 123). The measurement can be done by examining factors of fill rate (ability to fill the orders by due day), on-time deliveries, manufacturing frequency, reliability of supply, stability of supply, average time from order to delivery, total supply chain costs, number of delays of supply in inventory, responsiveness, supply chain response time, forecast accuracy and source/make cycle time, cash-to-cycle time, among many others (Laudon and Laudon 2005, p. 343).

6.5 Emerging Trends and Future Directions of Digital Supply Chains

The future supply chains have to be stronger and more agile, and are able to have the right people and skill sets, processes, and tools in the right places to drive efficiency and effectiveness of the supply chains; and in order to achieve those objectives, organizations need to work on such initiatives as focusing on better system and process standardization, building flexibility in the organizational model, enhancing sourcing capabilities in emerging markets (especially in the BRIC group of countries being Brazil, Russia, India, and China), better institutionalizing staff development, and restructuring the supply base (Houston et al. 2012).

Meanwhile, technologies such as cloud computing, social computing, mobile computing, Big Data, and The Internet of Things, will be adopted by more and more companies for managing supply chains. For example, in recent years, an explosion of serviced-based marketplaces, which help balancing global supply and demand, has been observed (London 2014). One of the interesting phenomenon is the evolution of the human cloud for acquiring external talent and expertise and outsourcing work tasks, and it can significantly help small buyers and small suppliers, who are the largely neglected long tail of global sourcing for such reasons as the lack of resources and/or the lack of expertise to outsource globally (Kaganer et al. 2013). The human clouds can be classified into four categories:

- Facilitators: matching suppliers and buyers through a direct bidding process (e.g., Freelancer, Elance, oDesk, Coffee and Power)
- Arbitrators: dealing with multiple suppliers through competitions (e.g., crowdSpring, 99desings, Witmart)
- Aggregators: aggregating many micro-tasks performed by multiple suppliers (e.g., MobileWorks, CrowdFlower, CloudFactory)
- Governor: supplying project governance and certifying supplier quality.

O'Brien and Marakas (2011, p. 341) believe that the trends in the use of supply chain management systems today are the adoption of three possible stages in a company's implementation of SCM systems. They are:

- First stage: improving internal supply chain processes and external processes and relationships with suppliers and customers
- Second stage: working on links among suppliers, distributors, customers, and other trading partners
- Third stage: developing and implementing collaborative supply chain management applications/systems.

Laudon and Laudon (2014, p. 380) present a view of future supply chain, which is more Internet-driven and includes multi-directional communications. Their Internet-driven supply chain functions like a digital nervous system and enables multidirectional communication among firms, networks of firms, and e-marketplaces so that the entire (global) supply chain could be more agile and could make immediate responses (e.g., adjustments to inventories and production capacities) to changes in demand.

Finally when more and more devices, objects, people, and organizations are connected, the integration of various internal and external systems and data sources will be a very challenging task.

References

Chaturvedi, N., Martich, M., Ruwadi, B., & Ulker, N. (2013, February). The future of retail supply chains. *Operations as a competitive advantage in retail* (pp. 59–67). McKinsey & Company.

Cohen, S. (2005). Moving to China. *Supply Chain Strategy (a Newsletter of Harvard Business Review), 1*(2), 4–6.

Dhawan, R., Singh, K., & Tuteja, A. (2014). When Big Data goes lean. *McKinsey Quarterly, 24* (2), 97–105.

Ebel, T., Larsen, E., & Shah, K. (2013, September). Strengthening health care's supply chain: A five-step plan. *McKinsey Quarterly*, 1–6.

Gill, B. (2013, June). E-mail: Not dead, evolving. *Harvard Business Review*, 32–33.

Glatzel, C., GroBpietsch, J., & Silva, I. (2011, January). Is you top team undermining your supply chain. *McKinsey Quarterly*, 1–6.

Haag, S., Baltzan, P., & Phillips, A. (2008). *Business driven technology* (2nd ed.). Boston: McGraw-Hill Irwin.

Harper, S., Kesteloo, M., Heinonen, P., & Kapoor, A. (2009). The collaboration game building value in the retail supply chain. *Perspective*, 1–5. (Booz & Company).

Hinze, G., Kaza, S., Sung Kown, O., Leopoldseder, M., & Weig, F. (2011, Autumn). From source to drain: Fixing the supply chain. *McKinsey on Semiconductors*, 42–49.

Houston, P., Turner, M. D., Miller, J., & Thelen, B. (2012). Supply management at a crossroads lessons for success in turbulent times. *Perspective*, 1–21. (Booz & Company)

Kaganer, E., Carmel, E., Hirscheim, R., & Olsen, T. (2013). Managing the human cloud. *MIT Sloan Management Review, 54*(2), 23–32.

Kauffeld, R., Mueller, C., & Michaels, A. (2011). The capable supply chain linked with strategy for superior performance. *Perspective*, 1–13. (Booz & Company).

Kirkland, R. (2014, May). The flow of trade: An interview with H. Ray Bingham. *Insights & Publications.* McKinsey & Company. Retrieved June 10, 2014, from http://www.mckinsey.com/insights/manufacturing/the_flow_of_trade_an_interview_with_h_ray_bingham.

Laudon, K. C., & Laudon, J. P. (2005). *Essentials of Management Information Systems: Managing the digital firm* (6th ed.). Prentice Hall.

Laudon, K. C., & Laudon, J. P. (2014). *Management Information Systems: Managing the digital firm* (13th ed.). Prentice Hall.

Lee, H. L. (2004, October). The triple—a supply chain. *Harvard Business Review*, 102–112.

London, S. (2014, April). Flow without friction: An interview with eBay's Devin Wenig. *Insights & Publications*, McKinsey & Company. Retrieved May 10, 2014, from http://www.mckinsey.com/insights/operations/flow_without_friction_an_interview_with_ebays_devin_wenig.

Manyika, J. (2014, April). The flow of value: An interview with Michael Spence. *Insights & Publications*, McKinsey & Company. Retrieved May 10, 2014, from http://www.mckinsey.com/insights/operations/the_flow_of_value_an_interview_with_michael_spence.

Martin, J., Dustman, E., Anderson, J., & Ram, R. (2013). Recapturing value in aerospace: Know your suppliers' cost and collaborate to lower them. *Perspective*, 1–12. (Booz & Company).

Niemeyer, A. (2014, June). Picking winning supply-chain technologies. *Interview*, McKinsey & Company. Retrieved June 14, 2014, from http://www.mckinsey.com/insights/operations/picking_winning_supply_chain_technologies.

O'Brien, J. A., & Marakas, G. M. (2011). *Management Information Systems* (10th ed.). New York: McGraw-Hill.

Paulonis, D., & Norton, S. (2008, July). McKinsey global survey results: Managing global supply chains. *McKinsey Quarterly*, 1–9.

Phillips, D., & Coghlan, P. (2013, November 4). Why you should create multiple supply chains. *Strategy + Business*, Retrieved April 7, 2014, from http://www.strategy-business.com/blog/Why-You-Should-Create-Multiple-Supply-Chains?gko=269a6.

Schwarting, D., Dutzer, H., Bauer, C., & Tenge, R. (2012). Managing multiple uncertainties: Building the capability to anticipate risks and prepare for them. *Perspective*, 1–13. (Booz & Company).

Sheffi, Y. (2005). Creating demand-responsive supply chains. *Supply Chain Strategy (a Newsletter of Harvard Business Review), 1*(2), 1–4.

Snow, C. C., Fjeldstad, Ǿ. D., Lettl, C., & Miles, R. E. (2011). Organizing continuous product development and commercialization: The collaborative community of firms model. *Journal of Product Innovation Management, 28*, 3–16.

Turban, E., King, D., Viehland, D., & Lee, J. (2006). *Electronic Commerce 2006: A managerial perspective, International Edition*. Upper Saddle River, NJ: Prentice Hall.

Turban, E., King, D., Liang, T. P., & Turban, D. (2012). *Electronic commerce: A managerial and social networks perspective, Global Edition* (7th ed.). UK.: Pearson Education.

World Trade Organization. (2013). *E-commerce in developing countries: Opportunities and challenges for small and medium-sized enterprises* (pp. 1–12). Switzerland: World Trade Organization.

Chapter 7
Digital Platforms

This chapter introduces the definition and different types of digital platforms, reviews social media platforms, and discusses some issues and success factors of digital platforms.

7.1 Definition and Classification of Digital Platforms

Digital platforms are multi-sided networks/markets, which provide the interface that brings together suppliers, customers and third parties (including platform providers) into a mutually-reinforcing synergy and are characteristized by network effects (developed from Gimpel and Westerman 2012; Parker and Van Alstyne 2012; Sarver 2013; Cusumano 2014; Bharadwaj et al. 2013; Hagiu and Wright 2013; Hagiu 2014). Digital platforms typically have two characteristics: (1) each participating side (could be a firm or a group of participants) is the customer of the platform and (2) there is direction interaction between the participating sides (Hagiu 2014); and they provide such services as providing connectivity, expanding variety, matching different users with each other (e.g., suppliers and customers), setting prices within the platform, and providing standards, governance and rules that mediate the transactions among users and regulate the behaviors of users. Digital platforms could significantly reduce search costs and/or transaction costs for participants; they have brought dramatic changes to the way different parts of the supply chain engage with each other thus improved the efficiency and value creation of the supply chain, have contributed in aggregating disconnected players in fragmented industries and unlocking new value from spare resources, and have increasingly become gateways through which businesses can transact with their customers (Gimpel and Westerman 2012; Parker and Van Alstyne 2012; Paul Choudary 2013; Hagiu and Wright 2013; Hagiu 2014).

Digital platforms can be typically classified into five categories:

- Business to Consumer (B2C) platforms (e.g., Apple's App Store-matching app providers with users).
- Business to Business (B2B) platforms (e.g., www.Alibaba.com-providing foreign buyers with Chinese suppliers).

J. Xu, *Managing Digital Enterprise*, DOI 10.2991/978-94-6239-094-2_7

- Consumer to Consumer (C2C) platforms (e.g., www.eBay.com-matching individual buyers with individual sellers).
- Peer to Peer (P2P) platforms (e.g., www.PayPal.com-facilitating money transfer between peers).
- Social Media platforms (e.g., social networks-connecting people).

7.2 Social Media Platforms

Kaplan and Haenlein (2010, p. 61) define social media as "a group of Internet-based applications that build on the ideological and technological foundations of Web 2.0, and that allow the creation and exchange of User Generated Content". Furthermore they classified social media, by looking at two perspectives of self-presentation/self-disclosure (SP/SD) and social presence/medium richness (SP/MR), into six categories: low SP/SD and low SP/MR collaborative projects (e.g., Wikipedia, Wikis), high SP/SD and low SP/MR blogs and microblogs (e.g., Techcrunch Blogs, Twitter), low SP/SD and medium SP/MR content communities (e.g., YouTube, Holu), medium SP/SD and medium SP/MR social networking sites (e.g., LinkedIn, Facebook), low SP/SD and high SP/MR virtual game worlds (e.g., World of Warcraft, Primary Games), and high SP/SD and high SP/MR virtual social worlds (e.g., Second Life, There Inc.). However it can be said that the lines between these categories have become increasingly blurred since many social media include more than one type of social media applications. On a related note, social business can be defined as using social media/social technologies to interact with customers, collaborate with customers, and facilitate internal communications. According to a recent survey of 1,100 business executives around the world along with extensive interviews with more than two dozen widely recognized social business leaders by IBM Institute for Business Value (reported in Cortada et al. 2012), organizations can apply social business in three major areas: creating valued customer experiences (e.g., engaging with and listening to customers, building the community, moving towards sales and service), driving workforce productivity and effectiveness (e.g., enhancing knowledge transparency and velocity, locating and developing expertise, leveraging external capabilities), and accelerating innovation (e.g., capturing new ideas widely, utilizing internal communities for innovation, enabling structured innovation efforts).

As a result of the wide adoption of mobile devices and the dramatic advancement to connectivity, more and more organizations are realizing the importance of digital platforms. Even though different social media applications have different emphases and functions, they have one thing in common: connecting people together and letting them do something they have common interest in (e.g., giving comments, sharing knowledge and exchanging experiences, making friends and networking, collaborating with others, and building communities). According to a recent global survey of 2,690 executives of organizations in various sizes, regions and industries (reported in Bughin et al. 2013), some social tools and technologies adopted by businesses include (in order): online video conferencing, social networking, collaborative document editing, video sharing, blogs, RSS (really simple syndication), Podcasts, Wikis, Microblogging, Tagging, Rating, Predication Markets, and Mash-ups.

A good example of social media is Wikipedia, which is an encyclopedia of the people, by the people, and for the people. The quality of the intellectual product created by people from all over the world voluntarily and collectively is very high (Kleiner 2014, p. 2). Wikipedia is a good example of democratization of knowledge versus monetization of knowledge. There are always people and organizations who would like to publish, develop, and share information and knowledge by looking at alternative publishing models other than the commercial model pursued by many for-profit businesses. On a related note, the Internet is inherently suitable to community business models.

Some uses of social media include: driving brand affinity (e.g., loyalty or trust building), providing customer services, marketing and lead generation, selling products directly to customers, monitoring and analyzing customer feedback and sentiment, crowdsourcing ideas and sharing knowledge, recruiting talent, managing projects, and facilitating external collaboration and internal cooperation (Kiron et al. 2013; Cortada et al. et al. 2012). Organizations can utilize social media to provide services to customers with lower costs (e.g., the average cost for handling an telephone call with a customer is US$6–8 while the average cost for interacting with a customer via social media is only US$1) (Benmark 2014). Many companies (could be as high as 70 % as suggested by Benmark 2014) have embarked on social media for customer care. Which department/function should manage social media is a tricky question to answer. While marketing or communication functions have been the traditional choice of owning the social media initiatives in the organization, especially for such activities of promotion and marketing, brand and reputation building, and customer engagement, they lack the required resources, expertise or institutional support to deal with customer services, especially on a large scale. It can be said that customer services (including social media customer services) should be dealt with by the operations functions, which are normally led by the Chief Operations Officer (COO) in the organization; and social media customer care should be integrated into the streamlined and coordinated operations across the organization. Meanwhile, some key skills for providing customer services via social media include: rich product knowledge and experience, excellent communication and writing skills, the ability to act as strong customer advocates, and good knowledge and skills of handling technical side of social media and the compliance issues associated with using social media (e.g., deciding the appropriate information and the appropriate approach to communication) (Benmark 2014).

Financial viability is the biggest challenge for social media. Some were very lucky to get support from Internet giants (e.g., Facebook's US$19 billion purchase of WhatsApp, Google's US$1.65 billion purchase of Youtube, Microsoft's acquisition of Webfives and its US$240 million investment in Facebook, Yahoo's US $30 million takeover of Flickr, and News Corporation's US$580 million buy of

MySpace), most of the social media companies need to work very hard to keep the business going. The digital world is full of opportunities (e.g., you may become someone, and a business may make its name rapidly) and challenges (for example, the huge costs of building up your large user base and developing technology infrastructure and the large bills of telecommunication networks are intangible and perishable; if you fail, you won't be able to see any tangible assets and you basically burn all the money you have invested). Facebook is the largest social network in numbers (e.g., 1.23 billion monthly users who have made 201.6 billion friend connections and clicked the 'like button' 3.4 trillion times) (Ross 2014), however users are spending less time on Facebook and some analysts have predicted doom future of Facebook (e.g., large reduction in user numbers, turning into an online yellow page or phone book). In addition, some mobile messaging services applications (e.g., WhatsApp, Line, SnapChat, WeChat, Kakao Talk) have becoming more and more popular among traditional users of Facebook (especially teenagers who keep in constant communication as this is what they really care about. And mobile messaging services apps could do a much better job than Facebook in that regard) (Sadauskas 2013).

Some ways social media can generate revenue include (Turban et al. 2012, pp. 409–410):

- Using social media for advertising, selling, and shopping (but it will take some time for business to figure out how to do it properly since it is still a new advertising model).
- Offering premium service for a monthly or per service fee.
- Earning a monthly service fee by partnering with organizations.
- Earning some income from members' offline gathering and other social activities: some social media companies have a network of thousands of local physical venues where members can meet. These venues, like coffee shops, may choose to pay a fee to be affiliated with the social network.

Generating revenue via advertising is becoming more and more important for social media. Some measures for social media advertising effectiveness include: click-through rates (CTR-click created per impression), cost per click (CPC-cost per click per an advertisement), cost per thousand (CPM-cost per thousand impressions of an advertisement), first-click-attribution (purchase attributed to the first click of consumer's purchasing), geo-targeting (post targeting a specific region), last-click attribution (purchase attributed to the last click of consumer's purchasing), return on investment (ROI-ratio of revenue to cost), return per visitor (RPV-revenue generated by per visit), social engagement (the volume of comments, likes, and shares received through social media), and social sentiment (social mentions ranked from 1 (negative) to 10 (positive) (Adobe Systems 2014). While the formula for successful social media is being developed, we should be confident that it is worth investing in social media. A recent study of customers of a wine retailers in the US by researchers from Texas A&M University, Aalto University, and State University of New York (reported in Strategy+Business 2013) indicates that customers who interact with the firm's social media sites (e.g., posting more messages) visited stores more often and spent more. The results of this study suggest that companies should tailor their social media efforts to specific types of customers (e.g., those who actively engage with the firm's social media sites) and focus on nurturing relationship with them. Tucker (2012), who studied advertising on Facebook, suggests that there exists evidence that social advertising (i.e., advertising via social media) is effective, and auto-mated (i.e., targeting customers with relevant advertisements automatically by the computing systems) social advertising is more effective than more explicit social advertising (e.g., when advertisers are trying to explicitly emulate or reinforce social influence, such as promoting social influence explicitly in the text of their advertisements).

Social media also can have implications for digital brand value and digital influence (especially real-time monitoring and comparison between different brands) of the organization (e.g., the number of Facebook Likes, the number of Twitter Followers) (Hodson et al. 2011). Big Data (e.g., creating growth and revenue opportunities from large volume information with large number of users) and global expansion (especially into more Asia Pacific and African regions where mobile initiatives are moving forward much faster) are two important growth opportunities for successful social media like Facebook, Twitter, LinkedIn, WhatsApp (Girotra and Netessine 2014; the author's own knowledge).

Content is very critical to the success of social media, and an effective content strategy involving content creation and sharing and dissemination is required (Dubois 2014). Content should be designed with specific goal the organization wants to achieve (e.g., production and service promotion, customer acquisition, customer relationship building, education of the customers, and brand and reputation development); and the delivery media of content is also important, videos being the more effective tools and are more viral and memorable (a good example is the recent automaker Volvo's video advertisement in Youtube, which shows action movie star Jean-Claude Van Damme's famous epic-split between two moving trucks). The approach for developing content should be innovative and should involve both internal and external knowledge resources (e.g., in-sourcing, outsourcing, co-creation/development, crowd-intelligence). While having great content is a necessity for hooking the audience, effective distribution and sharing of the creative content could be more important. Sharing the content frequently (e.g., several times in a day or week) can generate more clicks and exposure to your content (Kitschke 2014). Some good ways of doing this may involve using people with big influences (e.g., popular bloggers, online opinion leaders, celebrities), building a network of influencers (both offline and online) to disseminate the content, matching the content with the environment (e.g., producing content related to China during Chinese New Year), and linking with relevant content and sites (e.g., people can access the content via the links in different formats from other sites) (Dubois 2014; Kitschke 2014; the author's own knowledge).

According to a recent study by Georgia Institute of Technology and the University of Michigan (reported in Palmquist 2013), some effective ways to have more Twitter Followers include: providing information-based content but not focusing on self-focused messages (you only have up to 140 characters to spend in a Twitter message), posting happy messages (negativity won't be popular), not overusing hashtags that could distract readers from the messages, tweeting messages directly to other users (but not blanket broadcasting), exploring effective and strategic ways of having content retweeted (i.e., asking users to retweet to their networks where they are trusted), and increasing your digital visibility by linking to personal websites and identifying home locations. Chetty (reported in Palmquist 2013) points out that "If the whole point of social media is to be social, then some of the same factors that affect influence in live interactions should be reflected online-share valuable information, be positive and polite, lend credibility to those who earn it and understand what your network (and behavior) says about you." Meanwhile leadership is required for the organization's Twitter strategy. According to a recent survey by BRANDfog (reported in Palmquist 2013), 82 % of the survey respondents indicated that they are more likely to trust a firm whose top management team uses social media, and 77 % suggested that they prefer to buy products from a company whose leaders express the value and the mission of the organization via social networking sites like Twitter and Facebook. The results of a recent survey of more than 2,500 business executives from 99 countries and 25 industries by MIT Management Review and Deloitte (reported in Kiron et al. 2013) confirm the importance of effective leadership in the organization's social media/social business initiatives (especially in the early stage). Effective leadership means the need of committed executives who lead by example, play critical role in social media/social business strategy planning and implementation, invest time and effort in communicating the purpose and value of social media/social business initiatives, and provide the required organizational (e.g., cultural, structural, and business processes adjustments), human resources and financial support.

Another critical issue of social media (e.g., Twitter and Facebook) is dealing with negative comments. Some ways to handle negative comments include timely responses (within 24 h), demonstrating the organization's willingness to listen to criticism (there is a saying in Chinese, "we should listen willingly to all the criticisms, and take actions for those useful criticisms while closely examining other criticisms with appreciation"), and dealing with empathy and transparency. Another useful tool suggested by Rick Wilon, Director, Social Media at McDonald's (reported in Seijts 2014) is having "hater sessions" training to staff so they can better prepare for potential negative sessions (e.g., imagining possible negative comments and difficult questions and preparing corresponding responses beforehand). Rick Wilon also suggests that organizations should not take positive feedback/messages on social media for granted; they should appreciate the positivity towards the firm and have deeper engagement with their customers by such initiatives as sending thank-you notes, redistributing their positive messages about the firm, and even providing financial incentives to promote some of the best positive messages. Chui et al. (2013) suggest some principles of implementing social media initiatives, including adding value but not complexity (i.e., social technologies should be embedded the organization's way of doing business), having a systematic approach (i.e., defining objective, selecting a technology/solution, implementing the chosen technology/solution) and providing essential organizational support for social media initiatives (e.g., resources, mindset and behavioral changes, leadership), and taking the approach of experimenting and learning (e.g., starting small, testing and improving before expanding to a larger scale; encouraging new things by tolerating mistakes and believing mistakes make the best learning), and comprehensively examining the impacts of social media initiatives and developing robust measures of effectiveness of social media in a evolving way (i.e., it is very likely that robust metrics can't be developed in the beginning as a result of the lack of practical experience and the real-feel of using social media).

In addition, like any other businesses, understanding user diversity is also critical of social media/social business. For example, according to Finances Online (reported in Cater 2014a, b), men and women are different in using social media: men are more likely to use social media for business and dating while women are more likely to use social media for relationships, entertainment, and self-help; men prefer quick access to deals or information while women prefer to encounter with brands; women are less likely to take action on paid digital advertising; and men prefer video, news, and GPS while women favor sharing, camera, and games. Different generations of consumers tend to have different habits of adopting social media. According to a study of 1,056 consumers and 351 business executives in the US, Canada, the UK, France, Germany, India, China, Australia, and Brazil by IBM Institute for Business Value in October 2010 (reported in Baird and Parasnis 2011a, b), Generation Y (people born between 1975 and 1992: 18–35 years old), Generation X (people born between 1965 and 1974: 36–45 years old), and Baby Boomers (people born in or before 1946: 46 years and older) are different in adopting the following social media applications (in order): social networking sites (89 % of Generation Y, 79 % of Generation X, 72 % of Baby Boomers), media sharing sites (57, 42, 33 % respectively), microblogging sites (42, 37, 24 % respectively), blogging sites (30, 24, 12 % respectively), wikis (27, 22, 14 % respectively), social review sites (20, 16, 10 % respectively), social bookmarking sites (19, 12, 7 % respectively), and no accounts (5, 13, 20 % respectively). Meanwhile among the surveyed businesses, 79 % of them have presence on social networking sites, 55 % on media sharing sites, 52 % on microblogging sites, 48 % on wikis, 45 % on blogging sites, 36 % on social review sites, and 31 % on social marking sites; and they used social media to (in the order): communicate with customers (74 % of the participating firms), respond to customer questions (65 %), promote events (60 %), generate sales leads (52 %), sell products/services (50 %), solicit customer reviews(48 %), capture customer data (46 %), monitor brand (46 %), research customers (43 %), recruit employees (43 %), facilitate employee-to-employee interactions (41 %), solicit customer ideas (40 %), provide support (40 %), develop expert insights/thought leadership (38 %), provide training/education (37 %), facilitate customer-to-customer interactions (35 %), and communicate with vendors or partners (27 %). The identified responsible departments/functions for the firm's social media strategy are (in order): marketing (52 %), marketing communication (45 %), public relations (42 %), information technology (41 %), sales (32 %), web/e-commerce (29 %), social media (25 %), general management (22 %), customer service/other (17 %), customer insights (17 %), research and development (17 %), operations (17 %), risk management (15 %), product/service development (15 %), Finance (14 %), and supply chain management (10 %). Furthermore some identified top challenges of social media in the study include (in order): establishing ROI strategy (36 % of the participating firms), monitoring employees' social media use (30 %), negative brand exposure (28 %), lack of strategy (27 %), public concern over privacy (23 %), not realizing ROI (20 %), lack of support (19 %), lack of skills (19 %), industry regulation (19 %), tracking cross-channel interactions (16 %), lack of analytics (15 %), lack of employee participation (14 %), and employee concern over privacy (10 %).

According to a recent study by surveying 117 leading companies and a series of in-depth interviews with senior executives by Booz & Company and Buddy Media (reported in Vollmer and Premo 2012), some capabilities for social media success include: community engagement (e.g., monitoring, engaging, servicing and activating a social media presence and fan base; designing and executing the social media experience to drive participation and activation), content development (e.g., creating and sourcing brand and audience relevant content; tracking, cataloguing, storing, and serving content assets), and understanding of customers (e.g., ability to analyze and interpret social media activities in real time, understanding of drivers of community behavior and interest). The same study unveiled some top social media challenges are (in order): not enough cross-departmental collaboration (57 % respondents), insufficient resources dedicated to community management (52 %), lack of understanding among senior leaders (51 %), difficulty of proving ROI (48 %), and not core to overall strategy (43 %). In addition, while at the time of the study (2011) 67 % of participants indicated that their firms spent less than 5 % of their digital marketing spend on social media, 87 % of participants expected that their firms will spent more than 5 % of their digital marketing budget on social media in the next 3 years. Meanwhile it is suggested that in the future, companies will spend more on their own social media teams rather than buying advertising inventories from social networking sites such as Facebook, YouTube, or Twitter.

Meanwhile a recent report by Tata Consultancy Services (reported in Carter 2014b) suggest that while there is huge potential in social media, the impact of social media is still very limited at this stage and only 10 % of businesses are producing results with any kind of significance for the firm from social media. The same report also unveils some top mistakes of social media initiatives: (1) companies are not using the full spectrum of social channels; (2) companies are using social media less than Big Data and mobility; (3) companies are not using social media to replace traditional focus groups in customer research initiatives; (4) most companies simply don't spend enough on social media; (5) company cultures are not changing from the top down to embrace social media; (6) companies have been late to the game with social media; (7) companies are not staffing up on social; (8) companies might be watching, but they are not really listening and interpreting; and (9) companies aren't even tracking their social media ROI.

Bendall (2013) suggests some steps for embracing social media:

- Doing your intelligence by asking such questions as what are people saying about the organization? Where are your customers' social media ecosystems? What can their networking habits tell you? Her tip is to think niche and small and to have really rich understanding of your customers (especially via qualitative ways).
- Rethinking where you need to live in their digital ecosystems by looking at such perspectives as their habits, their best channels, the way they speak, their views of you, their engagement with you, their suggestions as to how you can become a better-networked connection for them. Her tip is to open up yourself to ideas and criticisms and challenge yourself to rethink.
- Working on required changes by identifying programs to begin with (but start with a limited number of programs-the suggested number is 3), being patient and giving yourself some time (you still need to focus on your core business when integrating social media into your business), examining and ensuring the suitability of internal processes, human resources, content, tools, and application development methods required for social media.

Social media need to build their business ecosystems for long term growth and prosperity. Some firms have actively pursued this approach (e.g., Facebook's mobile phone initiatives and its recent acquisitions of mobile messaging business WhatsApp and virtual-reality headset maker Oculus VR). Some other success factors of social media could include: user loyalty and engagement (e.g., ensuring users stick to your business and use it frequently), international growth (e.g., many social businesses are very successful in the home markets, but they need to be able to successful internationally for longer-term growth), revenue generation (e.g., how to generate new revenue sources and reduce reliance on advertising revenue?), having a dedicated social media officer and/or a social media team, innovation capability (e.g., in addition to the acquisition strategy, having better in-house innovation capabilities and co-invention abilities (with external partners and customers) abilities), effectively leveraging network effects, having a clear focus, and organically growing user community (Albergotti 2014; Sadauskas 2014; the author's own knowledge).

7.3 Challenges/Issues and Success Factors of Digital Platforms

Some identified main obstacles to digital platforms include: the difficulties in attracting sufficient numbers of suppliers and buyers to join the platform (especially the suppliers) as well as other important players who are not sure about or don't want to be beholden to or don't want to create potential competitors for themselves, the complexities of running a platform with conflicting interests to satisfy, and the uncertainties about product and service quality and the reliability of buyers and sellers who will damage the platform's reputation if not being managed properly

(Haigu and Wright 2013; Haigu 2014; the author's own knowledge). According to a recent survey of leading digital agencies and marketers of their use of digital platforms by Doubleclick (2013), some top barriers holding organizations back from leveraging their digital platforms include: lack of budget, lack of trained staff and expertise, culture of centralized decision making, and lack of support from senior management. Some other challenges to the success of digital platforms include: size of the platform (without sufficient number of suppliers and users, especially suppliers in the beginning, it is difficult to achieve financial viability) and the uniqueness of the platform (e.g., whether it is valuable, rare, inimitable, and non-substitute) (Gimpel and Westerman 2012).

Some suggested success factors include (Gimpel and Westerman 2012; Parker and Van Alstyne 2012; Haigu and Wright 2013; Haigu 2014; Hill 2014; the author's own knowledge):

- Deciding whether a digital platform is the right choice (e.g., selling direct to customers or providing a platform for sellers to sell to customers? The former could give the company more control, better profit (especially for high demand products and optimized bundling packages), and provide better experience to customers).
- Deciding the number of sides to bring on board (need to balance such issues as cost-benefit analysis, complexity, agility and flexibility to develop innovative products and services and respond to market changes, user experience, reputation of the platform; and it is recommended that organizations should start with fewer sides to establish the platform before expansion).
- Making the platform user-centric (for suppliers and customers as well as other participants) addressing their needs with great functionality and user friendliness and establishing a secure, reliable and dynamic platform.
- Having dynamic pricing strategy (e.g., free access but charging for value-added services, discounts for large groups and large orders/amounts, low fees for some basic services but charging more for additional services) and providing appropriate incentives to ensure the fluidity of the platform (e.g., offering free services or subsidized prices to at least one side of the platform and balance the loss from other sides).
- Establishing effective governance rules (e.g., rules regulating access to the platform, rules regulating interactions on the platform) and enforcing strict compliance with such rules.
- Ensuring transparency and sufficient information on the platform.
- Avoiding creating too much competition within one side of the platform.
- Opening the platform to the public or as widely as possible.
- Allocating sufficient resources (including financial and human resources) to the development and implementation of the digital platform.
- Effectively building up the large user base as quickly as possible and strategically leveraging the network effects (e.g., achieving large trading volume and generating new revenue sources from the large user base and the associated large information assets).

- Building an ecosystem with the growth and future larger scale in mind and ensure each one in the ecosystem gets enough of what they value to be satisfied (not only satisfying customers).
- Identifying, attracting and retaining influential suppliers and customers as well as third parties by offering special deals and tailored services.
- Adopting open standards and technologies and working hard on integration and interoperability issues (e.g., seamless interaction across various digital channels such as websites, mobile devices, social networks, e-mail, videos, messages, apps, search engines, and portals; and integration with systems of users and strategic partners).
- Developing creative content of the digital platform and treating it as mission-critical asset.
- Establishing and implementing effective strategy of data collection and data analytics as well as generating new opportunities and new revenue sources arising from them.

References

Adobe Systems. (2014). *Social Intelligence Report, Adobe Digital Index*, Q4 2013, 1–17. Retrieved March 28, 2014, from http://www.cmo.com/content/dam/CMO_Other/ADI/ADI_SocialIntelReport_Q413.pdf.

Albergotti, R. (2014, April 23). Facebook earnings: What to watch, Digits, Blog, *The Wall Street Journal*. Retrieved May 8, 2014, from http://blogs.wsj.com/digits/2014/04/23/facebook-earnings-what-to-watch-3/.

Baird, C. H., & Parasnis, G. (2011a). From social media to social CRM: What customers want-The first part of a two-part series. *Executive Report, IBM Global Business Services*, (pp. 1–16) IBM Institute for Business Value.

Baird, C. H., & Parasnis, G. (2011b). From social media to social CRM: What customers want-The first part of a two-part series. *Executive Report, IBM Global Business Services*, (pp. 1–18) IBM Institute for Business Value.

Bendall, F. (2013, September 11). Is social media fad. www.Smartcompany.com.au. Retrieved March 4, 2014, from http://www.smartcompany.com.au/technology/33644-is-social-media-a-fad.html.

Benmark, G. (2014). Why the COO should lead the social-media customer service. *McKinsey Quarterly, Number,* (1), 11–13.

Bharadwaj, A., El Sawy, O. A., Pavlou, P. A., & Venkatraman, N. (2013). Digital business strategy: Toward a next generation of insights. *MIS Quarterly, 37*(2), 471–482.

Bughin, J., Chui, M., & Pollak, L. (2013, November). Organizing for change through social technologies. *Insights & Publications*. McKinsey & Company. Retrieved January 20, 2014, from http://www.mckinsey.com/insights/high_tech_telecoms_internet/organizing_for_change_through_social_technologies_mckinsey_global_survey_results.

Carter, J. (2014a, 17 April). Infograhic: How do men use social media differently to women. www.Mycustomer.com. Retrieved April 20, 2014, from http://www.mycustomer.com/news/infographic-how-do-men-use-social-media-differently-women.

Carter, J. (2014b, 11 April). The top nine social faux pas: Is your brand socially awkward. www.Mycustomer.com. Retrieved April 20, 2014, from http://www.mycustomer.com/feature/social-crm/social-media-faux-pas-your-company-socially-awkward/166837.

Cortada, J. W., Lesser, E., & Kprsten, P. J. (2012). The business of social business: What works and how it's done. *Executive Report, IBM Global Business Services*, (pp. 1–16) IBM Institute for Business Value.

Chui, M., Dewhurst, M., & Pollak, L. (2013, November). Building the social enterprise. *McKinsey Quarterly*, 1–4.

Cusumano, M. (2014). Technology strategy and management: The evolution of platform thinking. *Communications of the ACM, 53*(1), 32–34.

Dubois, D. (2014, January 28). Content strategy is king in social media. *INSEAD Knowledge*. Retrieved March 7, 2014, from http://knowledge.insead.edu/marketing-advertising/content-strategy-is-king-in-social-media-3135.

Doubleclick. (2013, December).Unravelling the digital display industry: Understanding the tools and benefits of digital marketing. www.Thinkwithgoogle.com. Retrieved January 12, 2014, from http://www.thinkwithgoogle.com/research-studies/unraveling-digital-display.html.

Gimpel, G., & Westerman, G. (2012, October). Shaping the future: Seven enduring principles for fast-changing industries. *Working Paper*, (pp. 1–24) The MIT Center for Digital Business.

Girotra, K., & Netessine, S. (2014, February 21). What is Facebook up to, *INSEAD Knowledge*. Retrieved March 7, 2014, from http://knowledge.insead.edu/blog/insead-blog/whats-facebook-up-to-3186.

Hagiu, A. (2014). Strategic decisions for multisided platforms. *MIT Sloan Management Review, 55* (2), 71–80.

Hagiu, A., & Wright, J. (2013, March). Do you really want to be an eBay? *Harvard Business Review,* 103–108.

Hill, G. (2014, February 18). Customer-centric confusion: Why customer focus is not enough to succeed. www.Mycustomers.com. Retrieved April 10, 2014, from http://www.mycustomer.com/feature/experience/customer-centric-confusion-why-customer-focus-not-enough-succeed/166515.

Hodson, N., Aytekin, U. & Crawford, J. (2011, December 9). What is your company's Facebook LPM (Likes per million). *Strategy + Business* (pp. 1–6). Retrieved March 2, 2014, from http://www.strategy-business.com/media/file/00099-Whats-Your-Companys-Facebook-LPM-Likes-Per-Million.pdf.

Kaplan, A. M., & Haenlein, M. (2010). Users of the world, unite! The challenges and opportunities of social media. *Business Horizons, 53*, 59–68.

Kiron, D., Palmer, D., Nguyen Phillips, A., & Berkman, R. (2013). The executive's role in social business. *MIT Sloan Management Review*, *54*(4), 83–89.

Kitschke, Z. (2014, April 14). Three social media trends every business should know about. www.Smartcompany.com.au. Retrieved April 28, 2014, from http://www.smartcompany.com.au/technology/social-media/41518-three-social-media-trends-every-business-should-know-about.html.

Kleiner, A. (2014). The thought leader: Thomas Malone-The head of MIT's Center for Collective Intelligence explains how to build smarter and more successful teams. *Strategy+Business,* (75), 1–7.

Palmquist, M. (2013, July 11). How to win (Twitter) friends and influence people. *Strategy +Business* Blogs. Retrieved January 20, 2014, from http://www.strategy-business.com/article/How-to-Win-Twitter-Friends-and-Influence-People?gko=6fdbb.

Paul Choudary, S. (2013, October 19). The rise of the platform: A seismic shift in business models, *Platformed.info*. Retrieved January 10, 2014, from http://platformed.info/platform-economics/.

Parker, G., & Van Alstyne, M. (2012, January). A digital postal platform: Definitions and a Roadmap, *Working Paper*, (pp. 1–31) The MIT Center for Digital Business.

Ross, M. (2014, February 4). Facebook turns 10: The world's largest social network in numbers. *ABC News*. Retrieved March 27, 2014, from http://www.abc.net.au/news/2014-02-04/facebook-turns-10-the-social-network-in-numbers/5237128.

Sadauskas, A. (2013, November 20). Why users are visiting Facebook less often. www.Smartcompany.com.au. Retrieved March 2, 2014, from http://www.smartcompany.com.au/technology/34645-why-facebook-is-slowly-turning-into-a-phone-book-best-of-the-web.html.

Sadauskas, A. (2014, April 30). The inside story of why Google+ failed, www.Smartcompany.com.au. Retrieved on May 10, 2014, from http://www.smartcompany.com.au/technology/41726-the-inside-story-of-why-google-failed-best-of-the-web.html.

Sarver, R. (2013, September 26). What is a platform, technology. www.Sarver.org. Retrieved January 8, 2014, from http://www.sarver.org/2013/09/26/what-is-a-platform/.

Seijts, J. (2014, March) When the Twitter turns on you. *Harvard Business Review*, 117–121.

Strategy+Business. (2013, May 17). The dollar payoff from social media, Recent Research, *Strategy+Business*. Retrieved January 20, 2014, from http://www.strategy-business.com/article/re00236?gko=35f18.

Tucker, C. (2012, February 25). Social advertising, *Working Papers Series*, MIT Management Science. Retrieved March 8, 2014, from http://papers.ssrn.com/sol3/papers.cfm?abstract_id=1975897.

Turban, E., King, D. Liang, T. P., & Turban, D. (2012) *Electronic commerce: A managerial and social networks perspective*, Global Edition (7th ed.). New York: Pearson Education.

Vollmer, C., & Premo, K. (2012). *From campaigns to capabilities: The impact of social media on marketing and beyond* (pp. 1–25). Japan: Perspective, Booz & Company Inc.

Chapter 8
Digital Marketing and Advertising

This chapter highlights the importance of understanding digital customers, looks at digital advertising methods, presents measures for evaluating effectiveness of digital advertising, and discusses some issues and success factors of digital marketing and advertising.

8.1 Understanding Digital Customers

A critical aspect of successfully implementing a customer-focused strategy is to have a good understanding of customers. Organizations could develop a good understanding of customers' needs via applying good research (including both qualitative and quantitative methods) about customers, gaining market insights, and using intuition based on experiences (Edelman 2010b; Shaprio 2012).

In addition, a good understanding of the customer/consumer decision process and shopping/engagement journal with the organization and how technologies can assist in different parts/stages of the process/journey is essential as well, and the key is to engage with customers throughout their process/journey. The customer shopping/engaging journey with the organization could be a multiple-channel but all the one journey (Collins 2014), and it can be grouped into three categories (LivePerson 2013; Brandweiner 2013; Laudon and Traver 2012, pp. 397–398; Edelman 2010a, b; Divol et al. 2012; Turban et al. 2012, p. 433; Xu and Quaddus 2013, pp. 122–123; the author's own knowledge):

- Pre-purchase activities: including awareness/need recognition (e.g., considering something because of external influences (such as advertisements, peer-influence, word of mouth) and/or actual needs), and searching for suitable products and services, and evaluating alternative options. On top of the traditional media of TV, radio, newspapers, magazines, outdoor displays, and other things (such as in-store promotions), digital technologies and applications (e.g., ad banners, interstitials, video ads, e-mails, e-newsletters, social networks, search engines, blogs and micro-blogs, discussion forums, live chatting, click-to-call, virtual communities, online catalogues, and information intermediaries) could provide

J. Xu, *Managing Digital Enterprise*, DOI 10.2991/978-94-6239-094-2_8

assistance to customers and enable organizations to provide speedy responses and easy resolutions to issues. In addition,

- Purchase/Buy activities: including buying online (via firms' own sites or third-party platforms), buying in store, buying online, paying online and picking-up in store, buying online via kiosks or other computing devices in the store, and organizing delivery arrangements online. Digital technologies and applications (such as e-commerce sites, digital platforms, digital payment systems, online order tracking systems, online coupon and discount systems, and real-time dynamic pricing systems) could assist customers and enable organizations to provide speedy responses and easy resolutions to issues.
- Post-purchase activities: including enjoying/experiencing the product/service, advocating the product/service, having the bond with the product/service, and repurchasing the product/service. Digital technologies and applications (e.g., social networks, online communities, live chatting, click-to-call, blogs and micro-blogs, and discussion forums) could be useful and enable organizations to provide speedy responses and easy resolutions to issues.

It could be argued that the Internet and digital technologies have been particularly useful to customers in the areas of (pre-purchase) search and evaluation and (post-purchase) reviews and advocacy. Search engines (especially Google) have been effective in helping customers find information even though the results are not perfect-most of the search results (normally after first page) don't really match what we are looking for. There is just too much information on the web, and our (eyeball) attention is limited. Businesses that can effectively grasp our attention for information and advertisements at the right time at the right place will be doing fine. In fact, according to Hal Varian, Google's Chief Economist (reported in Manyika 2009), Google has developed its entire business model around the notion. Big Data and Data Analytics could be very useful in having better understanding of and getting closer to the customers. For example, through monitoring and analyzing actual online activities organizations could look at their customers in a more accurate and systematic way, and eliminate the discrepancy between what they say (e.g., responses to interviews, surveys, and other qualitative and quantitative research methods) and what they do or reduce the amount of field experiments (Ferguson 2013b; Cayla et al. 2014).

Data analytics could also provide information about an individual customer in a particular moment (via his/her activities and engagement with the organization), so organizations can create something (content and/or product offers and/or service offers) for each customer (i.e., mass customization and personalization) (Collins 2014) or even achieve "anticipatory shipping" initiatives (i.e., sending customers products or services before they even order them) by Amazon (Carter 2014). In addition, data analytics enables organizations to design more effective, timely, and responsive ads and achieve smarter decisions and better agility of reallocating advertising budgets to reflect the changes in customers' habits on very short notice (Bhandari et al. 2014).

In line with the popularity of Big Data and Data Analytics, having a test-and-learn mindset with appropriate testing process and capabilities is critical for understanding digital customers (Davenport 2009). Creating a testing mind-set is very much a culture thing, which needs senior management's leadership and commitment for its success. An effective testing process, which could include such steps as developing hypotheses, designing experiment, setting up the experiment, conducting the experiment, tracking and monitoring, and analyzing and discussing, is fundamental to any organizations' testing initiatives. Meanwhile testing capabilities could be built up via managerial training, development of software for managing experiments, learning capture and knowledge management, doing tests regularly to identify and reflect the changing needs of the customers, and establishing a core research group to lead and coordinate the testing initiatives in the organization (Davenport 2009).

One useful approach in gaining better understanding of customers is to look at their comments and opinions on the Internet; and online reviews could play an important role in customers' purchasing decision-making process (for example 70 % of consumers surveyed by Nielsen in 2012 suggested they trusted online reviews, and research done for Google in 2011 unveiled that the average shopper consults 10.4 information sources before they make purchase (almost twice as many as in 2010) (reported in Simonson and Rosen 2014a)). Organizations need to carefully examine customers' online views (including online ratings) since they could be biased and manipulated easily (Aral 2014). On a related note, some organizations have looked at using social media reputation management service, which is a US$5 billion industry, for their online reputation management (Stafford 2013). In addition, consumers would only use online reviews for certain product categories which are normally important to them (e.g., restaurant selections by online reviews from food critics and sites such as Yelp; buying a car by looking at reviews from various sites on cars; choosing electronics (especially brands not being adopted before) by checking with different review sites (including dedicated review sites to certain brands) and comments on such sites as Amazon, eBay; planning trips via reading comments and reviews on such sites as www.Lonelyplant.com, www.Tripadvisor.com); on the other hand, low-involvement habitual purchases (e.g., buying milk and bread) and decisions made largely based on prior experiences and emotions, preferences and beliefs (e.g., buying food from McDonald and KFC, buying luxury items) are less influenced by online reviews (Simonson and Rosen 2014b). Organizations could investigate to what extent and in what situation their products and services are influenced by online reviews and then implement relevant solutions (e.g., generating more in-pulse buying online and offline by more effective and persuasive marketing initiatives, time-limited and/or product limited online sales such as one product only sales and/or 1 day only sales adopted by some sites).

One important perspective associated with understanding customers is choosing the right customers who best fit your company's culture and traditions, most closely matched to your existing capabilities (such as technology excellence of Google and Apple, logistics excellence of Walmart and Amazon, superior brand marketing of

Ralph Lauren and Nestle), or industry specific capabilities (e.g., mining capabilities of BHP and Rio Tinto, original content production of HBO and Netflix)), and who provide the greatest direct and indirect profit potential (Simons 2014).

Meanwhile to effectively reach digital customers, organizations need to build its digital marketing capabilities. According to Künstner et al. (2013), three fundamental digital marketing capabilities for organizations are:

- Deciding market-back investment priorities via understanding market requirements: some questions to be considered include (1) how do customer segments match up with digital behavior segmentation? (2) how many segment-specific go-to-market approaches are required? (3) what is the state-of-the-art digital marketing in your industry? (4) Is it must have versus nice to have? and (5) which new digital channels are ultimately needed?.
- Establishing cross-channel transparency via managing the marketing and sales mix: some questions to be considered include (1) how should marketing budget be allocated across the multitude of new digital channels? (2) how do traditional and digital channels influence each other? and (3) how should marketing budget be balanced between traditional and new digital channels?.
- Becoming digital via laying the foundation for marketing and sales operations: some questions to considered include (1) how should you structure marketing and sales organizations in the digital age? (2) how can you better deliver the necessary innovation in digital marketing, given the limitations the traditional organizational setup? and (3) what type of culture is required to stay on top of the digital marketing evolution?.

In line with the rapid development of digital technologies, global connectedness, and the penetration of computing devices (especially mobile devices) around the world, organizations should have another look at the 4P's of their marketing model (such as focusing on solution for meeting customers' needs instead of *product*, focusing on access via multi-channel (e.g. contact center, in-store, social media, online, mobile, e-mail, live chat, click-to-call) instead of *place*, focusing on value instead of *price*, and focusing on education rather than *promotion*) (Ettenson et al. 2013). In addition, dynamic pricing systems, which are not new concepts and have been used by airlines for many years, could be adopted as well (Brandweiner 2013). Organizations could have different prices for different customers, for different periods (e.g., off-peak times vs. peak times), and for different times of the day or the week (for example, it is reported that old people, unemployed, young families are likely to shop in the morning while younger people and working people tend to shop in the afternoon and evening (Brandweiner 2013); and they can charge higher prices to customers who are willing to pay for more for some value-added services. Meanwhile with the ever increasing mobility and connectedness, real-time dynamic pricing systems are made possible.

Providing customers with consistent experience and communication across multiple channels and multiple touch points throughout their journey with the retailing organization is critical to the success and performance of the retailer. According to a recent study of 27,000 American consumers across 14 different industries (reported in Pulido et al. 2014), focusing on customer journey could deliver 35 % more predictive of customer satisfaction and 32 % more predictive of customer churn than performance on individual touch points; and maximizing customer satisfaction with the journey could potentially increase revenue by up to 15 % and reduce the cost of serving customers by up to 20 %. Consistent communication plays a very important role in achieving consistent customer experience; organizations need to fulfil their promises and then actively highlight the delivery of the made promises to reinforce their commitments and promote their successes of providing consistent customer experience.

8.2 Digital Advertising Methods

After understanding customers and their needs, organizations need to attract customers to their products and services via advertising. In line with the rapid development of digital technologies and networks, digital advertising has been growing significantly in recent years. Digital advertising now accounts for 22 % of global advertising market and will reach 27 % by 2017 (Brennan et al. 2013).

According to Interactive Advertising Bureau and Pricewaterhouse (2014), of the total US$175 billion advertising revenue in the US in 2013, 42.8 billion (24.5 % of 175 billion) came from the Internet, 40.1 billion (23 %) from Broadcast Television, 34.4 billion (19.7 %) from Cable Television, 18 billion (10.3 %) from Newspaper, 16.7 billion (9.5 %) from Radio, 13.4 billion (7.7 %) from Magazine(consumer), 7.9 billion (4.5 %) from Out of Home, 0.9 billion (0.5 %) from Video Game, and 0.8 billion (0.45 %) from Cinema.

Advertising on the Internet can take many forms (e.g., banners, pop-ups and similar ads, e-mail advertising, newspaper and classified ads, search engine advertisement, advertising in chat rooms, blogs, and social networks). The most common is the use of search engines and banners, and mobile has been popular in recent years. For example, according to Interactive Advertising Bureau and Pricewaterhouse (2014), of the total US$42.8 billion 2013 US Internet Ad revenue, 43 % came from Search, 19 % from Banner/Display, 17 % from Mobile, 7 % from Digital Video, 6 % from Classifieds, 4 % from Lead Generation, 3 % from Rich Media, and 2 % from Sponsorship. Table 8.1 presents advantages and disadvantages of major digital advertising methods.

8.3 Evaluating the Effectiveness of Digital Advertising

Various measures are used to evaluate the success of online advertising Table 8.2 presents some measures which can be used to evaluate online advertising effectiveness.

Table 8.1 Advantages and disadvantages of digital advertising methods

Advertising methods	Advantages	Disadvantages/limitations
Banners	Linking to buying opportunities; Wide reach; Effective targeting	Limited by their cost, space for information and user indifference
Pop-up and similar ads	Catch users' attention; Linking to buying opportunities	Could annoy users (actually very likely)
Search engine advertising (e.g., Google's Adwords and AdSense)	Good credibility; Good position/place available (in terms of being among the first few results or on the first page of the search results); Significant audiences	High competition among users (e.g., competing to be among the first few results or on the first page of the search results); Information overload (e.g., too many search results and most of them are not relevant. The current search engines only do some basic tasks comparing to the human brain)
E-mail adverting (directly by the organization or by third parties)	An effective method of advertising to large groups	May cause SPAM issue
Embedded advertising (e.g., text links and image links in the digital content)	A well-established advertising method	Limited to people who are interested in reading the specific content; Those people who may read the content could skip the embedded links
Digital video, digital TV and other digital rich media	A very large audience; Better way of communicating messages and getting the users' attention	Users would skip the digital videos and digital TV programs including too many ads, which annoy them very much; Could be effective in areas/regions where the Internet bandwidth or the telecommunication infrastructure is not adequate
Viral advertising (electronic version of word-of-mouth)	Could be more accepted and trusted; If properly used, could be more effective and cost-productive	Could lose users if it is overused and/or wrongly used
Directories and Classifieds	Could reach a large audience; Being very accessible	Could be difficult to measure the effectiveness of the ads
Advergaming (using computer games to advertise)	Could be very attractive to young generation and game lovers	Could have the difficulty of getting the attention of a mass audience
Social network/media advertising (advertising on social networks, blogs, wikis and online communities)	A very large audience; Better and more interactive way of communicating messages and getting the users' attention	Could require resources and dedication to engage with customers and keep the content relevant and current; May need to address complains and negative comments quickly and effectively; and still a challenge to make money from social media/network ads

(continued)

Table 8.1 (continued)

Advertising methods	Advantages	Disadvantages/limitations
Mobile advertising (advertising on mobile devices, including advertising through mob applications and location-based mobile advertising)	A very large audience; Mobility; Could be more targeted, more real-time, and more location specific	Technical limitations (e.g., small screen size, battery life, data transfer speed, bandwidth issues); Lack of user friendliness; Lack of interaction (mobile ads tend to more static); Lack of standards across different mobile platforms and devices; Lack of established measurement tools; and still a challenge to make money from mobile ads
Wearable devices and augment reality advertising	A very large audience; Mobility; Could be more targeted, more real-time, and more location specific	Technical limitations (e.g., small screen size, battery life, data transfer speed, bandwidth issues); Lack of user friendliness; Lack of standardisation across different platforms and devices; and still in the very early stage
Affiliate advertising	Could potentially reach a large audience (especially via affiliate networks); Leverage outside expertise which may not available in the firm	Could have the issue of low click-through rates
Ad exchanges	Could better meet the needs of the ad buyers by matching supply and demand; Better transparency	Could be only limited to firms who are aware of this
Ads as a commodity (paying people to watch ads)	Could be more attractive as a result of the incentive than other methods	The incentive is usually small and may not be able to attract a large audience; May not attract the intended customers since some people are simply viewing for the money regardless of the relevance of the content of the ad to their needs and interests
Advertising networks and ammediaries	Could potentially reach a large audience via advertising networks who normally have large databases of potential customers; Leverage outside expertise which may not available in the firm	Beyond the control of the organization; The loss of the internal advertising capabilities and customer data
Ads by sponsorships	Could be an effective way of advertising to the target segments and beyond the target segments (especially via television broadcasting); Could improve the brand awareness more quickly and broadly	Could be expensive; Could be perceived as only linking to certain activities, people, organizations, and agencies

(continued)

Table 8.1 (continued)

Advertising methods	Advantages	Disadvantages/limitations
Ads by collaborating with the crowd	Could be very popular and very innovative	Could have too many competing priorities and ideas; Could have quality control issues
Coupons, vouchers and discounts	Could be a very attractive advertising method	Could not be relevant to what customers really want; If not properly managed, they (coupons, vouchers and discounts) could damage the business for such reasons as lower profit margins and misuses by intermediaries who provide coupons and vouchers to the end customers
Dynamic, personalized and customized ads	Could be more effective and targeted	Could cause users' privacy concerns if they believe you know too much about them; Could require the firm to have detailed and accurate information about its customers-wrong personalized ads could annoy and turn away customers; More developed for the online channel so far but could be extended to mobile channel and other electronic media (including television) in the future
Native advertising	Could be less intrusive to and more acceptable by people; This could reach better advertising effectiveness	Still in the very early stage; Still in the process of trying to figure out how to commercialize it and implement it at a large scale
Promoting websites and mobile applications via traditional advertising channels (e.g., television, radio, catalogue, direct mail, newspapers, magazines, posters, billboards, stadium/scoreboard, airport display, in-store, shopping malls)	Could reach more customers and drive more customers to digital channels; Could help increase awareness and brand equity	Would need more upfront capital investments
Multi-channel advertising	Could reach more customers and have better advertising outcomes; Multi-channel strategy is so far the most powerful advertising strategy which leverages the strengths of different channels	Would need more resources and more capital investments

(*Source* Developed from Turban et al. 2012, pp. 454–465; Rayport 2013; Laudon and Traver 2014, pp. 379–408; Heiligtag and Xu 2006; Kirby 2013; Galloway 2014; Sealey 2014; Bommel et al. 2014; eMarketer 2014a; Interactive Advertising Bureau and Pricewaterhouse 2014; Yeh and Zhang 2013 the author's own knowledge)

Table 8.2 Digital advertising effectiveness measures

Measures	Specific measures
Hits	Number of hits on the site
Return customers	Number of re-purchases
Click-through rate	Percentage of times an ad is clicked
Page views	Number of pages viewed
Stickiness (duration)	Average length of stay at a website
Unique visitors	Number of unique visitors during a period
Impressions	Number of times an ad is served
Recency	Time elapsed since the last action taken by a buyer, such as a visit or purchase
Lead generation	Number of useful or qualified leads
Conversion rate	Percentage of visitors who become customers online
Cross-channel conversation rate	Percentage of online visitors of a retailer's site who purchases in the retailer's store
Abandonment rate	Percentage of shoppers who begin a shopping cart purchase but then leave the site without completing a purchase
Attrition rate	Percentage of customers who do not return during the next year after an initial purchase
Retention rate	Percentage of existing customers who continue to buy on a regular basis
Open rate (for e-mailing advertising)	Percentage of e-mail recipients who open the e-mail.
Delivery rate (for e-mailing advertising)	Percentage of e-mail recipients who receive the e-mail
Bounce back rate (for e-mailing advertising)	Percentage of e-mails that could be delivered
Unsubscribe rate (for e-mailing advertising)	Percentage of recipients who click unsubscribe
Number of participants (for social media advertising)	Number of users or/and contributors
Engagement (for social media and mobile advertising)	Number of posts, comments, response; Number of followers (however it is argued that we can at most actively follow 150–300 others online (Dubois 2013)); Number of map look-ups in the store/shopping areas; Number of searching for information in the store; Number of click-to-call
Amplification (reach) (for social media and mobile advertising)	Percentage of likes and/or shares or connections and/or posts to other sites; Number of SMSs received and shared; Number of mobile location-based messages received and shared
Community (for social media and mobile advertising)	Monthly total and/or average of posts, comments, and activities; Number of mobile voice messages
Brand strength/sales (for social media and mobile advertising)	Percentage of sales and/or revenue generated by social media; Percentage of sales and/or revenue generated by mobile channel; Comparison of revenue from different channels

(*Source* Developed from Laudon and Traver 2014, pp. 428–431; Turban et al. 2012, p. 453; Interactive Advertising Bureau and Pricewaterhouse 2014; Macri 2014; the author's own knowledge)

8.4 Issues and Success Factors of Digital Advertising

Even though digital/online advertising has been experiencing higher growth than other traditional advertising channels, online advertising to date is not as effective as off-line advertising. According to Laudon and Traver (2014, p. 433), typical click-through rates for various digital advertising tools are (in order): E-mail marketing in-house list 3–5 %, Google enhanced search ads (product listing ads) 1.66 %, Sponsorships 1.5–3 %, Search engine key word purchase 0.5–4 %, Video and rich media 0.5–2 %, Affiliate relationships 0.2–0.4 %, Mobile display ads 0.15–0.5 %, Social site display ads 0.15–0.25 %, Banner ads 0.03–0.3 %, and E-mail marketing purchased list 0.01–1.5 %. It is also suggested that the typical click-through rate to an e-commerce site is between 0.5 and 1.5 % (Ferguson 2013a). The response rate to hard copy mail campaigns is 3–4 % and the response rate for well-targeted direct mailing is 30 %. The Internet and digital technologies can be used to collate, store and manipulate consumer data in large databases and well-targeted use of such data can lead to 30 % response rates. Hence, digital advertising should be considered in relation to advertising using other media. Digital advertising is one avenue, but not necessarily the most effective one to obtain a response from the consumer. On a related note, even though mobile advertising has been enjoying fast growth, spending on mobile ads has been falling behind. For example, in 2014, US adults spent 23.3 % of their time with mobile devices and 3.5 % of their time on print media while ad spending is 7 cents per US adult per hour on mobile devices and 83 cents per US adult per hour on print media (eMarketer 2014b, c).

Offline advertising is still important because so far the marketing communications campaigns that have been the most successful at driving traffic to a website have combined both offline and online tactics. It can be said that the most powerful marketing campaigns include both online and offline advertising. Online companies need to learn how to use traditional marketing communications/media to drive traffic to the website and increase brand awareness and equity. In addition, consumers will more likely purchase via multi-channels (such as searching online then purchasing offline, purchasing offline then confirming online after purchasing, and searching online then experiencing offline then purchasing online).

Another important matter is the pricing strategy of digital advertising, which could be priced based on ad views (e.g., cost per 1,000 click per impression (CPM)), click-through rate (i.e., fees for clicks the ad received), action/interactivity of the user (e.g., fees for registration, becoming a member), actual purchase (e.g., payments for actual purchases), and fixed cost/subscription (e.g., payments for a certain period and/or certain space). In practice, organizations would use a combined approach by using two or more of those methods together. In addition, digital advertising costs are different to that of traditional advertising. For example Laudon and Traver (2014, p. 435) provide some indicative figures for traditional and digital advertising methods (such figures could have the US focus, but still could assist us understanding the overall pattern of cost comparison across different channels):

- Local television: US$4,000 for a 30 s commercial during a movie; US$45,000 for a highly rated show.
- Network television: the average is US$120,000–140,000 for 30 s commercial during a movie and the figure could go up to 600,000 during prime time.
- Radio: US$200–1,000 for a 60 s spot.
- Newspaper: US$120 per 1,000 circulation for a full-page ad.
- Magazine: US$50–120 per 1,000 circulation for an ad.
- Direct mail: US$15–40 per 1,000 deliveries.
- Billboard: US$5,000–25,000 for a 1–3 month rental of a highway sign.
- Banner ads: US$ 2–15 per 1,000 impressions.
- Video and rich media: US$20–25 per 1,000 ads.
- E-mail: US$5–15 per 1,000 targeted e-mail addresses.
- Sponsorships: US$30–75 per 1,000 viewers.
- Social network ads: US$0.5–3 per 1,000 impressions.

The development of digital advertising varies among different industries. For example, according to Interactive Advertising Bureau and Pricewaterhouse (2014) some major digital advertising spending by US industries in 2013 consist of (in order): Retail (21 % of total digital advertising spending in the US in 2013), Financial services (13 %), Auto (12 %), Telecom (9 %), Leisure travel (8 %), Consumer packaged goods (7 %), Computing products (6 %), Pharmacy and healthcare (5 %), Media (5 %), and Entertainment (4 %).

Meanwhile, the development of digital advertising varies across different countries/regions. For example, in 2011, the distribution of different advertising channels of the three largest advertising markets in the world of the US (US $156 billion), Japan (US$54 billion), and China (US$33 billion) was (Yeh and Zhang 2013): mobile (1 % of annual advertising spending in the US, 3 % in Japan, and 1 % in China), radio (10, 3, and 4 % respectively), Internet (18, 19, and 21 % respectively), out of home (i.e., billboards and posters) (4, 12, and 15 % respectively), Print (28, 21, and 21 % respectively), and TV (39, 42, and 38 % respectively). It can be seen from these figures that in 2011, TV was still the largest single category of ad spending in the world's three largest advertising markets (around 40 % for all three countries); Billboards and posters were more popular in Japan (12 %) and China (15 %) than in the US (4 %); and Radio was used more for advertising in the US (10 %) than in Japan (3 %) and China (4 %). On a related note, China's advertising market has been growing very quickly and spending will double the amount of 2011 and reach US$73 billion by 2016; while digital advertising has been on the upswing and print and TV shares have been declining, billboards and posters remains their popularity as a result of China's light and flexible regulations on such ads (for example, China's distribution of advertising channels in 2016 will consist of 4 % mobile (1 % in 2011), 3 % radio (3 % in 2011), 33 % Internet (21 % in 2011), 14 % billboards and posters (15 % in 2011), 11 % print (21 % in 2011), and 34 % TV (38 % in 2011).

Digital advertisers also need to understand factors associated with the trend of using multiple computing devices (such as the time of day, goal orientation (e.g., for work, or for communication, or for research), and location). According to recent research by Google (cited in Redrup 2013), more than 80 % of Australians used multiple screens sequentially in a 24 h period (e.g., using mobile phones in the morning, using laptops and PCs at work, and using iPads and tablets in the evening), so more effective, targeted, and integrated (i.e., integration of different computing devices) ads could be designed and delivered. In addition, while advertising via mobile, social and location-based platforms getting more and more popular, native advertising, which looks at placing ads which actually get consumers to pay attention and provide value to consumers via presenting ads in the context of the user's experience (e.g., placing ads in the flow of editorial content) (Galloway 2014; Wikepedia.org 2014; Hallett 2014), has started emerging as a future trend.

Finally, this chapter has been focusing on business to consumer (B2C) digital marketing and adverting. In fact, the buying process of organisations from their suppliers (business to business (B2B) transactions and interactions) and that of individuals from retailers is very similar. Organisations first recognise a need, then develop product specifications before they search for and evaluate suppliers, then select a particular supplier and purchase the product from the supplier. As a result, many of the above mentioned B2C digital marketing and advertising methods could be applied to B2B marketing and advertising, and many factors influencing B2C digital marketing and advertising are relevant to B2B digital marketing and advertising; meanwhile some different factors associated with B2B digital marketing and advertising include interpersonal influences (e.g., authority and status in the organization, decision making power and process, personal relations and persuasiveness) and organizational factors (e.g., purchasing and contracts guidelines, policies and procedures, organizational structure, and systems) (Turban et al. 2012, p. 220). Some other popular methods include: B2B portals and directories, E-distributors, B2B digital platforms (including single-sided (i.e., electronic storefronts) and multiple-sided platforms), B2B industry networks and consortia, B2B collaborative commerce, and B2B affiliate programs and ads exchanges, extranets; and using social media, virtual communities and forums, mobile channel and cloud computing for marking and advertising has been an emerging trend in recent years (Laudon and Traver 2014, pp.785–794; Turban et al. 2012, pp. 221–222; the author's own knowledge).

References

Aral, S. (2014). The problem with online ratings. *MIT Sloan Management Review, Winter, 55*(2), 47–52.

Bhandari, R., Singer, M., & Scheer, H. V. D. (2014, June). Using marketing analytics to drive superior growth. *Insights & Publications*. McKinsey & Company. Retrieved July 2, 2014, from http://www.mckinsey.com/insights/marketing_sales/using_marketing_analytics_to_drive_superior_growth.

Brandweiner, N. (2013, November 22). Dynamic pricing: The next frontier in customer relationship management, www.Mycustomer.com. Retrieved January 10, 2014, from http://www.mycustomer.com/feature/experience/bq/166027.

Bommel, E. V., Edelman, D., & Ungerman, K. (2014, June). Digitizing the consumer decision journey, *Insights & Publications*. McKinsey & Company. Retrieved July 8, 2014, from http://www.mckinsey.com/insights/marketing_sales/digitizing_the_consumer_decision_journey.

Brennan, J., Kelly, G., & Martinez, A. (2013, December). Tough choice for consumer goods companies, *Insights & Publications*. McKinsey & Company. Retrieved January 20, 2014, from http://www.mckinsey.com/insights/consumer_and_retail/tough_choices_for_consumer_goods_companies.

Cayla, J., Beers, R., & Arnould, E. (2014). Stories that deliver business insights. *MIT Sloan Management Review, 55*(2), 55–62.

Carter, J. (2014, February 20). Amazon's anticipatory shipping: Innovative or insane. www.Mycustomer.com. Retrieved April 12, 2014, from http://www.mycustomer.com/feature/technology/anticipatory-shipping-far-out-or-farfetched/166457.

Collins, L. (2014, June). Mastering digital marketing: Interview with McKinsey's David Edelman, *Insights & Publications*. McKinsey & Company. Retrieved July 8, 2014, from http://www.mckinsey.com/insights/marketing_sales/mastering_digital_marketing.

Davenport, T. H. (2009, February). How to design smart business experiments. *Harvard Business Review*, 69–76.

Divol, R., Edelman, D., & Sarrazin, H. (2012, April). Demystifying social media. *McKinsey Quarterly*, 1–11.

Dubois, D. (2013, June 21). Social media in B2B marketing: Publish or Perish, *INSEAD Knowledge*. Retrieved December 10, 2013, from http://knowledge.insead.edu/leadership-management/strategy/social-media-in-b2b-marketing-publish-or-perish-2508.

eMarketer. (2014a, April 28). Better creative, analytics, and reporting needed to improve mobile ad effectiveness. www.eMarketer.com. Retrieved May 8, 2014, from http://www.emarketer.com/Article/Better-Creative-Analytics-Reporting-Needed-Improve-Mobile-Ad-Effectiveness/1010790.

eMarketer. (2014b, April 22). Mobile continues to steal share of US adults' daily time spent with media, www.eMarketer.com. Retrieved May 8, 2014, from http://www.emarketer.com/Article/Mobile-Continues-Steal-Share-of-US-Adults-Daily-Time-Spent-with-Media/1010782.

eMarketer. (2014c, April 23). Despite time spent, mobile still lack of ad spending in the US, www.eMarketer.com. Retrieved May 8, 2014, from http://www.emarketer.com/Article/Despite-Time-Spent-Mobile-Still-Lacks-Ad-Spend-US/1010788.

Edelman, D. C. (2010a). Branding in digital age. *Harvard Business Review*, 62–69.

Edelman, D. C. (2010b, March). Four ways to get more value from digital marketing. *McKinsey Quarterly*, 1–8.

Ettenson, R., Conrado, E., & Knowles, J. (2013, January–February). Rethinking the 4 P's. *Harvard Business Review*, 26.

Ferguson, R. B. (2013a, September). How analytics is giving fashion a makeover. *MIT Sloan Management Review*, 1–5.

Ferguson, R. B. (2013b, June) How eBay uses data and analytics to get closer to its (massive) customer base. *MIT Sloan Management Review*, 1–4.

Galloway, R. (2014, March 2). The future of advertising: Is your business ready. www.Workintelligent.ly. Retrieved 13, 2014, from http://www.workintelligent.ly/information/trends-information/2014-3-2-future-advertising/.

Hallett, T. (2014, no date). What is native advertising anyway. www.Theguardian.com. Retrieved July 15, 2014, from http://www.theguardian.com/media-network-outbrain-partner-zone/native-advertising-quality-scalability.

Heiligtag, J., & Xu, J. (2006). Factors influencing the adoption of online advertising in SMEs: An Australian Study. In *Proceedings of the seventh international Working for E-Business (We-B) Conference*, November 29–30, (pp. 31–43), Melbourne, Australia.

Interactive Advertising Bureau (IAB) and Pricewaterhouse (PWC) (2014, April 2014). *IAB Internet Advertising Revenue Report: 2013 Full Year Results*, (1–28).

Kirby, J. (2013, March). Creative that cracks the code. *Harvard Business Review*, 86–89.

Künstner, T., Benzin, T. Blum, S., & Roschard, C. (2013). Create your own buzz: The promise and practice of digital marketing, *Perspective*, 1–13 Booz & Company.

Laudon, K. C., & Traver, C. G. (2012). *E-Commerce 2012: Business, technology, society* (7th ed.). Boston, USA: Addison Wesley.

Laudon, K. C., & Traver, C. G. (2014). *E-Commerce 2014: Business, technology, society* (Tenth ed.). Boston, USA: Addison Wesley.

LivePerson (2013, January). The connecting with customers report: A global in-depth study of the online customer experience. *LivePerson Inc. Report*, 1–23.

Macri, G. (2014, April 14). Google can now follow you from the computer to the store. *Dailycaller.com*. Retrieved May 8, 2014, from http://dailycaller.com/2014/04/14/google-can-now-follow-you-from-the-computer-to-the-store/.

Manyika, J. (2009, January). Hal Varian on how the Web challenges managers. *McKinsey Quarterly*. Retrieved July 23, 2012, from https://www.mckinseyquarterly.com/Strategy/Innovation/Hal_Varian_on_how_the_Web_challenges_managers_2286.

Pulido, A., Stone, D., & Strevel, J. (2014, March). The three Cs of customer satisfaction: Consistency, consistency, consistency. *Insights & Publications*. McKinsey & Company. Retrieved April 20, 2014, from http://www.mckinsey.com/insights/consumer_and_retail/the_three_cs_of_customer_satisfaction_consistency_consistency_consistency.

Rayport, J. F. (2013, March). Advertising's new medium: Human experience, *Harvard Business Review*, 77–84.

Redrup, Y. (2013, June 27). The new customer: Targeting new-age consumers in an e-Commerce environment, www.Smartcompany.com.au. Retrieved December 8, 2013, from http://www.smartcompany.com.au/growth/economy/32384-the-new-customer-targeting-new-age-consumers-in-an-ecommerce-environment.html.

Sealey, D. (2014, February 11). Omnichannel: How Domino's delivers a highly integrated customer experience. www.Mycustomer.com. Retrieved April 10, 2014, from http://www.mycustomer.com/feature/experience/how-dominos-delivers-highly-integrated-customer-experience/166466.

Shapiro, A. (2012, April). Are you making the most of your company's software layer. *McKinsey Quarterly*, 1–6.

Simons, R. (2014, March). Choosing the right customer: The first step in a winning strategy, *Harvard Business Review*, 49–55.

Simonson, I. & Rosen, E. (2014a). Is tech eroding consumer loyalty. *Strategy + Business*, Summer 2014, Issue 75, 1–3.

Simonson, I. & Rosen, E. (2014b, January-February). What marketers misunderstand about online reviews, *Harvard Business Review*, 23–25.

Stafford, P. (2013, July 3). How a convicted tax fraud changed his online reputation, www.Smartcompany.com.au. Retrieved December 10, 2013, from http://www.smartcompany.com.au/technology/information-technology/32482-best-of-the-web-how-a-convicted-tax-fraud-changed-his-online-reputation.html.

Turban, E., King, D., Lee, J. K., Liang, T. P., & Turban, D. (2012). *Electronic commerce 2012: A managerial and social networks perspective* (International ed.). Upper Saddle River, NJ: Prentice Hall.

Wikipedia.org (2014, July 15). Native Advertising, www.Wikipedia.org. Retrieved July 15, 2014, from http://en.wikipedia.org/wiki/Native_advertising.

Xu, J., & Quaddus, M. (2013). *Managing information systems: Ten essential topics*. Berlin, Amsterdam: Springer, Atlantis Press.

Yeh, J., & Zhang, M. (2013, June). Taking the pulse of China's ad spending, *McKinsey Quarterly*, 1–2.

Chapter 9
Digital Payment Systems

This chapter presents an overview of payment systems, discusses B2C and B2B digital payment systems, addresses mobile payment systems, highlights success factors and challenges/issues of digital payment systems, and suggests some emerging trends and future directions of digital payment systems.

9.1 Overview of Payment Systems

This chapter presents an overview of payment systems, discusses B2C and B2B digital payment systems, addresses mobile payment systems, highlights success factors and challenges/issues of digital payment systems, and suggests some emerging trends and future directions of digital payment systems.

Even though cash will still be the dominating payment method in coming years (e.g., around 85 % of all retail payment transactions or 60 % of retail transaction value (MasterCard 2013)), non-cash payments (especially digital payment systems) have grown dramatically in recent years and will be having even higher growth rates in the future. According to World Payments Report 2013 by French consulting firm Capgemini and The Royal Bank of Scotland (2013), Global non-cash payments transactions (volume-the number of transactions) reached 307 billion transactions in 2011 and are expected to reach 333 billion transactions in 2012, with the Central Europe, Middle East, CEMMA (including Central Europe, Middle East and Africa), Emerging Asia (including India, China, Hong Kong and other Asian countries) have the highest growth rates (more than 20 %). On a related note, through examining global payment market in 2011, MasterCard (2013) suggests that among 2.8 trillion transactions and US$592 trillion value of all payment types (cash and non-cash), 91 % transaction volume came from consumer spending while 89 % of transaction value were contributed by business and government sectors; and by looking at consumer payments only (2.6 trillion transactions and US$63 trillion transaction value in 2011), non-cash payments contributed to 34 % of transaction value and 85 % of transaction volume. Meanwhile digital payments have the lowest costs. For example, according to a McKinsey study (reported in McKinsey 2013), average

J. Xu, *Managing Digital Enterprise*, DOI 10.2991/978-94-6239-094-2_9

costs of different payment methods are: US$0.16 for digital, US$0.17 for ATM, US $0.61 for Call Center, US$0.75 for Mail, and US$2.36 for Branch.

Consumer to business (C2B or B2C) payments and P2P (peer to peer) mobile payments are the two largest digital payment methods (in terms of transaction volumes). In addition, mobile payment transactions will grow 58.5 % annually to 28.9 billion transactions (with the value of US$796 billion) in 2014 while online payments will grow 18.1 % yearly to 34.8 billion transactions (with the value of US $1,792.4 billion) in 2014. Some drivers of the rapid growth of digital payment systems include: the wide adoption of mobile phones (especially smart phones), the large number of global Internet users, advanced and more affordable technologies and computing devices, and more and more innovative digital products and services from traditional and non-traditional payment services providers.

Meanwhile according to a report by Juniper Research (2011) mobile payments will reach US$670 billion by 2015-an increase of about 200 % from US$240 billion in 2011. The same report also suggests the top 3 mobile payments regions (Far East & China, Western Europe, and North America) will contribute 75 % of the global mobile payment gross transaction value by 2015, and the purchase of physical goods will continually be the main driver of mobile purchases while digital goods payments will contribute almost 40 % of the market in 2015.

According to Javelin Strategy & Research and Digital Transactions (reported in Laudon and Traver 2014, pp. 288–289), global online payments will reach almost 1.2 trillion in 2013 and are expected to exceed 2 trillion by 2017. In the U.S., the dominating online payment methods are still the plastic cards (e.g., 71 % (including 42 % credit cards and 29 % debit cards) in 2012) even though their usage has been declining in recent years. Alternative payment methods (e.g., PayPal, Google Wallet, Amazon Checkout, and Bill-me-later (a part of PayPal now)) are the next biggest player of online payments in the U.S. in 2012 and contributed 16 % to online payment transactions in 2012, with the expectation of reaching 20 % of all online payments by 2017 in the U.S. The top 4 alternative online payment methods in the U.S. in 2012 are (in order): PayPal (84 % of all alternative payment methods), Amazon Checkout (26 %), Bill Me Later (21 %), and Google Wallet (11 %). Mobile payments are still relatively small in the U.S. (i.e., only 6.4 % in 2012) but have been and will be fast growing in coming years.

9.1.1 Country's Cashless Journey

MasterCard (2013) looked at the cashless journey of various countries by examining three perspectives/indicators of (1) the percentage of the value of all consumer payments that are presently done by non-cash methods (Share) (2) the shift of non-cash payments in the period of 2006–2011 (Trajectory), and (3) the future potential for conversion from cash payments to non-cash payments (Readiness) by looking at whether conditions in the country (e.g., access to financial services, macro-economic and cultural factors, merchant scale and competition, technology and infrastructure) exist for cash payments to move to electronic/digital non-cash payments.

Some most cashless countries, in which non-cash accounted for more than 80 % of the value of consumer payments include (in order): Belgium (93 % cashless), France (92 %), Canada (90 %), United Kingdom and Sweden (both 89 %), Australia (86 %), and Netherlands (85 %). Meanwhile China had the strongest growth of non-cash payments for such reasons as rapid urbanization and government's leadership in non-cash payments (e.g., implementing non-cash payments in the areas of payroll services, utilities, public services). South Africa and Poland are other notable countries in terms of a shift to non-cash payments in the period of 2006–2011 for their initiatives of working on user acceptance and nurturing non-cash culture. In addition, Countries such as (in order) Canada, Sweden, U.K. and the Netherlands, Australia, Belgium, Germany, and the United States have the highest readiness for non-cash payments (all have more than 80 Readiness score). It is unveiled that such factors as affordable and broadly available financial products, a vibrant and competitive merchant market place, a transparent and productive business environment (e.g., in Australia), payment product innovation (e.g., in Kenya), strong government non-cash initiatives leadership (e.g., in China), and a pro-non-cash culture and user acceptance (e.g., in South Africa and Poland), are closely associated with the progress of the country's cashless journey.

9.2 B2C and B2B Digital Payment Systems

When products and services are sold electronically, there has to be a means of paying for the transaction electronically. Paper-based payments cannot support the speed, security, privacy and internationalization necessary in the digital enterprise/ e-business environment. Hence, digital/electronic payment systems represent one of the pillars supporting digital enterprise/e-business.

There exist a number of B2C payment methods. According to a payments study of 2,000 Australian adults in September 2013 by HP & RFi (reported in Hewlett and Packard 2013), cash remains the most popular payment method while other payment methods have been increasingly used as well. The payment methods used by survey participants (in order) include: cash (70 % of participants used), BPAY (46 %), Credit Card (46 %), Visa/MasterCard Debit Card (45 %), EFTPOS/ATM card (42 %), PayPal (40 %), Direct Debit (39 %), Direct transfer (30 %), Store gift card (14 %), Check (6 %), EFTPOS prepaid card gift card (6 %), Visa/MasterCard reloadable prepaid card (4 %), Visa/MasterCard prepaid gift card (4 %), Charge card (3 %), Reloadable prepaid travel card (2 %), Bitcoin (2 %) and other (1 %).

Basically there are six major types of B2C (and C2C) digital payment systems: (1) cards (including credit cards, debit cards, pre-paid cards, stored-valued cards) (2) electronic funds transfers (3) born-on-Internet payment systems (4) e-checking (e-check) (5) e-billing, and (6) mobile payment systems (Laudon and Traver 2014; Turban et al. 2012; the author's own knowledge).

Cards (including credit cards, debit cards, and prepaid cards) are still the dominating digital payment systems. For example, in 2011, on average 62 % of global payments were made by cards (Capgemini and The Royal Bank of Scotland 2013). Some leading payment card services providers are (in order in terms of market share of payment card transactions worldwide in 2013): MasterCard (60.5 %), Visa (26.9 %), UnionPay (7.7 %), American Express (3.8 %), JCB (1.1 %), and Diners Club (0.1 %) (The Nelson Report 2014). Electronic funds transfer also plays an important role in global payments market. For example, in 2011, on average 30.5 % of global payments were made by direct debits and credit transfers (Capgemini and The Royal Bank of Scotland 2013). According to Booz & Company (reported in Venkateswaran et al. 2011), among US$157 billion U.S. payments transactions in 2008, 43.3 % were done by cards (including credit, debit, and pre-paid), 31.2 % by cash, 13.4 % by EFT (including P2P, wire, and bill pay), and 12.1 % by paper checks.

Born-on-the-Internet payment systems are typically developed by Internet firms for digital transactions. Such payment systems are particularly relevant to micropayments (i.e., small payments under US$10); credits cards do not work well for small payments under US$10 (e.g., purchasing music services online) since the fees associated with credit cards become quite significant for vendors who accept the credit cards (i.e., 25–35 cents transaction fee plus 2–3 % of the purchasing price). Some good examples of digital payment systems include Google Wallet, Amazon Payments, eBay's PayPal, Alibaba's AliPay, and Facebook Payments. Some new micropayment models (e.g., aggregation model adopted by iTune purchases, charging to mobile phone bill, using credits on prepaid/stored value cards, and subscription model adopted by online newspapers and magazines) have been developed in recent years.

E-billing facilitates both presenting and payment of bills electronically. E-billing is also known as electronic invoice presentment and payment (EIPP), which enables the online delivery, consolidation, and payment of boils (Laudon and Traver 2014, p. 294). E-billing (or EIPP) has been adopted by many consumers and businesses for such benefits as convenience, time and cost reduction, better record, and faster and easier bill payment. Meanwhile paper-based checks are still popular with some small and medium enterprises (for them paper-based checks contain useful data), with some consumers (they value paper-based checks as a free commodity), and with some charities and not-for-profit organizations (they are attracted to the better security control that dual signage offers by paper-based checks); their usage has been continually declining (i.e., 5 % of non-cash payments across Europe in 2011 from 9 % in 2007, 18 % in North America in 2011 from 27 % in 2007, 3 % of Mature APAC (including Australia, Japan, Singapore, and South Korea) in 2011 from 9 % in 2007, 7 % of Latin America in 2011 from 15 % in 2007, and 11 % of Emerging Asia in 2011 from 25 % in 2007) (Capgemini and The Royal Bank of Scotland 2013). On the other hand, the usage of e-check, which is the electronic version or representation of the paper check and is a good option for people who don't have credit cards or not willing to provide credit card information online, has been growing quickly. For example, e-check transactions reached 2.4 billion in 2009, with 9 % increase from 2008 (Turban et al. 2012, p. 562). E-checks contain the same information as a paper check, can be used wherever paper checks are used, and are based on the same legal framework.

B2B payments usually are much larger and significantly more complex than the payments made by individual consumers. B2B payments are part of a much larger financial supply chain which consists of activities such as procurement, contract administration, fulfilment, financing, insurance, credit ratings, shipment validation, order matching, payment authorization, remittance matching, and general ledger accounting (Turban et al. 2012, p. 569). Major e-payment methods for B2B include e-checks, purchase cards, e-letters of credit, and EFT. One popular B2B payment service in recent years is the enterprise invoice presentation and payment (EIPP) services, which consolidate, present and pay B2B invoices online and could save time and money involved in handling the large number of invoices and payments of enterprises.

9.3 Mobile Payment Systems

The number of mobile payment users worldwide is expected to surpass 212 million in 2012 (Capgemini and The Royal Bank of Scotland 2013). Garner (2013) says that worldwide mobile transaction value will reach 235.4 billion in 2013 from US $163 billion in 2012 (44 % increase) while the volume of transactions will achieve 22 % growth from 2012 and reach 245.2 million in 2012. Money transfers and merchandise purchases are the two largest contributors. These will contribute 71 and 21 % respectively to the value of global mobile transaction value in 2013; and these are expected to make 69 and 23 % individually in 2017. It also suggests that an average 35 % annual growth for the period of 2012–2017 is expected for both global mobile transaction value and global transaction volume and by 2017 the global mobile payment market will be worth US$721 billion with 450 million users. The top global payment markets in terms of transaction value in 2013 are: Africa (more than US$74 billion), Asia Pacific (US$74 billion), North America (US$37 billion), and Western Europe (US$29 billion); however it is expected that Asia Pacific will take over Africa as the largest mobile payment market in 2016 (i.e., US $165 billion vs. US$160 billion).

Meanwhile according to a report by Juniper Research (2011) mobile payments will reach US$670 billion by 2015-an increase of about 200 % from US$240 billion in 2011. The same report also suggests that the top 3 mobile payments regions (Far East and China, Western Europe, and North America) will contribute 75 % of the global mobile payment gross transaction value by 2015, and the purchase of physical goods will continually be the main driver of mobile purchases while digital goods payments will contribute almost 40 % of the market in 2015. In addition, according to a recent study by GSMA and ATKearney (reported in Page et al. 2013), total value of global mobile payments is predicted to reach US$13 trillion by 2017.

Some key mobile payment applications include (in order of estimated size of volumes): peer to peer (P2P) payments (e.g., domestic transfer and international remittances), consumer to business (C2B) payments, business to business (B2B) payments, and business/government to employee/consumer (e.g., salary disbursements, family benefits, pensions); and P2P payments in developing markets (e.g., Africa) and C2B payments in developed markets are the main drivers of mobile payments growth (Capgemini and The Royal Bank of Scotland 2013). One example of the most prominent mobile payment systems worldwide is Kenya's M-PESA (a peer to peer mobile money transfer system) with more than 15 million subscribers (more than 65 % of Kenya's population), and facilitates payment volume equal to 20 % of the country's GDP. Another notable example of P2P mobile money transfer is BelCash developed in Ethiopia, which has partnership agreements with the major financial institutions in the country (Longoni and Gâza 2013). An additional good example of popular mobile payment systems is Tencent's WeChat payments. Its 4 million plus active users can do such things as shopping, banking, checking and paying bills, ordering and paying taxi services, and booking and paying restaurants (Meeker 2014). Meanwhile some popular mobile payments apps include: Facebook, Amazon, MyBank's App, Alibaba's Alipay, Tencent's WetChat Payment, PayPal, eBay, Groupon, Apple Passbook, Starbucks, LivingSocial, Google Wallet, Foursquare, Square Wallet, Shopkick, GoPago, and LevelUp (Ewing et al. 2013). In addition, some mobile POS (point of sale) technologies include: mobile phone number at POS (e.g., PayPal at POS), mobile device reader (e.g., Square reader), QR code or barcode scanning (e.g., Starbucks prepaid), Self-checkout scanning (e.g., Apple's EasyPay), Near field communication (NFC) (e.g., Google Wallet), and m-commerce in-store (e.g., Pay with Square) (Bruno and Ewing 2013). In addition, some mobile payment enabling technologies include: Voice, DTMF, USSD, Audio, WAP, SMS, GPS, Bluetooth, Camera, Memory Card, MMS, GPRS, UMTS/3G, 4G, Mobile Internet, Network Location, USB, Gyro, WiFi, Push Message, Apps, NFC, and (Plug-in)Add-on (Longoni and Gâza 2013).

9.3.1 Contactless Cards/NFC Payments

An emerging trend is the NFC (near field communication) mobile payment systems. Some popular applications include Google Wallet, Visa Paywave, and Mastercard Paypass as well as cardless (mobile) ATM cash withdrawal applications, PayPal's Beacon, and Apple's iBeacon. According to a recent study in September 2013 by HP-RFi (reported in Hewlett and Packard 2013), younger consumers are more comfortable with mobile payments. The age group of 18–34 of research participants felt most comfortable making mobile payments for shopping, coffee and meals, public transportation, and money transfer.

According to a recent study by GSMA and ATKearney (reported in Page et al. 2013), 50 % of all smartphones will be NFC enabled by 2015, 85 % of POS terminals shipped in 2016 will be contactless, 1 billion SIM-based NFC handsets will be sold in 2016 and these handsets will support US$50 billion value of transactions. Even though the adoption of contactless cards (e.g., contactless cards for public transport and for replacing keys to rooms) and NFC (near field communication) payments (e.g., Visa's payWave, Mastercard's PayPass, American Express' Express Pay, Goolge Wallet, Osaifu-Keitai; PayPal Here, PayPal Beacon, LevelUp, PayLeven, JUSP, mPOWA, Clicks-in-Bricks, iZettle, Sqaure, Isis (by AT&T, T-Mobile & Verizon)) has continued, the adoption has not grown as fast as expected (Capgemini and The Royal Bank of Scotland 2013; Gartner 2013). In 2013, NFC payments contributed only 2 % of the global mobile payment transaction value and are expected to reach 5 % in 2017 (Gartner 2013). Some reasons for the slow adoption of NFC payments include: a lack of interest and awareness among customers, unattractive of the NFC business models to banks, the impacts of regulations on mobile payments in some countries (e.g., the imposition of services taxes on mobile money transfer in Kenya and Uganda), the required deployments of large-scale contactless infrastructure (but it is changing with the majority of point of sale (POS) terminals now shipping with contactless), the maturity of the required culture of paying via mobile (whether it is NFC, QR Codes, SMS, mobile web, mobile apps, mobile bill, or other mobile technologies), the development of more innovative design of systems and services (for more useful, more user-friendly and more integrated) NFC applications, the required patience for large-scale adoption, and the right inducements (e.g., charging less for using mobile devices to pay, especially for public transport and services) (Juniper 2014; Gartner 2013; MobiThinking 2013). Meanwhile according to a recent study by eDigital-Research (2013), some barriers of NFC and contactless mobile payments adoption include consumer's awareness (retailers need to improve trust and confidence of consumers), retailer's adoption (retailers need to be more active in implementing NFC and contactless payment systems and encouraging the use of them by providing such initiatives as developing apps and introducing payment points), and access to technology (many handsets are not NFC-enabled).

Contactless cards have been used for various types of purchases and payments. For example, according to a recent study by HP and RFi (reported in Hewlett and Packard 2013), research participants used contactless cards in September 2013 for such purchases as (in order): supermarket (79 % of the participants), petrol (42 %), liquor store (31 %), take-away/fast-food (28 %), other retailer (26 %), convenience store (22 %), café (17 %), small food store (16 %), restaurant/formal dining (11 %), and pub/bar (8 %).

Meanwhile mobile business is still in the early stage, especially in terms of the mobile purchase experience. Even though mobile merchandise purchases are a big contributor to the global mobile payments market (i.e., 21 % in 2013 and 23 % in 2017 (Gartner 2013)), its growth has not been as significant as expected and people are not purchasing via mobile devices as much since optimal mobile purchase experience has yet to be realized.

9.4 Challenges/Issues and Success Factors of Digital Payment Systems

Some characteristics of successful digital payment methods include (Turban et al. 2012, pp. 551–552; Capgemini and The Royal Bank of Scotland 2013; Infosecurity Magazine 2013; the author's own knowledge):

- Ease of use: those digital payment methods that require the payer to install specialized components (especially hardware) are less likely to succeed.
- Security: if the risk for the payer is higher than the risk for the payee, then the payer is not likely to accept the method. Meanwhile a balance between ease of use and security should be achieved. If it is secure but difficult to use, users will be less inclined to use it. And for mobile payments attention should be given to security of a payment transaction, security of the mobile device itself, and security of the payment acceptance solution.
- Anonymity: anonymity has to be guaranteed for digital payment systems (especially for e-cash and digital currencies).
- Divisibility: any method that can address the lower (e.g., the capacity of dealing with micropayments by accumulating the small payments) or higher end of the price continuum (e.g., the capacity of dealing with large payments by combining different payment accounts and divide the large payments into smaller ones) or that can span one of the extremes and the middle has a chance of being widely accepted.
- Integration: ensuring the integration with existing systems and applications, the interoperability between customers, partners, and suppliers; and ensuring the interoperability between different computing devices and platforms as well as preparing for the integration of various payment solutions into one payment system. The adoption of a standard computing platform and co-development with various stakeholders will definitely make the task of integration much easier.
- Agility: anticipating and addressing new/changing customer needs and preferences.
- Optimal pricing strategy: value-added and performance-linked pricing strategy for both users and businesses.
- Internationalization: to be successful at the global market, digital payment systems need to have both international best practices and local customization/adaption.
- Regulation compliance: complying with regulations (domestic and international) is essential for the success of digital payment systems.

9.4.1 Security of Digital Payment Systems

According to a payments study of 2,000 Australian adults in September 2013 by HP & RFi (reported in Hewlett and Packard 2013), the top factor influencing consumers' decision of adopting certain payment method is security. Many security measures and tools discussed in the Chap. 2 of this book could be applied to deal with security issues of digital payment systems, in particular secure socket layer (SSL) and digital certificates.

9.4.2 Payment Fraud Management

CyberSource Corporation (2013) reports that in 2012 companies in North America lost an average of 0.9 % of total online revenue to fraud. According to a 2012 study by the Merchant Risk Council and CyberSource Corporation (a Visa Company), the top digital payment frauds include (reported in Tucker and Donlea 2012):

- Clean fraud (e.g., seemingly legitimate transactions with (quite) accurate information at card-not-present situations).
- Account takeover (i.e., the account is taken over by the fraudster).
- Friendly fraud (e.g., denial of making purchases).
- Identity theft (e.g., the fraudster pretends to be someone else by assuming the person's identity).
- Affiliate fraud (e.g., an affiliate of a merchant attempts to cheat the merchant by creating false clicks or visits to the merchant site via software or human activities).
- Re-shipping scams (also called postal forwarding scams. In such events people (mules) could be lured to help (the victim pays the shipping fees) forward goods often purchased with stolen credit cards to overseas locations, with the payment of a fake check for compensating the victim).
- Botnets (e.g., computers are compromised by malicious software and controlled by third parties for illegal activities).
- Phishing/Pharming/Whaling (e.g., luring users to a fake website of a legitimate business).
- Triangulation schemes (e.g., the fraudster puts an item up for auction in an online auction site and uses a stolen credit card to purchase the item and send it to the auction winner, and the fraudster receives the money for the item from the auction winner. The real loser is the auction winner since he is in possession of goods purchased with a stolen credit card and once the stolen card is reported the auction winner will lose the purchased item).

What are some effective tools for managing digital payment frauds? Through surveying 312 firms of different sizes and across various industries in Canada and the U.S. in 2012, CyberSource (2013) identifies the following tools for managing digital payment frauds:

- Implementing a payment fraud management framework including activities of (1) automated screening (2) manual review (3) order dispositioning/decision making (i.e., accept or reject the payment) (4) fraud claim management (e.g., monitoring the pattern, the level, and the trend of frauds), and (5) tuning and analytics (making adjustment to fraud management strategies and required resources).
- Allocating sufficient resources for payment fraud management initiatives (e.g., 19 % for internal tools and systems, 29 % for third party tools, and 52 % for order review staff).
- Employing effective tools to deal with payment frauds:
  - Proprietary data/customer history including a fraud scoring model (firm specific), customer order, order velocity monitoring, negative list (in-house list), customer website behavior, positive lists.
  - Purchase device tracing including device fingerprint results, device fingerprinting, IP geolocation information.
  - Multi-Merchant data/Purchase history including multi-merchant purchase velocity, shared negative lists, shared hotlists.
  - Validation services including paid-for public records services, contact customer to verify order, card verification number (CVN), payer authentication (3D Secure), address verification services (AVS), social networking sites, Finger vein recognition, two-factor/two-step phone authentication, contact card issuer/Amex charge verification program (CVP), telephone number verification/reverse loop, and postal address validation services.

Meanwhile, Malick and Rudolph (2013) suggest that companies (especially data rich firms such as banks and retailers) should apply Big Data applications to safeguard payments (e.g., providing real time credit analysis and risk management and identifying transactions falling beyond the customer's behavioral profile). It is also suggested that dynamic data authentication, whereby a unique set of payment information is generated for each transaction, should be embedded in the payment systems so even if the payment information is intercepted or stolen or lost, it won't be useful for future unauthorized transactions (Federal Trade Commission 2013). Some innovative security measures also could be deployed by businesses. A good example is MasterCard's initiative of combing mobile phone's geolocation function to reduce credit fraud by requiring consumer's mobile phone to be in the same location as the consumer's credit card at the time of purchase (Peters 2014). Furthermore, consumers play the most important role in the security of their payment systems, they should not disclose their passwords to anyone else, and have different passwords for different payment systems/applications (on top of the password for the login of the computing device).

On a related note, according to a recent study of a Mobile Payments Consumer Panel consisting of 1,000 consumers randomly selected in the U.S. by McKinsey (reported in Ewing et al. 2013), networks, banks and established digital innovators have the highest levels of trust in mobile payments; and some trusted mobile payments players identified in the study include (in order): Visa, Banks, Amazon,

Paypal, MasterCard, American Express, Apple, National Merchants, Discover, Telcos, Google, Local merchants, Facebook, and Start-ups.

9.4.3 The Hype of Bitcoin

Bitcoin is a digital currency and is not regulated by any central authorities and/or federal banks (but countries like China, India and Russia have banned the trading of Bitcoin due to its association with shadow economy (Do 2014)), and is backed by no commodity but exists because a small numbers of users have decided to buy in its legitimacy (Ford 2014). Bitcoin is mined by solving algorithms by enormous computing power, and it will take roughly ten minutes for each mined Bitcoin (Hewlett and Packard 2013). The independence of Bitcoin from central authorities has helped reduce the transaction cost (e.g., typical 2–3 % fees of credit cards vs no fees or much smaller fees for Bitcoin, and even bypassing transaction fees of international money transfer, bill payments, check-cashing). Other perceived opportunities for Bitcoin include expanding banking, making digital art unique, and reinventing digital advertising (Ford 2014). On the other hand, the independence, the anonymity of the Bitcoin transactions, security issues, lack of policies for protection and dispute resolution, functionality issues, price volatility (especially after the crash of Japanese Bitcoin exchange company of Mt Gox in February 2014, which mysteriously lost 850,000 Bitcoins or around 7 % of all mined Bitcoins with a value of US$470 million), criminal activities channeled by Bitcoins have helped the digital currency gain the notoriety (Hewlett and Packard 2013; Wikepedia.org 2014).

According to a recent study of 2,000 Australian adults in September 2013 by HP and RFi (reported in Hewlett and Packard 2013), consumers adopted Bitcoin for such reasons as (in order): it was easy (50 % of the participants), it was fast (48 %), it was cheaper than other payment methods (40 %), it gave me greater control over spending (40 %), it was the only available payment option (33 %), it is believed to be more secure than other payment methods (31 %), just wanted to try it out (24 %), and Bitcoins are hard to trace (19 %). On the other hand, reasons for consumers not using Bitcoin include (in order): I have not had the need to, I don't know how to use Bitcoin, I don't know anyone who would accept Bitcoin, I don't know how to obtain Bitcoin, and I don't trust it. Meanwhile the results of the research also indicate that the adoption level of Bitcoin among consumers still very low (i.e., 2 % in September 2013), the average user of Bitcoin is a male in their late 20s, 80 % of Bitcoin users are with tertiary qualifications, and Bitcoin users are much more likely to be professionals working in the IT industry or studying.

There are no universal views on the future of Bitcoin. Some people believe it is a fad like other previously failed digital currencies (e.g., digital currency's difficulty in offering real utility to existing markets, such as how to achieve cryptographic certainty to a digital item paid by digital currency-meaning you have paid for it and own it, and you can hold on it and prove the transaction, the possession, the ownership, and the value of it) and others believe we may need to give it more time since it is in the early stage of its life cycle; however it is quite reasonable to argue that no matter what the destination of Bitcoin will be, it has certainly caused disruption to the existing payments market even though a claim of "Bitcoin is changing finance the same way the Web changed publishing" is too pre-mature and only for some people (Do 2014; Ford 2014; Wagstaff 2014). But do we have answers for such a question of: Will any digital currency ever be truly successful? There is no definite answer for this question, but maybe we can put more hope in such initiatives as Universal Digital Currency and after all "Money or what onc perceives as money, is just a form of disintermediated trust" (Wagstaff 2014).

9.4.4 Required Legal Framework and Policies

Another challenge in digital payment systems is the lack of a well-established legal framework and policies for digital payment systems, especially cross-border payments. For example, as a result of the complexities (e.g., questions such as when and how much taxes should be charged as a results of so many taxation systems across the globe), there is a lack of a well-established legal framework and policies as well as understanding and best practices of dealing with taxes associated with international digital transactions; many digital businesses (B2C and B2B) rely on specialized third-party software and services to calculate the taxes associated with a sale. Another concern is the need to develop and implement policies for resolving disputes involving fraudulent payments or unauthorized charges, especially for such mobile payments not funded by credit and debit cards and bank accounts (e.g., prepaid and stored-value cards, mobile phone accounts), which have statutory protections against fraudulent payments or unauthorized charges (Federal Trade Commission 2013); and policies for appropriately dealing with funds sitting on large payment platforms (i.e., facilitating payments between buyers and sellers) and compliance auditing with such policies are needed since those platforms could exploit the large amount of funds sitting on their payment platforms for their own benefits (e.g., delaying payments to sellers so earning more interest).

Another important area is a legal framework and policies for international digital payments issues. So far we are still in the very early stage; however organizations such as International Consumer Protection and Enforcement Network (ICPEN), The European Commission, and Organization for Economic Cooperation and Development (OECD) (via its Committee on Consumer Policy (CCP)), have started initiatives for finding solutions for such challenges (Federal Trade Commission 2013). In addition, when digital payments providers are expanding into foreign markets, they need to pay close attention to country/market specific payment considerations, including such things as mandates and regulations, checkout localization, fraud management, acquiring and processing, customer services & fulfilment, and settlement and reconciliation (CyberSource Corporation 2014).

9.4.5 Required Collaboration Among Stakeholders

The speed of adoption and the ultimate success of digital payment systems are heavily influenced by the collaborative efforts of all the stakeholders involved in the digital payments value chain. For example, the large-scale acceptance and use of mobile payment systems require close collaboration with relevant stakeholders of (1) merchants (2) consumers (3) mobile network operators (MNOs) (4) banks and financial institutions and payment card networks (5) handset manufacturers (OEMs) (6) software and technology providers (e.g., data brokers, trusted services providers, operating systems developers, payment applications developers, payment-specific devices providers) (7) coupon and loyalty program administrators (8) advertising agencies and networks, and (9) start-ups (e.g., Square, Stripe, LevelUp, Bowa, Dwolla) and corporations (e.g., Google, Apple, Amazon, Starbucks) venturing into mobile payments (Longoni and Gâza 2013; Federal Trade Commission 2013).

9.5 Emerging Trends and Future Directions

Digital payments support business processes and are an essential ingredient of the enterprise. Consumer to business (C2B) payments are moving towards 'any form', 'anywhere', 'any time', 'real-time customization and personalization', and 'real-time recognition and awards and relationship building' while business to business (B2B) payments are transforming from bi-lateral to multi-lateral models and from being silo, discrete, and inflexible to more integrated, cross-product/account, and agile approaches (ACI 2011; Venkateswaran et al. 2011). Many innovative players have appeared in the key areas of payments value chain. Table 9.1 presents some innovative C2B and B2B payment players in the key areas of payments value chain. In addition, there are a number of innovative consumer to consumer (also called peer-to-peer) digital payment systems, such as AliPay, TenPay, PayPal, M-PESA, among many others.

Another trend is that there will be more digital payment players from non-traditional financial institutions since they typically have a large user base and/or are involved with large volumes of payments (e.g., large e-commerce sites, digital content & services sites, social networks). Some good examples are Amazon, Google, Tencent, and Alibaba. Their payment systems of Amazon Payments, Google Wallet, Tencent's WeChat Payment and Alibaba's AliPay have been very successful (i.e., beating many traditional banks and financial institutions in terms of the number of users and the value of transactions in domestic and/or international markets). Social network sites (e.g., Facebook's e-money initiative) and Telecom operators (e.g., Vodafone's recent acquisition of an e-money license in Europe) have started to enter the payments market (Davies et al. 2014).

Convenience (e.g., one-stop services), 7 × 24 availability of services (especially comparing to traditional banks), flexibility, established trust and relationship before

Table 9.1 Examples of emerging innovative B2C and B2B payments

Area of payments value chain	B2C payments	B2B payments
Origination (trigging commercial transactions from anywhere, regardless of locations)	Amex TV Commerce, PayPal order Ahead, iDeal, My Bank, and Google Wallet	OB10, Tradeshift, Coface, ErsteConfirming, and RBS Paymode
Acceptance and capture (aggregating payment options by offering a single solution enabling merchants or suppliers to accept any mode of payments)	Square, iZettle, NCR Silver, MyPayMe, Ogone/Ingenico, WorldPay, Boku & Dwolla, and Starbucks & KFC Payment Applications	Chase Paymentech, Detsche Bank Autobahn App Market, JustPush Pay, SEPAmail, Bottomline, and Dwolla
Security and fraud (mitigating the risk and implementing security measures)	Experian, Chase Paymentech, and Visa (3DS)	CyberSource and SWIFT (3SKey)
Value added services (developing new services/new revenue streams via Big Data and data analytics capabilities)	Cardlytics, EDO Interactive, Barclaycard, LendingClub, Check, Chase Mobile, AliPay, and Tenpay	TradeCard GTNexus, RBS SmartCollect, and Global Payment Information Exchange (GPIE), LendingClub, AliPay, and Tenpay

Source Developed from Capgemini and The Royal Bank of Scotland (2013), ACI (2011), Meeker and Wu (2013), Federal Trade Commission (2013)

using the firm's payment systems, large traffic, large marketing and advertising platform (normally more cost effective), speed of response, lower costs, and better interest rates (in AliPay's case) are some success factors for these non-traditional payments players. Meanwhile on top of working on mobile payment systems (via mobile phones) and exploring the opportunities of location-based technologies (e.g., NFC and contactless systems, Apple's iBeacon), some financial institutions (e.g., Westpac in Australia and New Zealand) are exploring opportunities with wearable devices (e.g., Google Glass and iWatch) for payment-related activities (e.g., checking bank account balance, transfer money between own accounts, receiving messages in the branch, locating newest ATM and Westpac branch) (Timson 2014).

Furthermore there exist different opportunities for developed and emerging markets of digital payments. Let us look at the example of mobile payment systems. For developed markets, even though they have better infrastructure and more saturated/established mobile market, the commercial adoption of mobile payments is still not as commonly used as in emerging markets for such reasons as the lack of standardization and policies and the conflicting interests of the main stakeholders involved (e.g., telecom operators, banks and financial institutions). For the developed markets, some growth opportunities include: working on the interaction between the consumers and the merchant at the point of sale (e.g., via contactless/NFC payments), focusing on value-added services (e.g., loyalty and rewards programs, coupons and offers, and real-time personalized prices and services), providing seamless & integrated mobile payment experience (e.g., aggregating a wide array of payment tools & functionalities (such as banking, billing and payment, shopping, NFC applications, peer-to-peer transaction, web browsing, social networking, learning, and other routine tasks) across different platforms and devices, and focusing on nurturing consumers' attitude and willingness to use mobile payment systems (Longoni and Gâza 2013; the author's own knowledge). For the emerging markets, the emphasis should be on designing different products for target segments (e.g., different products for urban and rural areas, different products for middle class and affluent consumers and average-income consumers), implementing different strategies for different regions (e.g., providing new services to advanced and mature regions and pushing exiting services into inner areas and less advanced areas or other areas with less mobile payments penetration), and providing better digital banking infrastructure and more integrated digital banking services beyond the mobile channel (for example, quite a few countries in Africa are still in poor economic conditions and have very limited banking infrastructure, and many people are still living in poverty and have very limited or no access to formal retail banking. So questions such as how to provide real and safe branchless digital banking experience and how to provide integrated payments via digital channels need to be answered by the government and various stakeholders involved) (Longoni and Gâza 2013; the author's own knowledge).

References

ACI. (2011). Replacing legacy payment systems: An industry guide from ACI. *ACI worldwide*. Retrieved April 10, 2014, from http://www.aciworldwide.com/-/media/files/collateral/aci_guide_to_replacing_legacy_pymt_sys_tl_us_0411_4610.ashx.

Bruno, P., & Ewing, D. (2013, July). Driving merchant services and digital commerce: Findings from McKinsey's 2012 U.S. small business acquiring panel. *McKinsey on Payments*, 15–21.

Capgemini & The Royal Bank of Scotland. (RBS). (2013). *World Payments Report 2013*, 1–58.

CyberSource Corporation. (2013). *2013 online fraud report: Online payment fraud trends, merchant practices, and benchmarks* (pp. 1–27, 14 Annual Edition). CyberSource Corporation.

CyberSource Corporation. (2014). *Payment management insights for faster, safer global expansion* (pp. 1–21). CyberSource Corporation.

Davies, S., Robinson, D., & Kuchler, H. (2014, April 13). Facebook targets financial services. *Financial Times*. Retrieved on May 8, 2014, from http://www.ft.com/intl/cms/s/0/0e0ef050-c16a-11e3-97b2-00144feabdc0.html.

Do, E. (2014, April 16). Australia's first Bitcoin ATM raise questions, including: 'what?' 'why?' and 'really'. *Marketing Magazine*. Retrieved May 6, 2014, from http://www.marketingmag.com.au/news/australias-first-bitcoin-atm-raises-questions-including-what-why-and-really-51815/#.U36_4uLLO8A.

eDigitalResearch. (2013, May). *Mobile Payment Index Wave 3*, 1–37.

Ewing, D., Lebermab, D., Serrano, E., & Steitz, J. (2013, July). From solutions to adoption: The next phase of consumer mobile payments. *McKinsey on Payments*, July 2013, 15–21.

Federal Trade Commission. (FTC). (2013, March). Paper, plastic… or mobile? An FTC workshop on mobile payments. *FTC Staff Report*. Retrieved March 4, 2014, from http://www.ftc.gov/sites/default/files/documents/reports/paper-plastic-or-mobile-ftc-workshop-mobile-payments/p0124908_mobile_payments_workshop_report_02-28-13.pdf.

Ford, P. (2014, February 18). Marginally useful. *MIT Technology Review*. Retrieved April 26, 2014, from http://www.technologyreview.com/review/524691/marginally-useful/.

Gartner. (2013, June 4). Garnet says worldwide mobile payment transaction value to surpass $235 billion in 2013. *Press Release*. Retrieved May 2, 2014, from http://www.gartner.com/newsroom/id/2504915).

Hewlett & Packard (HP). (2013, September). *HP-RFi Australian payments research* (5 ed.). Retrieved May 6, 2014, from http://rfintelligence.com/downloads/HP-RFi-Australian-Payments-Research_Oct-13.pdf.

Infosecurity Magazine. (2013, February 14). News: PCI Council releases mobile payments security guidance for merchants. Infosecurity-magazine.com. Retrieved April 28, 2014, from http://www.infosecurity-magazine.com/view/30765/pci-council-releases-mobile-payments-security-guidance-for-merchants/.

Juniper Research. (2011, July 5). Mobile payments market to almost triple in value by 2015 Reaching $670bn. *Juniper Research*. Retrieved May 2, 2014, from http://www.marketwired.com/press-release/mobile-payments-market-almost-triple-value-2015-reaching-670bn-according-new-juniper-1534333.htm.

Juniper Research. (2014, April 8). Mobile payments to rise 40 % this year. *Juniper Research*. Retrieved May 2, 2014, from http://www.juniperresearch.com/viewpressrelease.php?pr=437.

Laudon, K. C., & Traver, C. G. (2014). *E-commerce 2014: Business, technology, society* (10th ed. Global Edition). London: Pearson.

Longoni, A., & Gâza, M. (2013). Mobile payments 2013: Changing checkout. *Innopay BV*, 1–110.

Malick, B., & Rudolph, S. (2013). The role of data analytics companies in mobile commerce. *McKinsey on Payments, 16*, 10–16.

MasterCard. (2013, September). MasterCard Advisors' cashless journey: The global journey from cash to cashless. *World Beyond Cash* (pp. 1–16). MasterCard. Retrieved May 2, 2014, from http://www.mastercardadvisors.com/cashlessjourney/MasterCard_Advisors_Global_Journey_From_Cash_To_Cashless.pdf.

McKinsey. (2013, September). Payments and financial inclusion: An interview with Rodger Voorhies of the Bill and Melinda Gates Foundation. *McKinsey on Payments*, 9–14.

Meeker, M., & Wu, L. (2013, May 29). "2013 Internet Trends", *2013 D11 Conference Presentation*. Kleiner, Perkins, Caufield & Byers. Retrieved April 2, 2014, from http://www.kpcb.com/insights/2013-internet-trends.

Meeker, M. (2014, May 28). "2014 Internet Trends", *2014 CODE Conference Presentation*. Kleiner, Perkins, Caufield & Byers. Retrieved July 10, 2014, from http://www.kpcb.com/internet-trends.

MobiThinking. (2013, June 6). Mobile payments will surpass $235 billion in 2013 (Gartner); NFC still disappointedly small, despite the hype. MobiThinking.com. Retrieved May 2, 2014, from http://mobithinking.com/blog/nfc2013.

Page, M., Molina, M., & Jones, G. (2013). *The mobile global economy*. ATKearney & GSMA. Retrieved April 15, 2014, from http://www.atkearney.com.au/documents/10192/760890/The_Mobile_Economy_2013.pdf/6ac11770-5a26-4fef-80bd-870ab83222f0.

Peters, J. (2014, March 27). What business can learn about mobile security from consumers. *Mobile Business Insights*. Retrieved April 25, 2014, from http://asmarterplanet.com/mobile-enterprise/blog/2014/03/businesses-can-learn-mobile-security-consumers.html.

Timson, L. (2014, February 4). Westpac trials Google Glass, iBeacon apps for wearable bank account access. Digital life. *The Sydney Morning Herald*. Retrieved April 10, 2014, from http://www.smh.com.au/digital-life/digital-life-news/westpac-trials-google-glass-ibeacon-apps-for-wearable-bank-account-access-20140204-31yj8.html.

The Nelson Report. (2014, March). Market shares of purchase transactions worldwide 2013. Nelsonreport.com. Retrieved May 2, 2014, from http://www.nilsonreport.com/publication_chart_and_graphs_archive.php.

Tucker, C., & Donlea, T. (2012). *Top 9 fraud attacks and winning mitigating strategies*. CyberSoruce Corporation 2012. Retrieved May 1, 2014, from http://www.cybersource.com/resources/collateral/pdf/CyberSource_MRC_Survey_Top_9_Fraud_Attacks.pdf.

Turban, E., King, D. Liang, T. P., & Turban, D. (2012). *Electronic commerce: A managerial and social networks perspective* (7th ed., Global Edition). London: Pearson Education.

Venkateswaran, S., Flamme, M., Lyman, S., & Sepulveda, J. (2011). *Driving profitable growth in payments* (pp. 1–17). Booz & Company. Retrieved April 20, 2014, from http://www.strategyand.pwc.com/media/file/Strategyand-Driving-Profitable-Growth-Payments.pdf.

Wagstaff, J. (2014, March 20). Bitcoin's promise: A financial revolution the web's been waiting for. *Reuters*. Retrieved April 28, 2104, from http://www.reuters.com/article/2014/03/20/us-bitcoin-future-idUSBREA2J27Y20140320.

Wikepedia.org. (2014, May 21). Bitcoin, version. Wikipedia.org. Retrieved May 22, 2014, from http://en.wikipedia.org/wiki/Bitcoin.

Chapter 10
Mobile Enterprise

This chapter introduces the mobile era, explains the concept of digital enterprise and its major applications, discusses key mobile technologies, examines some key issues and success factors of mobile enterprise, and points out some emerging trends and future directions of mobile enterprise.

10.1 The Mobile Era

10.1.1 The Mobility Culture

El-Darwiche et al. (2012) suggest that more people today have access to a mobile phone than to electricity. With more than 6 billion connections worldwide and US $1.3 trillion in revenue, mobile telephony has become the largest ICT industry in history and surpassed the landline Internet by more than 3.5 billion users (Dutta and Bilbao-Osorio 2012). Bold and Davidson (2012, p. 71) suggest that the installed base of smartphones exceeded that of PCs in 2011 and is growing more than three times faster than personal computers, and the expected shipment of smartphones between 2011 and 2015 could be around 4 billion. Today's smartphones deliver increasing rich experiences to consumers, including full web-browsing and computing capabilities, high-definition video, 3D gaming, access to social networks, and many other compelling services. Meanwhile tablets are getting popular among individual and business users. According to JP Morgan (reported in The Economist 2012), driven by the popularity of iPads, the tablet market will reach US$35 billion in 2012 (from virtually nothing in 2009). It is reported (by the end of 2011, smart phones and tablets will overtake personal computer shipments (Berman and Bell 2011).

Today, mobile devices have been an inseparable part of our life, and it is to say that many of us are addicted to our mobile devices. For example, a recent study commissioned by Nokia (reported in Spencer 2013) indicated that people are so dependent on their mobile phones that they will check their mobile phones every six-and-half minutes and up to 150 times a day. Meanwhile Flurry's examination of its data from 500,000 apps across 1.3 billion devices as at March 2014 (reported in Khalaf 2014b) reports a similar trend. It reports that in March 2014, there were:

J. Xu, *Managing Digital Enterprise*, DOI 10.2991/978-94-6239-094-2_10

- 176 million mobile addicts worldwide, who use mobile app more than 60 times daily; and 52 % of them are female while 48 % are male.
- 440 million global super users, who use mobile app between 16 and 60 times daily.
- 784 million global regular users, who use mobile app under 16 times daily.

In addition, according to mobile analytics firm Flurry (reported in Khalaf 2014a), in the U.S., time spent on a mobile device by the consumer has risen to 2 h and 42 min from 2 h and 38 min in March 2013 (one year ago). 86 % of the 2 h and 42 min was spent on mobile apps while 14 % was spent on mobile web browsers (the figures were 80 and 20 % respectively a year ago). The breakdowns of the average time the consumer spent on a mobile device between March 2013 and March 2014 are: gaming applications 32 %, web browsing 14 % (Apple Safari 7 %, Google Browsers 5 %), social and messaging applications 28 % (17 % for Facebook, 1.5 % for Twitter), entertainment apps 8 % (4 % for Youtube), utility applications 8 %, productivity apps 4 %, and news applications 3 %. On a related note, eMarket (2014c) says that mobile usage (share of time spend per day by US Adults) has been continually increasing while time spent online and with traditional media has been continually declining in recent years; mobile usage will reach 23 % in 2014 from 3.7 % in 2010, time spent online will decline to 18 % in 2014 from 22.0 % in 2010, time spent online will decline to 36.5 % in 2014 from 40.9 % in 2010, time spent on radio will decline to 10.9 % from 14.9 % in 2010, and time spent on print media (including magazines and newspapers) will decline to 3.5 % in 2014 from 7.7 % in 2010.

10.1.2 Mobile Workforce

It can be said that the use of mobile devices in the workplace is no longer a trend but a necessity for many organizations. International Data Corporation (2012a) suggests that by 2015, the world's mobile (remote) worker population will reach 1.3 billion (or 37.2 % of the global workforce) and increase by 300 million from 2010; and among the predicated 1.3 billion mobile workers, 877.3 million (67 % of the global total) will come from Asia Pacific, 244.6 million (19 %) from Europe, Middle East, Africa, and 212.1 million (16 %) from Americas. And by 2015, 1129 million smart phones will be shipped (305 million units shipped in 2010); 289 million notebooks (196 million units in 2010), 268 million tablets (32 million units in 2012), and 160 million desktop PCs (157 million in 2010) will be sold. Meanwhile according to a recent study by IBM (reported in IBM Corporation 2012), 74 % of 675 surveyed chief information officers and IT managers of large enterprises worldwide indicated that developing a flexible workplace is a top priority for their organizations and has been given greater priority than other investments over next 12 months. The majority of the participants of the study believed that the flexible workplace will result in productivity gains and nearly 50 % of the participants believe it will potentially increase revenue. The same trend is also identified by a recent McKinsey survey of 250 CIOs on their organizations' mobile strategies (reported in Akella et al. 2012):

56 % of respondents reported demand from employees to support a wide range of mobile devices, 77 % were going to allow staff to use personal mobile devices to access company data and applications, and nearly 100 % expected to deploy more than 25 mobile applications in the next 2 years. In addition, Gartner estimates (reported in IBM Corporation 2012) that by 2014 80 % of mobile professionals will use at least two mobile devices access corporate systems and data. At the same time, the mobile channel has lot of financial potential for organizations. The results of two recent studies by consulting firm McKinsey (reported in Bughin (2011); Bughin and Manyika (2014) respectively) indicate that the free digital services (e.g., free online and mobile services such as e-mail, search engines, social networks, instant messaging, internet phone, web mapping, comparison shopping, music, videos, wikis, yellow pages, podcasts, blogs, games, and directories) could be worth €250 billion in the United States and Europe in 2013 (i.e., the dollar amount consumers/users are willing to pay for these services), up from €100 billion in 2010; and the mobile channel contributes 75 % of the increase.

10.1.3 Mobile Economy

According to a report by ATKearney and GSMA (written by Page et al. 2013):

- The number of mobile subscribers will reach 3.94 billion by 2017 from 3.4 billion in 2013 and 2.3 billion in 2008.
- The total mobile connections (including machine to machine) will reach 9.7 billion by 2017 from 7.4 billion in 2013 and 4 billion in 2008.
- Mobile broadband connections will increase from 1.6 billion in 2012 to 5.2 billion by 2017.
- LTE/4G networks will account for 1 in 5 mobile broadband subscriptions by 2017 (1 in 25 in 2017) (i.e., 920 million subscriptions by 2017 compared to 62 million subscriptions in 2012).
- Mobile data volume will reach 11.2 hexabytes per month by 2017 from 0.9 hexabytes per month in 2012.
- 9.2 trillion messages were sent in 2012 and 28.2 trillion messages will be sent in 2017.
- By 2017, the total revenues created by the mobile ecosystem (including handset suppliers, infrastructure companies, distributors, and content providers) are forecast to reach US$2 trillion.
- By 2017, 1 in 9 lives saved (or 35,000 lives) will be saved through in-call emergency calling services.
- By 2017, M2M connections will reach 1.2 billion from 215 million in 2012.
- By 2017, mobile healthcare could help cut OECD countries healthcare costs by US$4,000 billion.
- By 2017, the total value of global mobile payments is predicted to reach US$13 trillion.

- By 2017, global annual smart grid spending will reach US$65 billion.
- Smart metering in major cities can reduce carbon emissions by 27 million tons or equivalent of 1.2 billion trees offset.

Reported by eMarket (2014a), in 2013, global mobile ad spending increased 105 % to total US$17.96 billion while in 2014 the total global ad spending will reach US$31.45 billion with 75.1 % increase from 2013. And the two major players are Google and Facebook; they attracted 66.8 % of the total mobile ad spending in 2013, and they will attract 68.5 % of the total mobile ad spending in 2014. It is noted that the dominating position of Google over Facebook in attracting mobile ad spending has been weaken in recent years (i.e., Google' percentages of 52.6 % in 2012, 49.3 % in 2013, 46.8 % in 2014 while Facebook's percentages of 5.4 % in 2012, 17.5 % in 2013, 21.7 % in 2014). In addition, some top players in attracting mobile ad spending in 2014 are: Google (46.8 %), Facebook (21.7 %), Twitter (2.6 %), Pandora (1.7 %), YP (1.6 %), and Millennial Media (0.7 %). Meanwhile Gartner (2014) says that global mobile advertising spending is projected to reach US$18 billion in 2014 and US$41.9 billion in 2017; and even though display formats will contribute most of the revenue, mobile video ads will have the highest growth. On a related note, mobile social network ads have the second highest growth after mobile video ads in 2013 and will be so in 2014 (eMarket 2014b). Search/map ad types will become more popular as a result of the increased use of location-based applications and data. And North America is where most of revenue will come from (for such reasons as the large scale of its advertising budgets, its advances in online advertising, the wide adoption of mobile devices, and its recognition and shift to the mobile channel) while growth will be seen in all regions. Furthermore leading high-growth economies (i.e., China and India) will contribute increasingly to mobile advertising growth while most mobile advertising mature countries like Japan and Korea as well as some other countries in the Asia-Pacific area will have relatively slow growth (i.e., 30 % per year) as a result of its early leading position and growth in mobile advertising.

Mobile in-app is an emerging area where organizations can realize mobile money. It is reported that mobile in-app advertising revenue has been increasing around 60 % a year, and by 2017, the mob in-app ad revenue will surpass online/web ad revenue (International Data Corporation 2014c). In 2013, 68 % of US$38 billion global mobile revenue came from mobile apps while 32 % came from mobile advertising (Meeker 2014). It is also estimated that mobile app-related revenue reached US$25 billion in 2013 and will reach more than US$70 billion by 2017 (Ajmera et al. 2014). In-app purchasing is a promising and sustainable monetization strategy for organizations since it encourages performance-based purchasing (e.g., users only pay when they are happy with the experience) even though they have or have not already paid for a mob application. The keys are good app design and performance (Gartner 2013).

10.2 Definition and Major Applications of Mobile Enterprise

As a result of factors such as the wide adoption of mobile devices (e.g., people in some developing countries may not have computers and access to the Internet but do have mobile phones and other mobile devices), the affordability of mobile devices (e.g., the price of Mozilla's upcoming smart phones could be as low as US $25), the availability of fast cabled and wireless networks, the explosion of innovative mobile applications, and better functionalities (e.g., camera, audio and video recording, payment systems, GPS, social networks, and other functions and mobile applications) and user friendliness (e.g., touch screen, larger screen, voice recognition tools, and being easy to learn and use), more and more organizations are embarking on mobile enterprise (m-commerce or m-business), which is any digital enterprise/e-business conducted over a wireless telecommunication network or from mobile devices (Turban et al. 2012, p. 277). Mobile Enterprise/Mobile Business is a natural extension of electronic business and adds additional dimensions on top of the opportunities arising from the Internet. Meanwhile it is argued that much as the Internet caused a rethinking of the nature of business and the way we do business almost two decades ago (and continues to do so today), organizations need to consider carefully how mobile channel and mobile devices could influence the future directions of the organization (Buckellew et al. 2013). Some major mobile enterprise applications include: B2C and B2B mobile business, location-based services, and pervasive computing.

B2C and B2B mobile business could enable organizations to provide products and services to customers (consumers and businesses). Mobile devices can be used to optimize an organization's supply chain (e.g., via timely, more accurate, more up-dated information). Mobile computing solutions enable organizations to respond faster and better to changes in the supply chain. Location-based services (e.g., location, navigation, tracking, mapping and timing (Turban et al. 2012, p. 304)), are mobile enterprise applications provided to customers (consumers and businesses) based on a user's specific location. It can be used to target advertising or services to a user based on location. Some widely used applications include GPS and GIS. A study by Juniper Research (cited in Wauters 2010) indicates that mobile location-based services could generate US$12.7 billion revenue by 2014.

Pervasive computing, also known as ubiquitous computing, embedded computing, or augmented computing, or wearable computing or everywhere computing is invisible and is embedded in the objects around us, such as wearable devices, smart cars, smart homes and buildings, and smart appliances. It is estimated that wearable devices (e.g., Apple's iWatches and Google's Google Glasses) alone in 2014 will be worth more than US$1.5 billion, and by 2018 between 300 and 485 million wearable devices will be sold (Buckellew et al. 2013). It has been predicted that wearable/everywhere computing is the next technology era/cycle from 2014 after previous technology eras/cycles of mobile Internet computing (2000s), desktop Internet computing (1990s), personal computing (1980s), mini computing (1970s), and mainframe computing (1960s) (Meeker and Wu 2013).

10.3 Key Mobile Technologies

Mobile enterprise, which is supported by the required hardware, software and telecommunication networks, eliminates the barrier of physical location by allowing individuals to communicate and do business from any location at any time. Mobile devices create an opportunity to deliver new services to existing customers. And wireless technologies promise to be the next major development in digital business/enterprise both for business and consumer markets (B2B and B2C). On top of the technical infrastructure discussed in Chap. 2, there are some specific technologies for mobile devices. Table 10.1 presents some key technologies for mobile phones (including both feature and smart phones) and for tablets and eReaders.

Meanwhile when existing mobile devices (especially mobile phones) enterprises are still holding onto their market position, emerging competitors (especially those ones from China including Xiaomi, Huawei, and ZTE) will no doubt have a big impact on the industry with their good quality, good functionality, ease of use, and cheaper price. Some other possible potential competitors are Internet-based

Table 10.1 Key technologies of mobile phones and tablets and eReadres

Mobile phones		Tablets and eReaders	
Category	Technologies	Category	Technologies
Operating systems	Google's Android, Microsoft's Windows Phone, Nokia's Symbian, Apple's iOS, Blackberry OS, Open Source's Linux, Mozilla's Firefox OS, and Samsung's Tizen	Operating systems	Android, Blackberry OS, iOS, Linux, webOS, and Windows
Generation	2G, 2.5G, 3G, and 4G	Connectivity	3G, 4G, WiFi, WiFi/3G, an dWiFi/4G
Air interfaces	CDMA EV-DO, GSM, GPRS, EDGE, UMTS, HSPA, LTE, and TD-SCDMA	CPU	ARM and X86
Other attributes	Input method, camera megapixel bands, GPS, bluetooth, WiFi, TV, Push2Talks, radio, VoIP, music player, video player, Java, BREW, MMS, display and screen size, primary memory card, screen size, NFC, Dual SIM, application processor information, and smartphone tiers	Other attributes	Screen size and resolution, storage, and detachable sub form factor

Source Developed from International Data Corporation (2014a, b)

enterprises such as Google, Facebook, Amazon, Mozilla, Alibaba, who have developed or are developing their own mobile phones; while entering into the mobile phone market could be a part of the firm's initiative of developing its business ecosystem, on the other hand, the counter argument is that Internet-based firms should focus on providing value-added services to customers and working with handset enterprises on installing and supporting services for the handsets. Tencent, China's largest and the world's fifth largest Internet company (Wikipedia.org 2014; Gittleson 2014), made such a choice (Sheng 2012).

On a different note, some breakthroughs and innovative ideas for improving batteries have been observed, and such breakthroughs and innovative ideas (e.g., wireless charging, charger capable of connecting with and powering up multiple mobile devices simultaneously, different shapes and sizes of battery to make the most of the available space inside mobile devices, a massive battery pack used for recharging multiple mobile devices a few times, using a super-capacitor which could be charged very quickly and store plenty of energy using one mobile device to charge another one, ultra-rapid charger (e.g., StoreDot's system), using our body heat to power mobile devices, clearly optimized software, mobile device screens with solar charging panels, Li-imide and silicon anode batteries (Boxall 2014)), will no doubt further increase the profile of mobile enterprises and the adoption and usage of mobile devices.

10.3.1 iOS, Windows Phone and Android

Android operating system is owned and managed by Google and is an open source mobile operating system. It has been adopted by many mobile device manufacturers. iOS (iPhone operating system) is a proprietary mobile operating system developed and managed by Apple, and it has been installed in iPhones and other Apple devices (e.g., iPods, iPads). So far Apple has not allowed it to be installed on the devices of other firms. Windows Phone system is a proprietary mobile operating system developed and managed by Microsoft. Some models including HTC, Samsung, and Nokia (Microsoft now owns Nokia handset business) mobile phones have used Windows Phone system. Android and iOS are the dominating mobile operating systems.

It is reported that in 2013, there were 1 billion smartphones shipped worldwide, and the top four smartphone operating systems in 2013 are: Android (78.6 %), iOS (15.2 %), Windows Phone (3.3 %), and Blackberry (1.9 %) (International Data Corporation 2014c). On a related note, according to a study of 98,285 iOS and Android devices (mobile phones and tablets) (reported in Gordon 2013), 88 % of Android devices are mobile phones (12 % tablets), 72 % of iOS devices are mobile phones (28 % tablets), and 91 % of Samsung devices are mobile phones (9 % tablets). In addition, the leading countries of smartphone penetration include: United Arab Emirates (UAE) (73.8 %), South Korea (73 %), Saudi Arabia (72.8 %), Singapore (71.7 %), Norway (67.5 %), Australia (64.6 %), Sweden

(62.9 %), Hong Kong (62.2 %), U.K. (62.2 %), and Denmark (59 %); and it is predicted that the penetration rates will reach 84 % or more for some countries by 2015 (Shehadi et al. 2014).

10.3.2 Bring Your Own Device

A recent trend is BYOD (bring your own device). The rise of BYOD programs has been argued as "the single most radical shift in the economics of client computing for business since PCs invaded the workplace" (IBM Corporation 2012, p. 2). It is reported that employed-owned devices in the workplace will grow from 2 billion to more than 5.25 billion by 2016 (IBM Corporation 2013). Organizations are now looking at allowing employees to use their personal mobile devices in the organization for work purposes. Such initiative can have benefits to both employees (e.g., only one device for both personal and work uses) and organizations (e.g., could reduce the costs of computing). One particular concern is the security issues associated with accessing the organization's applications and information from personal devices. BYOD programs could be more costly and complex as well due to the mix of corporate and personal data and the more complicated measures and thus more required resources for keeping personal mobile devices safe. It is estimated that an enterprise with 1,000 BYOD mobile devices will spend an average of US$170,000 more per year than an organization with only corporate owned mobile devices (IBM Corporation 2012).

10.3.3 Mobile Payment Systems

One significant element of mobile business is mobile payment systems (e.g., Google's Google Wallet, Amazon's Amazon Checkout, PayPal's mobile payment systems). For factors such as the wide adoption of mobile phones and devices (especially iPads), technologies such as NFC (near field communication), SMS, QR Codes, GPS applications, Augment reality (e.g., Google Goggles, Layar, and Wikitude), the popularity of mobile applications (e.g., i-tunes and games), and the convenience of paying anytime and anywhere without waiting in the checkout line, mobile payments have become an essential part of today's networked economy. NFC applications have increasingly been used in recent years for payment, retail, transport, mobile identity, ticketing, and information access (e.g., event news and schedules via NFC enabled Tap-n-Go points at the event venue) (Sadauskas 2014c). ABI Research (2014) says that over the period 2014–2019, 34 billion tickets will be delivered to mobile devices and authenticated by various mobile technologies including QR codes, NFC, SMS, mobile wallets, Bluetooth Smart, and dedicated apps; and among these mobile technologies NFC will have the fastest growth with annual compound growth rate (CAGR) in excess of 100 % and will account for 30 % of all tickets delivered, with QR codes for 48 % and SMS and other technologies for the remaining 22 % of the 34 billion mobile tickets.

10.3.4 Mobile Applications

Mobile applications/Mobile Apps, which are also called native applications, are typically developed for a specific mobile platform and/or mobile device and are normally installed via App stores (e.g., Apple's App Store, Google's Google Play Store, Blackberry World, and Windows Phone Store). They can take full advantage of the device's features (e.g., the camera, GPS, the compass, the contact list) as well as incorporating social media and other popular applications, allow for faster and more convenient access to content than web browsers. A range of mobile applications features can operate without an Internet connection while mobile browsers do need an Internet connection. Mobile websites in general provide one way communication to the users while mobile Apps facilitate two way communication and engagement (e.g., special offers, time critical messages or updates from apps which are not available from mobile websites) (Sadauskas 2014a; Budiu 2013; Benjamin 2014).

Gartner (2013) says that the annual mobile application downloads will reach 268.7 billion in 2017 from 102.6 billion in 2013 and the revenue from mobile applications will reach US$26 in 2013 up from US$18 billion in 2012. Free app downloads have been and will be dominating the mobile application downloads (e.g., 89.6 % of all downloads in 2012, 91 % in 2012, 92 % in 2013, and 94.5 % in 2017). iOS and Android app stores combined will account for 90 % of global mob app downloads in 2017. In addition, in-app purchases will account for 48 % of app store revenue in 2017 up from 17 % in 2013.

The Facebook's US$19 billion acquisition of WhatsApp has caused a lot of attention to mobile messaging Apps, which have been very popular in recent years (especially in some countries) for such reasons as (Clifford 2013; Chan 2014; Sadauskas 2014d):

- Good functionality with many features including text/voice chat, web chat, group chat, video chat, picture sharing, connections to social media, QR code, payment, mobile shop and others).
- Sending messages and having communications between mobile devices without paying for wireless network service.
- No need to rely on mobile operators/carriers and to pay for voice calls and messages.

According to social media agency tech news site READWRITE (reported in Chan 2014), the ten largest mobile messaging applications are:

- WhatsApp (U.S.A): 450 million monthly users.
- Line (Japan): 350 million registered users.

- WeChat (China): 272 million monthly users.
- Tango (U.S.A): more than 190 million registered users.
- NIMBUZZ (India): 150 million registered users.
- KIK (Canada): 130 million registered users.
- KAKAOTALK (South Korea): more than 100 million registered users.
- Viber (Cyprus): more than 100 million registered users.
- HIKE (India): 15 million registered users.
- MESSAGEME (U.S.A): 5 million registered users.

Meanwhile some other popular mobile messaging apps include Google's Hangouts, Blackberry Message, Snapshot, Skype, Ch@tON, Facebook Messager, and QQ.

In May 2013 two surveys on mobile apps use in Australia were commissioned by the Australian Communications and Media Authority (ACMA). One surveyed 2,400 consumers aged 18 years and over while the other surveyed 1,500 small and medium-sized enterprises (with less than 200 employees) with a fixed telephone line. The results of the two surveys indicated (reported in ACMA 2013):

- Young people tend to be early adopters of smartphone and users of mobile apps.
  - The adoption levels of smart ownership by different age groups are: 18–24 (89 %), 25–34 (85 %), 35–44 (81 %), 45–54 (65 %), 55–64 (49 %), and 65 plus (22 %).
  - The downloading levels of mobile apps by different age groups are: 18–24 (83 %), 25–34 (76 %), 35–44 (66 %), 45–54 (48 %), 55–64 (30 %), and 65 plus (9 %).
- Benefits of using mobile apps include:
  - It is easier to use online services on a mobile phone (53 %).
  - I have immediate access to the services I required (47 %).
  - Apps give me faster access to websites (17 %).
  - I have scheduled information at my fingertips (12 %).
  - I can access data offline via an app if out of network coverage (8 %).
- Barriers to using apps include:
  - Access to personal information (e.g., how will personal information be collected and used?).
  - Hidden costs of the app (e.g., in-app purchasing options, unauthorized or accidental in-app purchase, and data usage).
  - Content safeguards (e.g., in-app ads, linking to social networking sites and/or in-app chat features, location-based features).
- Types of apps downloaded:
  - Games (66 %), social networking (59 %), banking and finance (49 %), productivity and tools (48 %), travel and lifestyle (41 %), transport (35 %), education (33 %), shopping (33 %), and sports related (27 %).

- Frequency of app downloading:
  - 72 % once a month or less than once a month.
  - 27 % downloading an app on a weekly basis.
  - 7 % downloading a couple of times a week.
  - 2 % downloading on a daily basis.
- Apps and SMEs:
  - The app market and the benefits of applications are still to be effectively realized.
  - 18 % have developed a mobile optimized website.
  - 3 % have developed a business-related application.
  - 2 % have developed both a mobile-optimized website and a business-related app.

Meanwhile as per ACMA's 2013 May surveys, consumers use multiple devices to access the Internet from home: laptop (76 %), desktop PC (69 %), mobile phone (67 %), tablet (47 %), television (23 %), portable games console (7 %), MP3 player (15 %), and other games console (15 %). In addition, the mobile app market is still in the early development stage even though it is large and diverse. The apps will no doubt have increasing impact on the way consumers use and interact with traditional media, communications, entertainment and software (e.g., movies, television programs, games, social networking, task management and productivity, voice communications, SMS and texting) (ACMA 2013).

Some success factors for Apps development include (Shehadi et al. 2013; The author's own knowledge):

- The Apps must be intuitive and easy to use-the interface must be simple enough that the average user can figure it out on the first try with no assistance.
- The Apps must be bug free and reliable.
- Adopting proven mechanisms for loyalty programs (i.e., rewarding frequent use of Apps), gamification (i.e., increasing the usage of Apps by introducing a sense of fun), and social media (i.e., using the popularity of social media, the pervasiveness of social media and their ease of use on mobile platforms to better engage with customers) should be taken into consideration when organizations are developing mobile Apps.
- Utilizing both internal skills and external expertise as most organizations are not in the technology business thus their internal technological skills and expertise as well as resources are limited or insufficient (e.g., the central federal government could utilises the expertise of sectorial agencies and the capabilities of the private sector to develop mobile government Apps).
- Organizations could look at developing organization-specific Apps stores to increase the brand awareness of the organization and have the potential to generate revenue from the store when possible or necessary.

- Organizations could implement the approach of co-invention/co-development of mobile Apps by sharing data with customers and partners (e.g., government agencies could share data with the private sector and citizens for co-inventing/ co-developing mobile government Apps).

10.4 Issues and Success Factors of Mobile Enterprise

10.4.1 Key Issues

A recent McKinsey survey of 250 CIOs on their organizations' mobile strategies (reported in Akella et al. 2012), identified these top three challenges for mobile computing: (1) security concerns (wireless communication is more vulnerable than a wired one, and mobile devices have a higher chance of getting lost or stolen because of their smaller size); (2) costs (including costs for devices, connectivity, applications, maintenance and support); and (3) associated organizational challenges (i.e., fit with existing structure, process, information systems development and management, infrastructure, and governance required for mobile computing). In another recent survey of 675 chief information officers and IT managers of large enterprises worldwide by IBM (reported in IBM Corporation 2012), 71 % of the participants indicated that security was the most significant mobile enterprise challenge. One specific security issue of mobile enterprise is the security concerns associated with the emerging trend of BYOD. Organizations need to effectively deal with such issues as data access, data protection and recovery, data deletion (when people are leaving the organization or changing roles in the organization or their mobile devices are being lost, stolen, and hacked), and the separation of corporate data from personal data (Peters 2014). In addition, as a result of the relative smaller size (especially mobile phones) and the portability of mobile devices, the physical loss of mobile devices is another major security concern.

However it should be noted that the security and privacy issues for mobile enterprise/mobile business are just as they are for any type of digital enterprise/e-business. As a result, solutions for digital enterprise discussed in Chap. 2 can also be applied effectively to mobile businesses. On a related note, after looking at the securability of some major mobile platforms (including Apple's iOS, Google's Android operating system, Microsoft's Windows Phone OS, Nokia's Symbian, and RIM's Blackberry OS), Gruman (2013b) suggests that with appropriate security tools most organizations should feel confident that many of today's mobile devices are capable to meet with core corporate security needs (from dealing with routine business information to important business information to sensitive business information to top-secret information).

Furthermore the shift to mobile approach is a transformational one and has dramatically changed the way people work and organizations conduct their business (IBM Corporation 2013). IBM Institute for Business Value, in partnership with

Oxford Economics, surveyed 600 companies across various industries from 29 countries, with 33 % having annual revenue of US$500 million to 1 billion, 33 % of US$1 to 5 billion, and 33 % over US$5 billion. The findings of the survey indicated that (reported in Buckellew et al. 2013) generally speaking:

- There is a lack of a well-defined enterprise-wide mobile strategy.
- There is a lack of a systematic and coordinated approach in developing and implementing mobile strategy in the organization. There are many one-off, disconnected, and poorly-planned activities, efforts, and projects. One reason is the immature stage of mobile strategy development similar to that experienced in the early days of the Internet and electronic business/electronic commerce in the 1980s/1990s.
- There is a lack of leadership or a dedicated senior position for leading mobile strategy development and implementation.
- There is a lack of alignment with the enterprise-wide strategy and integration with existing business processes and infrastructure.
- There is a lack of a governance structure for mobile initiatives.
- There is a lack of required skills and expertise and dedicated resources for mobile initiatives.
- There is a lack of close cooperation and collaboration between multiple stakeholders of mobile initiatives.

10.4.2 Success Factors

In line with the above identified issues of mobile initiatives in the organization, some suggestions (or success factors) are proposed to address those issues (see Table 10.2).

10.5 Emerging Trends and Future Directors

After the Internet-based business era, the next battle will be over the mobile. Major technology and/or Internet-based companies (e.g., Google, Apple, Microsoft, Twitter, Amazon, Facebook, eBay, Tencent, Alibaba) are fighting hard to win the dominating position in the global mobile market. For example, Facebook declares (quoted in Bendall 2014) that "We are a mobile business" (57 % of its revenue is due to mobile and its three main business areas of social media (via Facebook social networks), photo-sharing (via acquired Instagram in 2012), and mobile messaging (via acquired WhatsApp in 2014) are desirable for mobile platforms). Meanwhile the wide adoption of mobile messaging apps have seriously challenged the business of mobile carriers and telecommunication operators), and they need to find ways to deal with the falling revenue from voice calls and text messages. One possible

Table 10.2 Suggestions for developing and implementing mobile initiatives in the organization

Suggestions	Explanations
Establishing a systematic approach for mobile strategy planning and implementation	Following a generic process of identifying mobile initiatives for improvement and new opportunities; prioritising and selecting suitable initiative; implementing the chosen initiative; and monitoring the performance of the chosen initiative
	Identifying priority user segments and meeting their needs (e.g., sales and marketing people)
	Ensuring the chosen mobile initiative is supporting strategic goals of the organization
	Collecting valuable information and reach consensus on a strategic and unified mobile strategy by getting the input from the people in the organization via different approaches (e.g., interviews, workshops, surveys, observations, focus-group, internal documents)
	Establishing and executing effective change management, project management and risk management strategies associated with chosen mobile initiatives
	Understanding the total of costs (including costs for devices, connectivity, applications, maintenance and support) of the chosen mobile initiative
	Examining closely how mobile initiatives can be prioritized and integrated with other digital initiatives/investments in the organization
	Pilot testing before full-scale implementation
	Planning for the future (i.e., required capabilities for the next 2–3 years)
	Providing ongoing support for mobile enterprise initiatives
	Implementing a team/cross-functional approach for mobile initiatives crossing the internal and external boundaries
Providing adequate support and resources	Appointing a dedicated senior position for leading the organization's mobile initiatives
	Allocating sufficient funding and having a clear funding mechanism for mobile initiatives
	Demonstrating the visible support and role model from top management
	Providing appropriate training to users

(continued)

Table 10.2 (continued)

Suggestions	Explanations
Putting required policies and measures for BYOD in place	Creating policies for bringing your own devices (BYOD)
	Developing security and privacy measures using personal mobile devices for work purposes (e.g., device wipe and lockdown for lost devices, hardware and software encryption, installing and regularly updating anti-virus applications, two-step user-based authentication process with first logging onto the device and then onto the corporate network)
Taking a collaborative and cooperative approach	Developing a collaborative governance structure for managing mobile initiatives and involving people from different parts of the organization and external stakeholders (e.g., customers, suppliers, and partners) from the beginning
Collecting and utilizing mobile data effectively	Collecting structured and non-structured data from mobile phones, other mobile devices, equipment and vehicles and combining such data with other information (e.g., activities on the website of the business, activities in the store)
	Putting more emphasis on using location-based data (or contextually relevant data including both timing and location data of mobile interactions) for enhancing customer experience and improving employee productivity and effectiveness
	Effectively analysing the collected data and applying the identified relations, patterns and trends to improve the performance of the organization
Creating mobile experience for both customers and employees	While organizations are focusing on improving customer experience via the mobile channel, the right mobile experience also needs to be developed for employees (e.g., appropriate mobile applications, access and permissions relevant to their specific job needs). The employees have to feel comfortable with the mobile channel before they can interact with customers via the mobile channel
	Developing branded mobile applications (e.g., applications with the organization's brands) for customers and internal task-specific applications for employees and internal purposes
	Deploying enterprise app stores and actually using them

(continued)

Table 10.2 (continued)

Suggestions	Explanations
Managing mobile devices like other corporate assets	For many organizations, in the past mobile devices have not been managed to the same extent as other IS/IT assets. As these devices are becoming a more integral part of the business, specific processes for dealing with procurement, distribution, and maintenance as well as security, privacy, and risk management of mobile devices need to be put in place
Building required skills and talents for mobile initiatives	Developing required internal skills and expertise for planning and implementing mobile strategy
	Developing required internal skills and expertise for developing and integrating mobile applications (especially skills and expertise for agile development, lean management, service-oriented architecture, application programming interface, HTML5)
	Developing required internal skills and expertise for collecting and especially analysing mobile data
Utilizing both in-sourcing and outsourcing approaches for developing and managing mobile applications	While it is essential to building internal skills and expertise, organizations need to actively look for assistance and expertise as well as services from outside of the organization to speed up the process of product development, innovation, and customer services. Cloud services should be definitely taken into consideration
Creating seamless mobile experience	Movement across devices need to be seamless, with data and transactions being preserved as end users (customers and employees) move between mobile phones, tablets, wearable devices, laptops, PCs, televisions, and other devices
	Providing end users with consistent experience across different channels (online, mobile and physical)
	Ensuring the organization's network is adequate for mobile initiatives (e.g., 24/7 availability, sufficient bandwidth for faster communications and transactions)
	Recognizing the personal nature of mobiles and having a good understanding of the motivations and patterns of customers' mobile time, and using customers' mobile devices to glue all customer touch points and bridge the digital and physical worlds for the purpose of providing customers with personalized and seamless whole/total experience with the organization

(continued)

Table 10.2 (continued)

Suggestions	Explanations
Working hard on integration, security and privacy, data governance issues	Ensuring interoperability of mobile applications with other systems and technical infrastructure of the organization and of the external partners
	Addressing mobile security and privacy issues (e.g., data protection, secure connectivity, device management, threat detection, mobile application and data usage, mobile application security, user security)
	Putting a data governance structure and policies into place
	Paying close attention to mobile device management (as a result of its relatively higher risk of being stolen or misplaced) by working on such areas as data loss prevention (e.g., traffic monitoring, managed data storage), device management, and application management (e. g., secure app development and management, application content management and secure app containers)
Making required organizational adjustments	Developing a pro-mobility culture in the organization
	Having a suitable structure for mobile strategy in the organization
	Examining and changing business processes and roles to take advantage of mobility
Developing mobile applications with the thinking of generating new revenue streams and improving the internal operation efficiency	Developing task-specific mobile applications for improving employees' productivity, reducing the response time to customers, and speeding up the innovation process
	Developing mobile applications which are linked with location-based data and/or social media for new and/or improved product/service and for new revenue generation. For example Tesco's Home Plus lets commuters do shopping while waiting for transport through virtual shelves displayed on the walls of stations. Commuters use a mobile application to scan the QR codes of the products/services and complete the purchase (including delivery arrangement)
	Developing free mobile applications for customers to use but with the inclusion of the opportunities to generate revenue (applying the freemium model) via in-app adverting and in-app shopping which has been becoming more and more popular and has been proven

(continued)

Table 10.2 (continued)

Suggestions	Explanations
	effective for organizations to generate revenue. Meanwhile the significant efforts have to be put into ensure good design and performance of mobile applications since customers are only willing to pay when they are having a good experience and are happy with the mobile applications
Taking a strategic approach towards mobile infrastructure development	Making mobile computing an integral part of the organization's IT infrastructure
	Having an enterprise-wide and strategic approach to mobile infrastructure supporting mobile strategy and mobile initiatives
	Optimizing the performance of network infrastructure to support increased access, workloads, volume and velocity generated by the move to mobile
	Looking at new technologies (e.g., virtualization, service-oriented architecture and cloud computing) and new standards (e.g., HTML5 and CSS) to support mobile capabilities and delivery of mobile applications

Source Buckellew et al. (2013), International Data Corporation (2012a, b), eMarket (2014a, b, c), Gartner (2013), IBM Corporation (2012, 2013), Havard Business Review (2013), Egol et al. (2013), Friedrich et al. (2008), Akella et al. (2012), Gupta (2013), Gruman (2013a), (2014), Violino (2014), the author's own knowledge

direction is that along with providing network and data storage infrastructure, mobile carriers and telecommunication operators need to provide value-added services (e.g., bill consolidation and payment functions, specific apps development and distribution, mobile big data and mobile intelligence services, more attractive packages bundling various services, and dynamic pricing strategies) by working with partners across various industries. Another interesting point organizations need to pay attention to is consumers' "me time". For example, according to a study by marketing research firm Insightsnow (reported in Harvard Business Review 2013), 68 % of consumers' smartphone use happens at home (not on the go), seeking relaxation or entertainment (e.g., watching video, reading news, playing games) (the "me time") is the most common activity on the mobile phone (not shopping or socializing). How to attract attention to the offerings of products and services during their "me time" is definitely worth exploring.

Organizations also need to consider whether going mobile only is the ideal solution for them. Instead of having both fixed line communication tools and mobile devices, some businesses (especially small businesses) have abandoned fixed line communication tools and have gone mobile only for the reason of cost saving. However before such a decision is made, organizations need to look at such issues as (Sadauskas 2104b; the author's own knowledge):

- Can mobile applications and mobile web browsers really have the same functions on desk PCs and laptops (e.g., how do you know enterprise systems such as ERP systems, SCM systems, CRM systems, KM systems work on mobile devices?)
- Can the organization successfully operate on mobile devices only (e.g., can you reach customers or can customers use all your services via mobile channel only)? Can all the business processes be supported by mobile devices?
- Are your customers and business partners ready for the organization's shift to going mobile only? Even if they are ready, are they going to embark on it when many other businesses are offering the three interaction channels of mobile, online and in-store?
- What is the proportion of mobile and remote staff in the organization?
- What is the proportion of the organization's activities requiring mobility and mobile support?
- Has the total cost of going mobile including network access, data storage and backup, software, hardware, support services, security and privacy measures, maintenance, and only been understood correctly?

For very small businesses (micro-business with less than five employees), going mobile only could be a good option, but not so for other businesses. One simple reason could be the costs for wireless broadband and mobile data storage could be too expensive to meet the needs of 5–10 employees and mobile services are generally more expensive than fixed line (i.e., telephone line and cable) services (Sadauskas 2014b).

On a related note, even though mobile data has been growing dramatically in recent years, it is argued that the fixed-line (i.e., fixed broadband) will still be dominating media for data downloading in the foreseeable future if not in our lifetimes; and unless there is a breakthrough in technology the fixed-line option (i.e., optic fiber) is the only known approach to provide high-speed broadband including traffic class management and quality of service (Stilghjerrian 2013). In addition, Duckett (2013) tells that for the period from June 2010 to June 2013, despite massive growth of mobile data in Australia, mobile data only made up 3 % of all data downloaded by Australians, as the domination of fixed-line broadband (accounting for more than 90 % of all the data downloaded) goes unchallenged. In the current environment (or in the foreseeable future), mobile bandwidth will not be sufficient and economical for the users of mobile devices. For example, looking at an example of 15 GB per month, it can't really allow you to do too much and last you for too long (i.e., 200–300 MB per hour for watching streaming video, 100 MB for audio-only conference on Skype, 1,000 MB (1 GB) for updating the device's operating system, and up to 100 MB per day for simple and cloud-based services of mapping services, chatting, emails) (Stilghjerrian 2013). Meanwhile, the increased use of mobile devices and services on a large scale has a dramatic impact on the environment. For example, according to the Center for Energy-Efficient Telecommunications in Melbourne (reported in Stilghjerrian 2013), currently the Internet uses about 1–2 % of the world's electricity but with the proliferation of many millions of energy-inefficient wireless/mobile devices the usage could reach 10 % by 2025. Furthermore, we are now in a world of multi-device employees. According to a recent survey of 9,766 global information workers by Forrest Research (reported in Gruman 2014), 84 % of employees/workers will use desktops at least weekly for work, 63 % will use laptops at least weekly for work, 59 % will use desk phones at least weekly for work, 48 % will use smartphones at least weekly for work, 21 % will use tablets at least weekly for work, and 21 % will use shared workstations at least weekly for work.

Finally organizations should be aware that developed countries may not always trump emerging economies in digital business. For example, by surveying 354 companies from 19 countries including both emerging and developed economies in 2012, Weill and Woerner (2013) unveil that emerging economies are investing more in digitization, digitizing more core-business activities, achieving better outcomes (i.e., being more innovative and faster to market, delivering better financial performance). Some possible reasons could be the firms in emerging economies jumped on the technology curve at a later point so they could invest lesser on developing and maintaining legacy systems, spend more on building new systems (e.g., cloud computing and mobile computing) and digitizing core business activities, use more modules, learn the lessons from the developed world and effectively apply the learned lessons, and realize better outcomes. The survey results also indicate that emerging market firms grew three times faster than firms in the same industries of developed countries. On top of the above mentioned reasons, such factors as the large population, the large number of mobile phone users, the good digital infrastructure, the favorable government policies, leading firms and entrepreneurs venturing into mobile business, good research and development capabilities, good supply of technical talent, has made China one of the leaders of mobile business. Another example is the adoption of mobile business in Africa. There are more than 500 million mobile phone subscribers in Africa (Mainardi 2012). According to ABI Research (reported in Van Dyk 2012), in comparison to developed economies, Africa has much fewer banks and ever fewer ATMS, and is a leader in mobile commerce. Mobile banking and mobile transactions is a standard there. Kenya only started its mobile commerce program in 2007, and already 20 % of the country's GDP are transacted via simple text messages from mobile phones.

References

ABI Research (2014, February 14). NFC playing catch up to QR codes and SMS in 34 billion mobile ticketing market. *Research News*, ABI Research. Retrieved April 30, 2014, from https://www.abiresearch.com/press/nfc-playing-catch-up-to-qr-codes-and-sms-in-34-bil.

Ajmera, N., Sato, L., & Stafford, B. (2014). Monetizing mobile apps: Striking the right balance. *McKinsey Quarterly*, *2*(2), 1–2.

Akella, J., Brown, B., Gilbert, G., & Wong, L. (2012, September). Mobility disruption: A CIO perspective. *Insights & Publications*, McKinsey & Company. Retrieved April 20, 2014, from http://www.mckinsey.com/insights/business_technology/mobility_disruption_a_cio_perspective.

Australian Communications and Media Authority (ACMA) (2013, November 29). Mobile apps: Putting the 'smart' in smartphones. *Research Snapshots*. Retrieved April 28, 2014, from http://www.acma.gov.au/theACMA/engage-blogs/engage-blogs/Research-snapshots/Mobile-apps-putting-the-smart-in-smartphones.

Bendall, F. (2014, February 27). Facebook's next stop to global domination: What is the deal with WhatsApp. *Bendalls.com.au*. Retrieved April 15, 2014, from http://www.bendalls.com.au/2014/02/.

Benjamin, D. (2014). Mobile revolution means apps have become must-have items for business. Technology Section, *Smartcompany.com.au*. Retrieved April 12, 2014, from http://www.smartcompany.com.au/technology/35895-mobile-revolution-means-apps-have-become-must-have-items-for-business.html.

Berman, S. J., & Bell, R. (2011). *Digital transformation: Creating new business models where digital meets physical* (pp. 1–17). IBM Global Business Service Executive Report, IBM Institute for Business Value.

Bold, W., & Davidson, W. (2012). Mobile broadband: Redefining internet access and empowering individuals. In S. Dutta & B. Bilbao-Osorio (Eds.), *The global information technology report 2012: Living in a hyper-connected world* (pp. 67–77). INSEAD & World Economic Forum.

Boxall, A. (2014, April 20). 10 Breakthroughs that will greatly improve phone batteries. *Digitaltrends.com*. Retrieved April 24, 2014, from http://www.digitaltrends.com/mobile/smartphone-battery-improvements/#!FJdWM.

Buckellew, P., Custis, K., Esposito, R., & Lesser, E. (2013). The upwardly mobile enterprise: Setting the strategic agenda. *Executive Report of Mobile Enterprise,* 1–20. IBM Institute for Business Value, IBM Global Business Services.

Budiu, R. (2013, September 14). Mobile: Native apps, web apps, and hybrid apps. Articles, *Nngroup.com*. Retrieved April 14, 2014, from http://www.nngroup.com/articles/mobile-native-apps/.

Bughin, J. (2011). The Web's €100 billion surplus. *McKinsey Quarterly*, *2*(4), 1–4.

Bughin, J., & Manyika, J. (2014). The mobile internet's consumer divided. *McKinsey Quarterly, 1*, 7–10.

Chan, S. (2014, March 6). The 10 most popular mobile messaging apps in the world. *Readwrite.com*. Retrieved May 1, 2014, from http://readwrite.com/2014/03/06/10-biggest-popular-mobile-messaging-apps-world-whatsapp#awesm=~oCXRiodHe0Pg0U.

Clifford, C. (2013, December 12). Top 10 apps for instant messaging (Infographic). *Entrepreneur.com*. Retrieved May 1, 2014, from http://www.entrepreneur.com/article/230335.

Duckett, C. (2013, October 8). Mobile data continues growth, fixed line remains download king. *Zdnet.com*. Retrieved April 26, 2014, from http://www.zdnet.com/mobile-data-continues-growth-fixed-line-remains-download-king-7000021675/.

Dutta, S., & Bilbao-Osorio, B. (2012). Executive summary. In S. Dutta & B. Bilbao-Osorio (Eds.,) *The global information technology report 2012: Living in a hyper-connected world* (pp. xi–xix). INSEAD & World Economic Forum.

El-Darwiche, B., Singh, M., & Genediwalla, S. (2012, Autumn). Digitization and prosperity. *Strategy + Business*, (68), 1–10.

eMarket (2014a, March 19). Driven by Facebook and Google, mobile ad market soars 105 % in 2013: Mobile ad spending on pace to reach $31.45 billion this year. *eMarket.com*. Retrieved April 14, 2014, from http://www.emarketer.com/Article/Driven-by-Facebook-Google-Mobile-Ad-Market-Soars-10537-2013/1010690.

eMarket (2014b, April 23). Despite time spent, mobile still lacks for ad spend in the U.S. *eMarket.com*. Retrieved April 24, 2014, from http://www.emarketer.com/Article/Despite-Time-Spent-Mobile-Still-Lacks-Ad-Spend-US/1010788.

eMarket (2014c, April 22). Mobile continues to steal share of US adults' daily time spent with media. *eMarket.com*. Retrieved April 28, 2014, from http://www.emarketer.com/Article/Mobile-Continues-Steal-Share-of-US-Adults-Daily-Time-Spent-with-Media/1010782.

Egol, M., Seelbach, F., & Sayani, N. (2013, June 10). Mobile now. *Strategy + Business*. Retrieved January 20, 2014, from http://www.zdnet.com/mobile-data-continues-growth-fixed-line-remains-download-king-7000021675/.

Friedrich, R., Grone, F., Holbling, K., & Peterson, M. (2008). The rise of mobile marketing: New opportunities for consumer companies and mobile operators. *Perspective*, 1–13. Booz & Co.

Gartner, G. (2013). Gartner says mobile app stores will see annual downloads reach 102 billion in 2013. *Press Release*, January 21, 2014. Retrieved April 28, 2014, from http://www.gartner.com/newsroom/id/2653121.

Gartner, G. (2014). Gartner says mobile advertising spending will reach $18 billion in 2014. *Press Release,* September 19, 2013. Retrieved April 8, 2014, from http://www.gartner.com/newsroom/id/2592315.

Gittleson, K. (2014, March 18). Tencent and Alibaba battle for internet dominance in China. *BBC Business News*. Retrieved May 3, 2104, from http://www.bbc.com/news/business-26540666.

Gordon, M. E. (2013, August 20). Samsung, the true ruler of the android kingdom. *Flurry Blog*. Retrieved April 29, 2014, from http://www.flurry.com/bid/100089/Samsung-The-True-Ruler-of-the-Android-Kingdom#.U2x48-IkSSo.

Gruman, G. (2013a). Mobile management's landscape. *Mobile device management: How to navigate the ever-changing mobile device landscape*, 2–5. InfoWorld Media Group.

Gruman, G. (2013b). Say yes to (almost) any device. *Mobile device management: How to navigate the ever-changing mobile device landscape*, 24–30. InfoWorld Media Group.

Gruman, G. (2014). Forget control-the mobile action is enablement. *Digital spotlight: Mobile enablement*, 4–6. Winter 2014, InfoWorld Media Group.

Gupta, S. (2013). For mobile devices, think apps, not ads. *Harvard Business Review*, *91*, 1–7.

Harvard Business Review (2013). How people really use mobile. *Harvard Business Review*, 30–31.

IBM Corporation (2012). Developing more effective mobile enterprise programs: A practical "how-to" guide for creating mobile enterprise programs with help from partners. *Thought Leadership White Paper*, 1–14. IBM Global Technology Services.

IBM Corporation (2013). Putting mobile first: Best practices of mobile technology. *Research Paper*, 1–14. IBM Mobile First.

International Data Corporation (IDC) (2012a). The rise of mobility. *IDC Infograhic Library*. Retrieved April 10, 2014, from http://www.idc.asia/microsites/infographics/mobility/Rise_of_mobility.asp.

International Data Corporation (IDC) (2012b). Enterprise mobility in Asia Pacific. *IDC Infograhic Library*. Retrieved April 10, 2014, from http://www.idc.asia/microsites/infographics/mobility/EnterpriseMobility-in-APAC.asp.

International Data Corporation (IDC) (2014a). *Production information: Worldwide quarterly mobile phone tracker*. Retrieved April 28, 2014, from http://www.idc.com/tracker/showproductinfo.jsp?prod_id=37.

International Data Corporation (IDC) (2014b). *Production information: Worldwide quarterly tablet tracker*. Retrieved April 28, 2014, from http://www.idc.com/tracker/showproductinfo.jsp?prod_id=81.

International Data Corporation (IDC) (2014c). *Android and iOS continue to dominate the Worldwide smartphone market with android shipments just shy of 800 million in 2013,* February 12, 2014 (Retrieved April 28, 2014, from http://www.idc.com/getdoc.jsp?containerId=prUS24676414.

Khalaf, S. (2014a, April 1). Apps solidify leadership six years into the mobile revolution. *Flurry.com*. Retrieved August 18, 2014, from http://www.flurry.com/bid/109749/Apps-Solidify-Leadership-Six-Years-into-the-Mobile-Revolution#.VCNb_OKaW8A.

Khalaf, S. (2014b, April 22). The rise of the mobile addict. *Flurry Blog*. Retrieved April 29, 2014, from http://www.flurry.com/bid/110166/The-Rise-of-the-Mobile-Addict#.U2xvvuIkSSo.

Mainardi, C. (2012). Forward. In S. Dutta & B. Bilbao-Osorio (Eds.), *The global information technology report 2012: Living in a hyper-connected world* (p. vii). INSEAD & World Economic Forum.

Meeker, M., & Wu, L. (2013, May 29). 2013 internet trends. 2013 D11 Conference Presentation, Kleiner, Perkins, Caufield & Byers. Retrieved April 2, 2014, from http://www.kpcb.com/insights/2013-internet-trends.

Meeker, M. (2014, May 28). 2014 internet trends. 2014 CODE Conference Presentation, Kleiner, Perkins, Caufield & Byers. Retrieved July 10, 2014, from http://www.kpcb.com/internet-trends.

Page, M., Molina, M., & Jones, G. (2013). *The mobile global economy*. ATKearney & GSMA. Retrieved April 15, 2014, from http://www.atkearney.com.au/documents/10192/760890/The_Mobile_Economy_2013.pdf/6ac11770-5a26-4fef-80bd-870ab83222f0.

Peters, J. (2014, March 27). What business can learn about mobile security from consumers. *Mobile Business Insights*. Retrieved April 25, 2014, from http://asmarterplanet.com/mobile-enterprise/blog/2014/03/businesses-can-learn-mobile-security-consumers.html.

Sadauskas, A. (2014a, April 4). $28 billion mobile gold rush: Consumers spend two hours and 19 minutes each day using apps. Technology Section, *Startupsmart.com.au*. Retrieved April 18, 2014, from http://www.startupsmart.com.au/technology/28-billion-mobile-gold-rush-consumers-spend-two-hours-and-19-minutes-each-day-using-apps/2014040412053.html).

Sadauskas, A. (2014b, March 26). Going mobile: Should your small business ditch the landline. Technology Section, *Startupsmart.com.au*. Retrieved April 20, 2014, from http://www.smartcompany.com.au/technology/41265-going-mobile-should-your-small-business-ditch-the-landline.html.

Sadauskas, A. (2014c, February 26). Eight major announcements from the 2014 Mobile World Congress. Technology Section, *Startupsmart.com.au*. Retrieved April 29, 2014, from http://www.smartcompany.com.au/technology/35794-eight-major-announcements-from-the-2014-mobile-world-congress.html?start=1.

Sadauskas, A. (2014d, February 26). Why Facebook paid $US16 billion for WhatsApp- and why Telestra, Optus, and Vadafone should be worried. Technology Section, *Startupsmart.com.au*. Retrieved April 30, 2014, from http://www.smartcompany.com.au/technology/35795-why-facebook-paid-us16-billion-for-whatsapp-and-why-telstra-optus-and-vodafone-should-be-worried-control-shift.html.

Shehadi, R. T., Acker, O., Karam, D., & Lee, K. K. (2014, February). Building next-generation sustainable cities: A road map for economic, social, and environmental sustainability. *Strategy*, 1–19.

Shehadi, R. T., Khoury, R., Kassatly, F., & Lamaa, A. (2013). Winning the mobile government game mechanisms for better customer engagement. *Perspective*, 1–9. Booz & Company Ltd.

Sheng, C. (2012, July 20). Tencent: We will not make smart phones. *Technode.com*. Retrieved May 2, 2014, from http://technode.com/2012/07/20/tencent-we-will-not-make-smart-phones/.

Spencer, B. (2013, February 11). Mobile users can't leave their phone alone for 6 min and check it up to 150 times a day. *Dailymail.co.uk*. Retrieved December 18, 2014, from http://www.dailymail.co.uk/news/article-2276752/Mobile-users-leave-phone-minutes-check-150-times-day.html.

Stilghjerrian (2013, October 9). Internet use: We are more mobile: But we still need a cable. *Crikey.com.au*. Retrieved April 26, 2014, from http://www.crikey.com.au/2013/10/09/internet-use-were-more-mobile-but-we-still-need-a-cable/.

Turban, E., King, D., Liang, T. P., & Turban, D. (2012). *Electronic commerce: A managerial and social networks perspective*. U.K.: Pearson Education.

Van Dyk, D. (2012). The end of cash. *Time*, *179*(1), 34–35.

Violino, G. (2014). An app strategy for the mobile era. *Digital Spotlight: Mobile Enablement, Winter, 2014*, 17–21.

Wauters, R. (2010, February 23). Mobile location-based services could rake in $12.7 billion by 2014. *Techcrunch.com*. Retrieved May 1, 2014, from http://techcrunch.com/2010/02/23/location-based-services-revenue/.

Weill, P., & Woerner, S. L. (2013, October). The new digital divide: Emerging trump developed economies. *Research Briefing*, *XIII*(10), 1–4. MIT Sloan Center for Information Systems Research.

Wikipedia.org (2014). Tencent. *Wikepedia.org*. Retrieved May 3, 2014, from http://en.wikipedia.org/wiki/Tencent.

MIX
Papier aus verantwortungsvollen Quellen
Paper from responsible sources
FSC® C105338

If you have any concerns about our products,
you can contact us on
ProductSafety@springernature.com

In case Publisher is established outside the EU,
the EU authorized representative is:
Springer Nature Customer Service Center GmbH
Europaplatz 3, 69115 Heidelberg, Germany

Printed by Libri Plureos GmbH
in Hamburg, Germany